I, Pierre Rivière,

having slaughtered my mother, my sister, and my brother . . .

I, Pierre Rivière

my sister, and my brother...

BY MICHEL FOUCAULT

Madness and Civilization: *A History of Insanity in the Age of Reason*

The Order of Things: *An Archaeology of the Human Sciences*

The Archaeology of Knowledge (and The Discourse on Language)

The Birth of the Clinic: *An Archaeology of Medical Perception*

aving slaughtered my mother,

Case of Parricide in the 19th Century

Edited by

Michel Foucault

Translated by Frank Jellinek

Pantheon Books

A Division of Random House, New York

Library of Congress Cataloging in Publication Data

Main entry under title:

I, Pierre Rivière, having slaughtered my mother, my sister, and my brother . . . : A Case of Parricide in the 19th Century.

Translation of Moi, Pierre Rivière, ayant égorgé ma mère, ma soeur et mon frère . . . : un cas de parricide au XIXe siècle.

"This work is the outcome of a joint research project by a team engaged in a seminar at the Collège de France. The authors are Blandine Barret-Kriegel . . . [et al.]"

    1. Rivière, Pierre, 1815-1840. 2. Parricide—France—Case studies. 3. Medical jurisprudence—France—Case studies. I. Foucault, Michel, ed. II. Barret-Kriegel, Blandine.

HV6248.R57M6413 1975   364.1′523   74-26205

ISBN 0-394-49310-9

Manufactured in the United States of America

FIRST AMERICAN EDITION

Contents

Foreword

WE HAD IN MIND a study of the practical aspects of the relations between psychiatry and criminal justice. In the course of our research we came across Pierre Rivière's case.

It was reported in the *Annales d'hygiène publique et de médecine légale* in 1836. Like all the other reports published in that journal, this comprised a summary of the facts and the medico-legal experts' reports. There were, however, a number of unusual features about it.

1. A series of three medical reports which did not reach similar conclusions and did not use exactly the same kind of analysis, each coming from a different source and each with a different status within the medical institution: a report by a country general practitioner, a report by an urban physician in charge of a large asylum, and a report signed by the leading figures in contemporary psychiatry and forensic medicine (Esquirol, Marc, Orfila, etc.).

2. A fairly large collection of court exhibits including statements by witnesses—all of them from a small village in Normandy—when questioned about the life, behavior, character, *madness* or *idiocy* of the author of the crime.

3. Lastly, and most notably, a memoir, or rather the fragment of a memoir, written by the accused himself, a peasant some twenty years of age who claimed that he could "only barely read and write" and who had undertaken

during his detention on remand to give "particulars and an explanation" of his crime, the premeditated murder of his mother, his sister, and his brother.

A collection of this sort seemed to us unique among the contemporary printed documentation. To what do we owe it?

Almost certainly not to the sensation caused by the case itself. Cases of parricide were fairly common in the assize courts in that period (ten to fifteen yearly, sometimes more). Moreover, Fieschi's attempted assassination of the king and his trial and the sentencing and execution of Lacenaire and the publication of his memoirs practically monopolized the space devoted to criminal cases in the press at the time. The *Gazette des Tribunaux* never gave the Rivière case more than a brief mention, in the main reproducing the *Pilote du Calvados*. The Rivière case never became a classic of criminal psychiatry like those of Henriette Cornier, Papavoine, or Léger. Apart from the article in the *Annales d'hygiène*, we have found practically no references to Rivière.[1] And Rivière's counsel, Berthauld, who was later to become fairly well known, seems never to have alluded to his former client in his writings.

Rivière's case was not, then, a "notable crime." The unusually full treatment in the *Annales* may be accounted for by a combination of chance circumstances and general considerations. Probably a doctor or some local notable in the Caen area drew the contemporary Paris experts' attention to the sentencing to death on November 12, 1835, of a parricide considered by many to be a madman. They must have agreed to intervene when the petition of mercy was presented, on the basis of the records compiled for the purpose; in any event, they drew up their certificate on the

---

[1] The *Journal de médecine et de chirurgie pratique* in 1836 summarized the article in the *Annales;* Vingtrinier briefly mentioned Pierre Rivière's case in the *Examen des comptes de l'Administration de la justice criminelle* (1846, p. 9).

basis of the material evidence without ever seeing Pierre Rivière. And once the commutation of the sentence had been granted, what they published in the *Annales d'hygiène* was the whole or part of the dossier on the case.

Over and above these circumstances, however, a more general debate emerges, in which the publication of this dossier by Esquirol and his colleagues was to have its effect. In 1836 they were in the very midst of the debate on the use of psychiatric concepts in criminal justice. To be more precise, they were at a specific point in this debate, for lawyers such as Collard de Montigny, doctors such as Urbain Coste, and more especially the judges and the courts had been very strongly resisting (especially since 1827) the concept of "monomania" advanced by Esquirol (in 1808). So much so that medical experts and counsel for the defense hesitated to use a concept which had a somewhat dubious connotation of "materialism" in the minds of the courts and some juries. Around 1835 it looks as if doctors rather tended to produce medical reports based less directly on the concept of monomania, as if they wished to show simultaneously that reluctance to use it might lead to serious miscarriages of justice and that mental illness could be manifested through a far wider symptomatology. In any case, the Rivière dossier as published by the *Annales* is extremely discreet in its references to "monomania"; on the other hand, it makes very considerable use of signs, symptoms, the depositions of witnesses, and very diverse types of evidence.

There is, however, one fact about all this that is truly surprising, that while "local" or general circumstances led to the publication of a remarkably full documentation, full not only for that period, but even our own, on it and on the unique document that is Rivière's memoir, an immediate and complete silence ensued. What could have disconcerted the doctors and their knowledge after so strongly eliciting their attention?

To be frank, however, it was not this, perhaps, that led us to spend more than a year on these documents. It was simply the beauty of Rivière's memoir. The utter astonishment it produced in us was the starting point.

But we were still faced with the question of publication. I think that what committed us to the work, despite all our differences of interests and approaches, was that it was a "dossier," that is to say, a case, an affair, an event that provided the intersection of discourses that differed in origin, form, organization, and function—the discourses of the cantonal judge, the prosecutor, the presiding judge of the assize court, and the Minister of Justice; those too of the country general practitioner and of Esquirol; and those of the villagers, with their mayor and parish priest; and, last but not least, that of the murderer himself. All of them speak, or appear to be speaking, of one and the same thing; at any rate, the burden of all these discourses is the occurrence on June 3. But in their totality and their variety they form neither a composite work nor an exemplary text, but rather a strange contest, a confrontation, a power relation, a battle among discourses and through discourses. And yet, it cannot simply be described as a single battle; for several separate combats were being fought out at the same time and intersected each other: The doctors were engaged in a combat, among themselves, with the judges and prosecution, and with Rivière himself (who had trapped them by saying that he had feigned madness); the crown lawyers had their own separate combat as regards the testimony of the medical experts, the comparatively novel use of extenuating circumstances, and a range of cases of parricide that had been coupled with regicide (Fieschi and Louis-Philippe stand in the wings); the villagers of Aunay had their own combat to defuse the terror of a crime committed in their midst and to "preserve the honor of a family" by ascribing the crime to bizarre behavior or singularity; and, lastly, at the very center, there was Pierre Rivière, with his innumerable and complicated engines of war; his crime, made to be written and talked about and thereby to secure him glory in death, his narrative, prepared in advance and for the purpose of leading on to the crime, his oral explanations to obtain credence for his madness, his text, written to dispel this lie, to explain, and to summon death, a text in whose beauty some were to see a proof of rationality (and hence grounds for condemning him to death) and others a sign of madness (and hence grounds for shutting him up for life).

I think the reason we decided to publish these documents was to draw a map, so to speak, of those combats, to reconstruct these confrontations and battles, to rediscover the interaction of those discourses as weapons of attack and defense in the relations of power and knowledge.

More specifically, we thought that the publication of the dossier might furnish an example of existing records that are available for potential analysis.

(a) Since the principle governing their existence and coherence is neither that of a composite work nor a legal text, the outdated academic methods of textual analysis and all the concepts which are the appanage of the dreary and scholastic prestige of writing on writing can very well be eschewed in studying them.

(b) Documents like those in the Rivière case should provide material for a thorough examination of the way in which a particular kind of knowledge (e.g. medicine, psychiatry, psychology) is formed and acts in relation to institutions and the roles prescribed in them (e.g., the law with respect to the expert, the accused, the criminally insane, and so on).

(c) They give us a key to the relations of power, domination, and conflict within which discourses emerge and function, and hence provide material for a potential analysis of discourse (even of scientific discourses) which may be both tactical and political, and therefore strategic.

(d) Lastly, they furnish a means for grasping the power of derangement peculiar to a discourse such as Rivière's and the whole range of tactics by which we can try to reconstitute it, situate it, and give it its status as the discourse of either a madman or a criminal.

Our approach to this publication can be explained as follows:

1. We have tried to discover all the material evidence in the case, and by this we mean not only the exhibits in evidence (only some of which were published in the *Annales d'hygiène publique*), but also newspaper articles and especially Rivière's memoir in its entirety. (The *Annales* reprinted only the second part of it.) Most of these documents were to be found in the Departmental Archives at Caen; Jean-Pierre Peter did most of the research. (With the exception of a few documents of minor interest, we are therefore publishing everything we could find written by or about Pierre Rivière, whether in print or in manuscript.)

2. In presenting the documents, we have refrained from employing a typological method (the court file followed by the medical file). We have rearranged them more or less in chronological order around the events they are bound up with—the crime, the examining judge's investigation, the proceedings in the assize court, and the commutation of the sentence. This throws a good deal of light on the confrontation of various types of discourse and the rules and results of this confrontation.

And, placed as it is at the time of its writing, Rivière's memoir comes to assume the central position which is its due, as a mechanism which holds the whole together; triggered secretly beforehand, it leads on to all the earlier episodes; then, once it comes into the open, it lays a trap for everyone, including its contriver, since it is first taken as proof that Rivière is not mad and then becomes, in the hands of Esquirol, Marc, and Orfila, a means of averting that death penalty which Rivière had gone to such lengths to call down upon himself.

3. As to Rivière's discourse, we decided not to interpret it and not to subject it to any psychiatric or psychoanalytic commentary. In the first place because it was what we used as the zero benchmark to gauge the distance between the other discourses and the relations arising among them. Secondly, because we could hardly speak of it without involving it in one of the discourses (medical, legal, psychological, criminological) which we wished to use as our starting point in talking about it. If we had done so, we should have brought it within the power relation whose reductive effect we wished to show, and we ourselves should have fallen into the trap it set.

Thirdly, and most importantly, owing to a sort of reverence and perhaps, too, terror for a text which was to carry off four corpses along with it, we were unwilling to superimpose our own text on Rivière's memoir. We fell under the spell of the parricide with the reddish-brown eyes.

4. We have assembled a number of notes at the end of the volume, some on the psychiatric knowledge at work in the doctors' reports, others on the legal aspects of the case (extenuating circumstances, the jurisprudence of parricide), yet others on the relations between the documentary levels (depositions, records, expert opinions), and others again on the narrative of the crimes.

We are aware that we have neglected many major aspects. We could have gone into the marvelous document of peasant ethnology provided by the first part of Rivière's narrative. Or we could have brought out the popular knowledge and definition of madness whose outlines emerge through the villagers' testimony.

But the main point for us was to have the documents published.

This work is the outcome of a joint research project by a team engaged in a seminar at the Collège de France. The authors are Blandine Barret-Kriegel, Gilbert Burlet-Torvic, Robert Castel, Jeanne Favret, Alexandre Fontana, Georgette Legée, Patricia Moulin, Jean-Pierre Peter, Philippe Riot, Maryvonne Saison, and myself.

We were aided in our research by Mme. Coisel and M. Bruno at the Bibliothèque Nationale, M. Bercé at the Archives Nationales, M. G. Bernard and Mlle. Gral at the Archives départementales du Calvados, and Mme. Anne Sohier of the Centre de Recherches historiques.

Pierre Rivière's memoir was published in pamphlet form in the same year as the trial. There is no copy in the Bibliothèque Nationale. The pamphlet contains the version published in the *Annales d'hygiène publique*, but published there only in part and with some errors.

The whole file is to be found in the Archives du Calvados, 2 U 907, Assises Calvados, Procès criminels, 4th quarter 1835.

M.F.

I

The Dossier

I

Crime and Arrest

1. REPORT BY THE CANTONAL JUDGE

THIS DAY, June 3, 1835, at one o'clock in the afternoon,

We, François-Edouard Baudouin, cantonal judge of Aunay, Louis-Léandre Langliney, our clerk, attending,

Being informed by the mayor of the commune of Aunay that a fearful murder had just been committed in the said commune of Aunay, at the village of la Faucterie, at the residence of one Pierre-Margrin Rivière, property owner and farmer, absent from home since morning, as we were told, we forthwith proceeded to the said residence accompanied by the mayor of Aunay and Messrs. Morin, doctor, and Cordier, local health officer, both resident at Aunay, duly summoned by us in accordance with the law. Having entered the ground floor used as a large room in a house bounded on the north by the local road from Aunay to Saint-Vignal, lighted on the south by a casement window and a door and to the north by a glazed door, we there found three bodies lying on the ground, viz. (1) a woman about forty years of age lying on her back opposite the fireplace at which she had seemingly been busied at the time she was murdered cooking a gruel which was still in a pot on the hearth. The woman was dressed in her ordinary clothes, her hair in disorder; the neck and the back of the skull were slashed and "cutlassed"; (2) a small boy aged seven or eight, dressed in a blue smock, trousers, stockings, and shoes, lying prone face to the ground, with his head split behind to a very great depth; (3) a girl dressed in a calico print, stockings, no shoes or clogs, lying on her back, her feet on the threshold of the door giving on to the yard, pointing toward the south, her lace bobbins resting on her stomach, her cotton cap at her feet as well as a large fistful of her hair which seems to have been torn out at the time of the murder; the right side of the face and the neck "cutlassed" to a very great depth. It would appear that the unfortunate young person was working at her lace near the glazed door opposite to that where she fell, since her clogs were still at the foot of the chair standing there.

This triple murder seems to have been committed with an instrument with a cutting edge.

The names of these victims are: the first, Victoire Brion, wife of Pierre-Margrin Rivière; the second, Jules Rivière; the third, Victoire Rivière; the latter two being children of the first-named.

Since the general rumor accused the man Pierre Rivière, son and brother of the murdered persons, as the perpetrator of this crime, we informed the sergeant of the gendarmerie stationed at Le Mesnil Auzouf of this occurrence, after ascertaining that the presumed culprit had escaped immediately after the crime imputed to him, and required this officer forthwith to seek and apprehend him if possible.

We requested Messrs. Morin and Cordier to take all steps they deemed necessary to investigate and certify the causes of death, with which request they complied after duly taking the oath required in such circumstances, drawing their attention to the fact that it was common knowledge that the mother was pregnant.

The medical officers completed their examination in our

presence and handed their report to us, which we have attached to these presents after countersigning it and sealing it with the seal of the cantonal court.

2. DEATH CERTIFICATE BY THE DOCTORS WHO EXAMINED THE BODIES

This day, June 3, 1835,

We, Théodore Morin, doctor, and Thomas-Adrien Cordière, health officer, residing at Aunay,

Proceeded at about two o'clock in the afternoon, duly summoned by the cantonal judge of Aunay and the mayor of the village of la Faucterie in the commune of Aunay to the house of one Pierre-Margrin Rivière, and having entered it found three bodies in the following condition:

1. A woman who we were told was a certain Victoire Brion, wife of the said Rivière, lying on her back, her feet resting against the hearth and slightly inclined, the right hand at her side, the fingers contracted, the left hand clenched on the breast, the clothes in fairly good order except for the headdress, a cotton cap spread under the corpse's head; a huge pool of blood extended around the head; the right side and the front part of the neck as well as the face were so slashed that the cervical vertebrae were wholly severed from the trunk, the skin and the muscles on the left side still retaining the head; the parietal bone on the right side was completely crushed; the blow extended toward the crown of the skull and so deeply that the greater part of cerebral substance was separated from it; several other blows had been struck all over the face and with such violence that the bones and muscles appeared as reduced to a mere pulp. Since the woman was with child, we proceeded, at the request of the authorities, to conduct an autopsy; an incision having been made and the uterus opened, we

found a female fetus which had reached about six and a half months of gestation. When opened, the stomach was found to be completely empty. We did not carry our examination further, the cause of death being positive since, as we have said, the head was almost separated from the trunk; as the jugular and carotid arteries had been severed, death must have been instantaneous.

2. Lying beyond the corpse described above was a child seven or eight years of age who we were told was Jules Rivière; he was lying face downward, still wearing his clothes, the head in a great pool of blood; on both lateral and posterior surfaces we observed broad and deep incisions which penetrated the brain to a considerable depth in several directions as well as many blows which must have been struck on the cerebellum, since the crown of the skull could easily be detached; a blow had also been struck on the nape of the neck without damaging the cervical vertebrae; several other blows had been struck on the shoulders and had cut through the smock and other clothing; these last-mentioned injuries, however, were not in themselves very serious; we did not consider that we needed to proceed to examine the splanchnic and thoracic cavities, the cause of death being positive—the brain and cerebellum being completely mangled, the arteries traversing them had been entirely severed.

3. To the south of the room and near the corpse described above was a young girl about eighteen years of age lying on her back, shod only in her stockings, her lace bobbins still lying at her left side, her garments disordered, her head bare; some of her spreading hair had been pulled out and was lying at her feet, her arms were almost crossed on her breast; the bib and kerchief had been torn away, which showed that the victim had put up some resistance to her murderer. At the right side of the neck were to be observed two broad and deep incisions; the first and lower one had severed not only the skin and muscles but also the carotid artery, the second cervical vertebra had been com-

pletely cut through. Above this first incision there were several others in the same direction, but not so deep; they had been arrested by the ascending branch of the lower jaw; the face was scored in various directions with broad and deep wounds, the lower jaw was almost severed toward the symphysis of the chin, the upper jaw was also severed by a blow which, struck above the orbits, almost penetrated the brain; an oblique incision from right to left completely severed the nasal fossae. In accordance with these observations, we consider that these many wounds, most of them mortal, made it unnecessary to conduct an autopsy of this body. It is practically certain that these wounds were caused by a sharp instrument with a cutting edge.

This report, completed and drawn up on the day, month, and year aforesaid, which we hereby certify to be true and authentic throughout, was delivered to the cantonal judge immediately following our examinations.

(signed)

3. STATEMENTS TO THE CANTONAL JUDGE BY WITNESSES OF THE CRIME

Marie Rivière, seventy-four:
Today, between about eleven o'clock and half-past twelve, being at the door of my house which, as you see, gives on to the same yard as the house in which the crime was committed, on the further side of the said yard to the left I saw the girl Victoire Rivière at her door facing our yard being held by her brother by the hair. She seemed to be trying to run away. When I approached them Pierre Rivière was holding a pruning bill in his hand and was raising it against his sister. I cried out: "Oh wretched boy, what are you about to do," and tried to seize his arm, but at the same instant he gave his sister several blows on the

head with the bill and stretched her dead at his feet. All this happened in less than a minute. He fled by the door giving on the local road going toward the town of Aunay, at the same instant I put my head inside the house and saw the corpses of his mother and his little brother, I lost my senses and set to crying out my god what a terrible thing my god what a terrible thing. Several people ran up, but all those who live in the houses on our yard were absent from their homes at that time.

Jean Postel, fifty, servant at M. Lerot's:

About noon today coming back from gathering clover which I was carrying on my head I heard in the road the widow Pierre Rivière crying out "oh my god what a terrible thing! oh my god what a terrible thing!" At the same instant I also heard another voice which I did not know cry out They are all dead; and on coming to the door of our stable I saw Pierre Rivière. He held a bloodstained bill in his hand, his hand was also bloody. He said to me as he went off toward the village: take care that nothing happens to my mother. I heard this injunction without knowing what it meant but as soon as I was given knowledge of the murder, I thought that it was his grandmother he meant.

Victoire Aimée Lerot, forty, wife of Jean André:

About noon today as I was about to enter my brother's house, which is opposite the house of Pierre Margrin Rivière, I saw Pierre Rivière, the son of the aforesaid, leaving his house by the glazed door giving on the local road which goes to the village of Aunay. He held a bloodstained bill in his hand; as he passed me, he said to me: "I have just delivered my father from all his tribulations. I know that they will put me to death, but no matter," adding, "I commend my mother to you."

4. REPORT OF THE DISTRICT PROSECUTOR ROYAL AT VIRE

We, the District Prosecutor Royal at the civil court at Vire, alerted by public report that a crime of deliberate murder had just been committed in the commune of Aunay, immediately proceeded to the scene accompanied by the lieutenant of gendarmerie, after notifying the examining judge of our proceedings, and there did as follows:

The cantonal judge of Aunay having, as he informed us, certified the material fact of the crime by his report dated the day before yesterday, we considered it unnecessary to proceed to an inquiry, which had become superfluous; but since the most manifest evidence established that the man Pierre Rivière, aged twenty, farmer at Aunay, deliberately put to death: (1) Marie-Anne Brion, wife of Rivière, his mother; (2) Marguerite Rivière, and (3) Jules Rivière, his brother and sister, we forthwith set about securing his apprehension; in consequence, we required the mayors of the communes of Aunay, Roucamps, Plessis, and other neighboring communes to alert a number of national guards with instructions to proceed to the apprehension of the said Pierre Rivière.

Thereafter, we proceeded to the village of la Fauctrie, where we collected the information on the said Pierre Rivière set out below.

We deemed it proper to hear the father, the grandmother, and one of the sisters of the accused person without administering the oath to them, and the following is a summary of their statements.

From his childhood Pierre Rivière was an affliction to his family, he was obstinate and taciturn; even being with his parents was a burden to him. Never did he show a son's affection for his father and mother. His mother especially

9

was odious to him. At times he felt a wave of something like repulsion and frenzy when she approached him.

Pierre Rivière displayed a harshness of character in all his habits which much distressed his family. He is remembered to have been seen in his childhood taking pleasure in crushing young birds between two stones and pursuing children of his age with instruments with which he threatened to kill them.

Sometimes he fled his parents' house and sought refuge in quarries and spent the night there. Returning from these nocturnal excursions he said that he had seen the devil and had made a pact with him.

His aversion to women was constantly noted.

At times he talked to himself and became excited and passionate.

When he grew older, he eagerly took to the reading of certain books, and his memory served him admirably in his reading . . . It seems that at one period he would spend all night reading philosophical works.

From irreligion he turned to great piety, or at least to an outward show of devotion.

The jubilee held two years ago seems to have wrought this change.

His father caught him reading at night the Montpellier Catechism (a work lent him by the parish priest of Aunay).

In the past year he twice took communion and took the sacrament at Easter.

On Saturday, the thirtieth of last month, he put on his best clothes, and on the day of the crime, after changing his clothes three times, he donned his Sunday best. Seeing which, his grandmother said to him: "But what are you doing dressed up so fine?" To which he replied: "you will know this evening . . ." That morning Pierre Rivière had complained of feeling very unwell; his heart was paining him, he said.

Solitary, wild, and cruel, that is Pierre Rivière as seen from the moral point of view; he is, so to speak, a being apart, a savage not subject to the ordinary laws of sympathy and sociability, for society was as odious to him as his family, thus he asked his father whether a man could not live in the woods on plants and roots.

Some notable traits emerge from a study of Pierre Rivière's physique: He is short, his forehead is narrow and low; his black eyebrows arch and meet, he constantly keeps his head down, and his furtive glances seem to shun meeting the gaze of others, as if for fear of betraying his secret thoughts; his gait is jerky and he moves in bounds, he leaps rather than walks.

After committing his crime, Pierre Rivière did not take to flight; he went out unconcernedly and, his hands stained with blood, went up to two persons to whom he said: "I have just delivered my father, now he will no longer be unhappy," and he then went on his way calmly as if nothing had happened; his pruning bill was dripping with blood.

Such is the information which we gathered at the scene of the crime itself, in the presence of the cantonal judge of Aunay, M. Morin, doctor and member of the municipal council, Angot, tax collector at Aunay and captain in the national guard, and Benoît, lieutenant of gendarmerie, who have signed this report together with us, this June 5, 1835.

(signed)

And forasmuch as after completing our report we learned that the said Pierre Rivière was seen in the wood at la Fontenelle, we summoned one Charles Denis, who, having sworn to speak the truth, declared as follows:

The woman Guillemette, known as the dame of Hamard (canton of Evrecy), told me that she had spoken with a person who had given her circumstantial details about the murder committed in the village of la Faucterie; according to the information given her by one Villemet and the girl Bonnemaison, this person is none other than the said Pierre Rivière.

(signed)

5. PERSONAL PARTICULARS OF PIERRE RIVIÈRE, CHARGED WITH MURDER

The District Prosecutor Royal of the district of Vire hereby calls upon the officers of the criminal investigation department to conduct the most urgent investigation in order to proceed to the apprehension of the man Pierre Rivière, suspected of murdering his mother, his brother, and one of his sisters.

His description follows:

Age	20
Height	5 feet 6 inches
Hair and eyebrows	black
Whiskers	black and thin
Forehead	narrow
Nose	ordinary
Mouth	ordinary
Chin	round
Face	oval and full
Complexion	swarthy
Gaze	furtive
Head lowered, gait jerky	

Dressed in a blue linen smock, cap, and ankle boots.

RIVIÈRE is without means; he begs.

He was seen on the 21st of this month in the canton of Flers, district of Domfront.

A warrant of arrest was issued for Pierre RIVIÈRE on the tenth of this month by the examining judge of Vire, and if apprehended he is to be brought before this judge.

At the district prosecutor's office, June 23, 1835.

ROBERT
District Prosecutor Royal

Note. The District Prosecutor Royal hereby requests cantonal judges to transmit these particulars to the mayors and rural police of their canton.

6. LETTER FROM THE MAYOR OF AUNAY TO THE DISTRICT PROSECUTOR ROYAL

Aunay, June 24, 1835

Sir,

I have the honor to send you herewith the report which has just been handed to me by the rural guard of my commune on his return from the search for the murderer Pierre Rivière of whom I informed you in my letter of the 23rd instant. The attempt to seize and apprehend the said Rivière, though carried on with the utmost possible vigor, has been unavailing.

Had the gendarmerie at Flers been sufficiently informed about this occurrence, there is every reason to believe that he would by now have been arrested, since he openly sat before the door of an innkeeper at the entry to the market town of Flers for at least three or four hours reading a book. His aspect was such that there could be no doubt that he would have been capable of committing the murder. But he was taken for a mental defective, according to local report when they learned of the search being made for him; and now that he is known throughout the district, it is safely to be presumed that it will not be long before he is brought to justice.

Harson, Mayor of Aunay

The rural guard's report states that Pierre Rivière was seen by a cider seller outside Flers on the road to Domfront.

He was looking in the hedges and hay fields for wild saffron bulbs to eat. The Flers rural guard's boy invited him in to give him a piece of bread. He declined with thanks several times and then accepted. He asked him where he came from; he replied that he was from everywhere and afterwards said that he was from Aunay.

7. REPORT BY THE SERGEANT OF GENDARMERIE AT LANGANNERIE GIVING PARTICULARS OF THE ARREST OF PIERRE RIVIÈRE

This day, July 2, 1835, at five o'clock in the morning,

We the undersigned, le Courtois, sergeant of gendarmerie at the post at Langannerie, department of Calvados, hereby certify that being on the road in Langannerie we met a person who appeared to us suspect; having approached him, we asked him where he was from; he replied from everywhere; where are you going? where God commands me. Having examined him, we recognized him as the man Pierre Rivière, of the commune of Aunay, murderer of his mother, his brother, and his sister, as described in the wanted notice circulated by our superior officers and issued at the district prosecutor's office at Vire on June 10, 1835, stating that a warrant was issued for the said Pierre Rivière. Having secured his person, we took him to our barracks and we asked his surname, first names, and place of residence and he replied he was named Rivière, Pierre, residing at Aunay; having asked him why he had killed his mother, he replied that she had sinned in the sight of God. Having further asked him the same question regarding his brother and his sister, he said they had sinned by remaining with their mother. He was carrying a piece of wood to both ends of which there was attached a cord in the form of a bow, and another piece of wood in the style of an arrow, having a brad nail at one end. We found in his cap a gun license issued on October 30, 1829, to Lefèvre, Jean-Denis, residing at la Bigue; the said Rivière stated that he had found it on the road at Jurques; we asked him what he had done with the pruning bill he had used to commit the crime, he said he had thrown it into a wheatfield not far from Aunay. Whereafter we locked him into our cell to be brought before the proper authority, himself, two knives, a penknife, a stick of sulphur, and a piece of string.

Langannerie, the day and year aforesaid.

(signed)

8. LETTER FROM THE DISTRICT PROSECUTOR ROYAL AT FALAISE TO THE DISTRICT PROSECUTOR ROYAL AT VIRE

July 3, 1835
Sir,

I have the honor to inform you that the man Pierre Rivière whose particulars you sent me was apprehended yesterday in one of the communes of my district. Today he is in the local jail. No sooner had he arrived than he tried to escape from the jail, but steps have been taken to forestall and prevent such escape. He had several objects in his possession. I saw him this morning, but he did not wish to answer any of the questions I put to him. I shall order that he be transferred to you and that the objects in his possession be taken with him.

Renault, assistant,
p.p. the District Prosecutor Royal

9. NEWSPAPER ARTICLES

Pilote du Calvados, June 5, 1835

Our correspondent at Aunay sur Odon wrote yesterday, June 3: An occurrence, or rather a dreadful crime, a triple crime, has spread alarm and dismay in our district: one Rivière, a carter, lived unhappily with his wife, something of a shrew who was unwilling to live with him. As a result of these domestic broils, the Rivières set up house separately, and of their five issue the wife had taken two children and the husband three, the eldest of whom is the perpetrator of the crime I have to report. This young man who, it is said, has for some time seemed not to be in full possession of his mental faculties, which were not very strong to begin with, seeing his father constantly plagued by his wife and wishing to relieve him, went to his mother's house this morning and killed her with a pruning bill. The woman was seven months pregnant. Then he flung himself on his sister aged about eighteen and then on his seven-year-old brother and slaughtered them. The head of this raving madman's mother was almost severed from her trunk. After committing this triple murder, the maniac took to flight, but will probably have been arrested by the time you receive my dispatch. He is aged twenty. While the son was perpetrating his atrocious deed, his father, who is well thought of in the district, was working his fields. As soon as they were apprised of the crime, the local authorities proceeded to the scene of this frightful occurrence and drew up a report. (Article reproduced practically word for word in the *Gazette des Tribunaux,* June 8-9, 1835.)

Pilote du Calvados, June 7, 1835

Though he has been sought throughout the district, the man Rivière, of whose triple crime committed on Wednesday morning we sent you an account, the police have not yet been able to lay hands on him. He has probably taken refuge in the woods near Aunay, from which he will be compelled to emerge for want of sustenance, and he cannot fail to be arrested at any moment now.

Pilote du Calvados, June 17, 1835

Young Rivière, of Aunay, the perpetrator of the triple murder we have reported, has not yet been arrested. It is said that he was met a few days ago in a commune near Aunay by a fish vendor who recognized him and notified the police of the encounter, but too late to enable them to arrest him. This, however, is simply a rumor. Many people in the district believe that the wretched man has killed himself and that his body will be found in some pond or stream any day now.

Pilote du Calvados, July 5, 1835

Pierre Rivière, of Aunay, the perpetrator of the triple murder of which we have had occasion to speak, was arrested the day before yesterday, the second of July, by the sergeant of gendarmerie at Langannerie. At the time of his arrest he had on him a bow and arrow, two knives, and a penknife. A stick of sulphur was also found in his possession.

Journal de Falaise, July 8, 1935

Pierre Rivière, of Aunay, murderer of his mother, his brother, and his sister, was arrested by the gendarmerie at Langannerie on Thursday and was taken the same day to the jail at Falaise. The man had lived for a month in the woods and fields. It seems that he bought bread for some days with some coins which he happened to be carrying at the time of the crime. Thereafter he fed on plants, leaves, and wild fruits. He states that he spent three days and three nights in the wood at Cingalis before his arrest. He had made a bow and arrow there with which he tried to kill birds, but he had not managed to hit any. This bow was found on him when he was arrested. He claims that he committed the crime by command of heaven; that God the father appeared to him amid his angels; that he was ablaze with light; that he told him to do what he did and promised not to abandon him. He shows no sign of emotion or repentance at the recollection of his crime. He says that it was fated to happen. To judge from what he says, he had thought out the deed beforehand and had sharpened his ax several days before, awaiting the right moment. He claims to believe that he will be set free and be sent back to the woods.

Rivière is of medium height, brown-haired, of a ruddy complexion. He keeps his eyes on the ground, furtively, and seems to be afraid to look those who speak to him in the face. He replies only in monosyllables. His answers evince religious mania or madness, but of a serious kind. He is a dour fanatic. He says that he read a great deal, especially religious books. He has mentioned as his main reading the Montpellier Catechism, lent him by his parish priest. He followed the divine service with great exactitude, never played with young people of his own age, and had no mistress and no wish for one. He is eating a great deal at present, like someone who has suffered a great deal from hunger. His sleep seems to be calm and his soul without remorse.

Such are the observations made at Falaise on this person who is a monster of our time, if the act which he committed is not the result of some mental derangement. He left this morning for Vire where the preliminary investigation is nearly completed. He will probably be tried at the next Calvados assizes. (Article reproduced in large part by the *Gazette des Tribunaux*, July 18, 1835.)

2

The Preliminary
Investigation

1. FIRST INTERROGATION OF
PIERRE RIVIÈRE (JULY 9, 1835)

ON THIS NINTH DAY of July in the year one thousand eight hundred and thirty-five, in the division of criminal investigation of the court of first instance of the district of Vire, before us Exupère Legrain, the examining judge of the district aforesaid, assisted by Théodore Lebouleux, assistant to the clerk of court; in Execution of the warrant of arrest from us issuing on the tenth day of June one thousand eight hundred and thirty-five against one Pierre Rivière,

There appeared the said Rivière, whom we interrogated orally as follows:

Question. What are your surname, first name, age, occupation, and place of residence?

Answer. Pierre Rivière, aged twenty, farmer, born in the commune of Courvaudon and resident in that of Aunay.

Q. For what motive did you murder your mother, your sister Victoire, and your brother Jules?

A. Because God ordered me to justify His providence, they were united.

Q. What do you mean by saying they were united?

A. All three of them were in league to persecute my father.

Q. You just told me that God had ordered you to commit the three murders of which you are accused, but you knew full well that God never orders a crime.

A. God ordered Moses to slay the adorers of the golden calf, sparing neither friends nor father nor son.

Q. Who taught you such things?

A. I read them in Deuteronomy. When he gave his blessing to the tribe of Levi Moses said: your grace and your fullness have been given to the holy man whom you have chosen, who said to his father and his mother: I know you not, and to his brother: I know not who thou art. Those they are Lord who have kept thy laws and thine alliance and will offer up incense to thee to appease thy wrath.

Q. You have read the Bible many times, then?

A. Yes, I have read Deuteronomy many times, and Numbers.

Q. You drew most lamentable conclusions from passages in a book which you did not understand?

A. My father was being persecuted, it was fit to make one doubt God's providence.

Q. When did you first become accustomed to read the Bible?

A. A long time ago, two or three years.

Q. Did you also habitually read books of devotion?

A. Yes I read the *Montpellier Catechism*.

Q. Before that you had read works of quite a different sort?

A. Yes, I leafed through the book called the *Good Sense of Curé Meslier* for about two hours.

Q. What impression did reading that work make on you and what did you see in it?

A. I did not believe in religion at one time. I doubted it. That was not the work that took away my religion, but it confirmed my doubts.

Q. To what other book do you refer?

A. I had read in the almanacs and geography books that the earth is divided into several parts and I doubted that if Adam was created on one of these parts it would have been possible for his posterity to people the others.

Q. When did you conceive the execrable project which you put into effect on the third of June?

A. Two weeks before.

Q. Why and on what occasion did you frame such a design?

A. Because my father was persecuted and I saw God who ordered me to do it.

Q. Explain to me what you saw?

A. I was unable to work because of the persecutions my father was suffering. I was in a field when God appeared to me in the company of angels and gave me the order to justify his providence.

Q. Long before the period of which you are telling me, you had displayed hatred toward your mother, your brothers and sisters, and even toward your father.

A. I could not love my mother because of what she was doing, but I had no evil design against her, and besides, God's commandments forbade me to do her harm.

Q. How did you come to believe later that there existed quite contrary commandments?

A. Because I was specially inspired by God as the Levites were, although those same commandments existed.

Q. You claim to excuse your crimes by saying, which is absurd and impious, that they were ordered by God; confess rather that, being unluckily born with a ferocious character, you wished to steep yourself in the blood of your mother whom you had long abominated, whom you abominated above all after she had conceived the idea of obtaining a separation from your father's bed and board.

A. I repeat: God ordered me to do what I did. The priest had told my father to pray to God, assuring him that

God would help him out of his tribulations. If he had not helped him, the existence of God and his justice would have been in doubt.

Q. Did you disclose to anyone what you claim happened in a field two weeks before your crime?

A. No.

Q. For fear that you might be deceived by a flight of imagination why did you not think that it might be wise to apply to some enlightened person for advice on your notions?

A. I did not think that I should do so.

Q. You had however, as it seems, gone to confession some time before, you had taken the sacrament at Easter, it was quite simple for you to consult your confessor, why did you not do so, your three victims would still be alive if you had been wise enough to do that?

A. I did not do it and I did not think I should.

Q. Is it not true that you sometimes displayed hatred of your father?

A. That is not true.

Q. You are accused of having in your childhood committed various acts of cold-blooded and deliberate cruelty, of having, for instance, crushed young birds between two stones and pursued your young playmates threatening to put them to death with instruments you carried?

A. I do not remember doing that, I only happened sometimes to kill birds by throwing stones at them, as schoolboys do to kill cocks.

Q. What have you done with a book you were seen reading in the village of Flers after you ran away?

A. I had no book with me. I read none.

Q. You are trying to deceive the law on this point, for you were seen in the village of Flers with a book in your hand.

A. It may perhaps have been an old almanac, the one I described to you. I also had some sheets of paper.

Q. What were you going to do with the so-called bow and

so-called arrow you were carrying when you were
arrested?

A. I was going to try to kill birds with it.

Q. And what were you going to do with the sulphur you
had on you?

A. Use it for lighting fires in the woods.

Q. So you were going to live in the woods?

A. Yes.

Q. You also had two knives in your possession?

A. Yes, I usually kept two of them at my father's house and
of the two taken on me, I used one to grub up roots and
the other to scrape them.

Q. You are intelligent enough to know that you could not
possibly avoid the penalty inflicted by law on murderers
and parricides, how is it that this idea did not deter you
from the crimes you committed?

A. I obeyed God, I did not think there was anything wrong
in justifying his providence.

Q. You knew quite well that you were doing wrong since
you took to flight immediately after your crimes, you
eluded all search for a long time and you even made
preparations to live in the woods?

A. I retired into the woods to live there as a solitary.

Q. Why did you not retire into the woods, if that was your
intention, before murdering your relations?

A. I did not have that intention before my deed; by my
deed I was consecrated to God and it was then that I
wished to become a solitary.

Q. So far you have tried to deceive the law, you have not
given truth its due, you seemed to be in a better frame
of mind yesterday, so tell us frankly today, what cause
could have led you to murder your mother, your sister,
and your brother.

A. I wish no longer to maintain the system of defense and
the part which I have been acting. I shall tell the truth,
I did it to help my father out of his difficulties. I wished
to deliver him from an evil woman who had plagued

him continually ever since she became his wife, who was ruining him, who was driving him to such despair that he was sometimes tempted to commit suicide. I killed my sister Victoire because she took my mother's part. I killed my brother by reason of his love for my mother and my sister.

Here the accused gives in an orderly and methodical manner a very detailed account which lasts for over two hours. It is the account of the innumerable afflictions which, according to him, his father suffered from his wife. Rivière promises to communicate to us in writing what he has stated to us by word of mouth.

2. STATEMENTS BY WITNESSES

July 15, 1835
Michel Harson, fifty-seven, property owner, mayor of the commune of Aunay:
I hardly knew Pierre Rivière before his crime, I have not seen him for two years, or saw him without remarking him; I have often heard about him as a hothead, an obstinate fellow who could not be turned from a thing by the remonstrances of his father and his family if he was set on it. The young man had no friend, according to what I have heard about him, he did not go to the inn three times in his life.

I have no personal knowledge of any quarrels which there may have been between the accused's father and mother, but I have long heard that they did not get on well together. They were living apart at the time of the crime. Rivière the father is of a very mild disposition, and those who witnessed his many quarrels with his wife always said she was in the wrong.

I have not heard either before the crime or after it that the accused was blamed for acts which showed any sign of a propensity to cruelty.

I knew he was not living with his mother, but with his father, but I had no knowledge that he took part in his parents' quarrels; I had never heard that his mother was odious to him. I must point out that I live in the market town of Aunay, whereas the Rivière family lives in a hamlet a quarter of a league away, so that I have not been able to get any other information except what I have just given you.

Zéphyr Théodore Morin, thirty-one, doctor of medicine:

I had never heard of Rivière before his crime; when I saw him in the jail today, I did not recollect having ever seen him before; since his crime I have heard from people and from his father himself that he is of an obstinate character, and that when he had resolved to do something, nothing could turn him from it, not even the respect he bore his father. It is said that the accused was constantly alone and had no ties whatsoever with the children of his age.

I have no personal knowledge of any quarrels which may have arisen between the accused's father and mother, but everyone knows that they were on very bad terms, and the general opinion has always been that the wife was in the wrong.

One Hamel of Beauquay told me that a few days before the crime he had heard the accused speaking bizarrely, giving him the impression that he was either mad or was trying to pass himself off as mad in order to avoid military service.

I can give no other information; the law might perhaps obtain some from the Rivière family's neighbors in the village of la Faucterie.

Jean-Louis Suriray, forty-three, parish priest of the commune of Aunay:

The accused had always seemed to me a very gentle character, he was held to be an idiot in his village and even throughout the parish, but having talked to him sometimes, I did not think he was. On the contrary, I have always noted in him an aptitude for science and a most remarkable memory; but he seemed to have *a skew in his imagination.*

I have certainly heard people say that on occasion he chased with a scythe a child who happened to be in his yard; but people also said that it was only in jest. Certainly no one would have thought anything more of it had it not been for the murders he has committed.

It seems that several of the accused's neighbors have seen him do things at various times which could have been signs of a state of mental derangement. I can refer as witnesses to Gabriel-Pierre Retout, former mayor of Aunay, Nicolas Rivière, Charles Grelley, Lami Binet, the wife of Louis Hébert, the widow Quesnel, and Pierre Fortin.

July 16, 1835
*Gabriel-Pierre Retout, sixty-three, property owner
and farmer:*
I hardly know the accused, and I cannot give you any useful information about his character and past. I remember only that some six or seven years ago, when I was resting in a field beside a road, I heard in the road something like the voices of two men in a fury with one another and saying to one another: you are a rogue, I'll cut your throat, and other such things; I was frightened and I got up to look through a gap in the hedge. I saw Pierre Rivière all by himself walking quietly by, making the frightful sound I have mentioned. What are you about then? I said to him; the accused broke off his conversation, looked at me, and went on without answering me. When he was a short way away, I heard him begin carrying on again, but not so loudly.

Pierre Fortin, fifty, carpenter:
I knew Rivière when he was a child, he seemed very eager to learn to read and write. When he was ten to twelve years old he did not seem the same any more, he appeared

26

to become an idiot, he displayed very great obstinacy, did not answer when called; he went to church alone and came back alone, he always looked as if he were ashamed, and almost never talked to anyone, he constantly held his head down and looked askance, he sometimes swore at his horse for no good reason; I sometimes felt that his father was distressed at his character, he used to say that he would never be able to make anything of him.

To my knowledge the accused showed no signs of cruelty before his crime.

One of my children (my daughter) told me that she saw Pierre Rivière in our loft about three years ago talking loudly and twisting himself about in a strange way; she saw him kissing the ground and waving his arms about. When the accused noticed that he was observed, he ran off and climbed down the back of the building, no doubt so as not to go back through the house, and then scaled a back wall enclosing the yard.

Rivière the father is the mildest of men; in the quarrels between him and his wife it was the wife who was in the wrong.

I had not heard at all before June third that Rivière was at odds with his mother. But his father did tell me one day that the accused was more ill-disposed toward his wife than he was and that if he had his son Pierre's character, Victoire Brun would not be so easy in her mind.

That is all I can tell you.

Pierre, known as Lami Binet, fifty-nine, day-laborer:
I have worked with Rivière the father for a long time (about five or six years); Rivière the father carted pebbles which I dug from a quarry; his son helped him to put them into a cart; when the father decided the cart was fully enough loaded, he told his son, do not put any more stones in; the accused went on as if he had not heard, the father repeated it, but to no avail; he had to reach into the cart

himself and throw out the pebbles he thought were too much; but as soon as he had moved a little way off from the cart, to get his horses ready to drive away, for instance, Rivière the son put back into the cart the stones his father had thrown out. The father complained a great deal about this obstinacy and said it was a great misfortune to have a son like that.

About the same time, one day I was there, the accused's father having told him to go and water his horse, the accused put the horse to the gallop straight across the fields, the father ran after him and managed to bring him back. Half an hour later, and in spite of his parent's remonstrances, he again took the horse, though his father needed it at the time, and again rode off; Rivière the father told me that shortly before this when he was in a field with his son, the son told him that he was going to do like the horned beasts, that he was going to "scamper about"; and he said that indeed the accused set off running across the fields, he lost sight of him, and, after looking for him, found him in his stable, without any clothes on; his father asked him why he was in such a state, it seems that he answered that he had taken his shirt off because it was too wet.

I can give you no more information.

Marguerite Colleville, fifty-eight, wife of Louis Hébert, known as Laviolette, farmer:
I am a neighbor of the Rivière family, I have several times seen the accused doing senseless and foolish things; I saw him one day cutting off the heads of cabbages in his father's garden with a stick, and as he did so, he shouted out the words: right, left, left, right; he did this again on several other occasions.

Pierre Rivière often went out in the evening and passed in front of our house, crying out very loud and lamentably, ah, ah! When asked why he cried out so, he replied in a tone of voice which seemed to denote fright, euh! the devil! the devil! and forthwith began to laugh.

Three or four months ago, the accused, helped by his grandmother, was carting manure; instead of putting it at the foot of another dung heap, as his father had told him to, he set himself to drive the loaded cart to the top of the heap; the heap was about four feet high, and furthermore it was on the edge of a hollow. I told the accused that he would kill his horse. "I have said he was going to get up it," he replied, "and up he must get"; "you're going to get up there," he told his horse, "for I have said you must." And indeed he urged up his horse and managed to get the cart up, the horse was foundered, I really thought it was injured; my husband and Rivière the father ran up and promptly unharnessed the horse, which was in great danger; the father scolded the son, who made no reply.

About two years ago, one day when I sat down beside the accused to talk to his grandmother, who had just spoken to me, Rivière drew back abruptly as if very much alarmed. His grandmother said to him: "What is the matter with you?" "Eh," he replied, "the devil! the devil!" He was asked what he meant, he answered that the devil was in the fireplace. It seems that Rivière had often behaved in the same way toward other women, of whom he had seemed very much frightened.

The accused, to my knowledge, has always loved solitude, he often retired into places where he could not be seen and only answered after he had been called many times. One evening, his father looked for him for a long time, not knowing what had become of him; he found him at last in his loft. I must point out that the father, very patient and very mild by nature, never beat him.

About two years ago, the accused was alone in the house with the widow Quesnel during his parents' absence; a jay belonging to his brother Prosper to which he, who was then unwell, was much attached, was found dead one morning. The widow Quesnel accused Pierre Rivière of killing the jay, he maintained that that was not true. Pierre Rivière gathered together some small children from the village and

540

conducted a mock funeral, he buried the jay a few steps from the house; he put on the grave an inscription of which I remember these words: "Here lies the body of the jay Charlo, belonging to Prosper Rivière"; there were some more words which I do not remember; the accused was then eighteen years old.

I cannot give any other information, I will only add that the accused was considered in the village to be an idiot.

Geneviève Rivière, thirty-six, widow of Jean Quesnel, housewife:

Rivière was constantly accustomed to retire into out-of-the-way places, he avoided company so much that when *going to church or coming back, he did not go by the same path as the other people*; he talked to himself with his head lifted, as if speaking to the trees; sometimes he uttered terrifying cries. When asked what he was doing, he sometimes answered that he was conversing with the fairies, sometimes that he was conversing with the devil. Several times when he was by the fireplace, he called to me: come and see, come and see, when I went over, he said to me: see the devil there. Other times, he said: see, look at Mourelle grinding her teeth (Mourelle was an old mare belonging to his father; he often talked of her). His parents concealed his bizarre behavior as much as they could; he seemed to be afraid of cats and hens, and above all of women; often when I approached him, he drew back abruptly as if frightened; if I asked him the reason for this behavior, he replied with a peal of laughter. It was the reply he made whenever he was asked questions about his peculiar doings or was reproached for them.

Two weeks before the crime Rivière called to me as he was passing by my door: what do you want? I asked him. I am going to see the devil, he answered; he burst out laughing loudly and went on toward a spinney owned by his father.

Two years ago, I was keeping the Rivière house during his parents' absence; his brother Prosper had asked me to take great care of a jay to which he was much attached. I told Pierre to give him something to eat, which he did in my presence; the jay seemed to me to be quite well, at five o'clock next morning I found it dead in its cage. I accused Pierre of killing it, he said that was not so, but he laughed as he denied it; his tone and his looks convinced me that I was right in accusing him. That evening he gathered together some little children, made a wooden cross, and buried the jay after going through the motions of a funeral ceremony.

For nearly two years, Rivière worked in his loft, using a knife and some small tools he got from the neighbors and some pieces of wood whose use one could not guess at; however, my children told me that it was a little like a gun; Rivière named this instrument "Calibine." He went one day, followed by the village children, and buried it in a meadow. Two or three months later he went, again followed by children, and dug it up again: this latter scene occurred about two years ago.

Victor Marie, twenty-six, servant to Charles Grelley:
About two years ago, I saw Pierre Rivière threaten one of his brothers, who died eight or nine months ago, with a scythe he was holding; the child was weeping and crying out; What are you doing? I asked Pierre. Pierre stopped pointing the scythe at his brother, but did not answer me; the child said to me: Pierre said he wanted to cut off my legs.

The accused, to my knowledge, often made a game of frightening children. One day, about a year ago, he took the son of Charles Grelley, in whose house I am a servant, and carried him into the manger where his horse was feeding, saying he was going to give him to his horse to eat; the child came back to the house in tears and immediately told what had happened: the child had been so frightened that for a long time he did not dare pass Rivière's door.

I have heard people say that the accused often displayed cruelty toward birds and frogs, he flayed the frogs and nailed the birds alive to trees.

Michel Nativel, thirty-eight, tow maker:
Five or six years ago, I was at the Rivières' and found Prosper Rivière, then six or seven years old, sitting in front of the fire on a chair, his feet tied to the pothook and beneath his feet a flame that was drawing and would soon burn him; the child was already feeling the heat and was weeping; his father's aunt, who had her back to the fireplace, was so deaf that she heard nothing; Pierre Rivière was walking round the room laughing heartily, a strange laugh, the laugh of idiots. I hastened to untie or cut the cord binding the child's feet to the pothook, the fire had already singed his stockings, and I saw that if I had not arrived in time, the unfortunate child's legs would soon have been burned. I fiercely upbraided Pierre (since the child had told me that it was Pierre who had tied him up) for what he had done, he did not answer me and went on laughing strangely.

On several occasions I saw him laughing, but always with an idiot's laugh, for a quarter of an hour on end.

He was accustomed to try to frighten children, and I was afraid he would hurt them; when I went away, I always told people to take great care not to leave them in his way, I had several times seen him put children on the edge of the well and frighten them by telling them, I am going to drop you in or I am going to throw you in.

Rivière did not like cats, one day he killed one belonging to me and he used a dung hook to do it; I do not know what he did with the body, but I have heard his brothers and sisters say that he amused himself by torturing animals and when he had killed one he set to laughing at it like an idiot. I have been told that he crucified frogs and young birds and then stood in front of these poor beasts staring at them and laughing.

Pierre Armand Quevillon, twenty-four, farmer:
   I have often seen Rivière laughing without any reason, I have seen him rolling on the ground, and when he was asked why he was doing this, his only answer was to laugh; I have not known Rivière long. That is all I know.

Louis Hamel, fifty-eight, pumphand:
   I happened to see the accused about three weeks ago; it seemed to me that there was something extraordinary about the way he looked at me that betokened *madness*, he refused to sit down at table with us, though he was to help us that day with his horse. A rope had to be tied to the top of a tree we wanted to fell; I said to the accused jokingly, it is you Pierre who are going to tie the rope; I hardly supposed he could do that, the more so as rain was falling, and the workman who had climbed other trees to tie the rope would himself have refused to climb that one at that time. Rivière, however, did not need further urging and nimbly climbed to the top of the beech, which was thirty foot high and almost without branches; he climbed a good way beyond the point where the rope had to be fixed and climbed down the tree very fast, letting himself fall ten or twelve feet. What he had done confirmed my idea that he was mad.
   That afternoon as he was driving his cart, I noticed that he was ill-treating his horses for no reason; when we got to the top of the hill at Roncamps, I noticed that the tree on Rivière's cart had slipped on the horses' side and that if the cart went down the slope (which is very steep) like that, the horses would be killed or maimed. I shouted to him to stop; instead of obeying, he whipped up his horses and he was so obstinate about it that I had to fling myself on him to stop him; to all my upbraidings he answered only by laughing, with his head down and with the air of a

33

madman. My son has told me that when he went to school with Rivière, he saw him crucify frogs and birds and stand before them laughing until they were dead; he habitually carried nails and brads in his pocket for this purpose.

July 17, 1835
Charles Grelley, forty-nine, merchant:
I can give you very little information about Rivière's character and past, for where I live is fairly far from his family's. I will tell you only that he was generally held to be mad and that when people talked of him, they commonly called him Rivière's idiot. I once saw him, he was then ten or twelve years old, tear his pocket handkerchief by beating it against a thorn, he did it as if he was shredding tow. I have heard (but I have no personal knowledge of it) that he amused himself by torturing frogs and field mice when he found them in the meadows.

3. SECOND INTERROGATION OF PIERRE RIVIÈRE (JULY 18, 1835)

We, Exupère Legrain, examining judge as aforesaid, assisted by M. Bidaux, clerk of court,

Had brought before us from prison the man Rivière and interrogated him as follows:

Q. Do the manuscript which you have handed to me and the composition on which you have been engaged since your interrogation on the ninth day of this month contain nothing but the truth?

A. Yes.

Q. There are some facts which you have not mentioned in your memoir; for example, you have not said that one day you tied to the pothook when there was a fair blaze in the hearth the legs of your brother Prosper, and his stockings were scorched and he would probably have suffered a very dangerous burn if a neighbor had not cut the cord attaching his feet to the pothook?

A. That has been exaggerated: my brother was not hurt at all and was not in danger; it is possible that I tried to frighten him, but that was all. I must point out that I was accustomed to warm myself like that by putting my feet in a cord which I tied to the pothook; my little brother wanted to do the same and I helped him when he was seven.

Q. It seems that you long amused yourself by frightening the little children who came near you?

A. Yes, that often happened, but I did not mean them any harm.

Q. That often happened; so one may think that you took pleasure in seeing their fright and hearing their cries?

A. That amused me a little; but I repeat I did not wish to do them any harm.

Q. The investigation has proved against you certain acts which would denote an instinct of ferocity in your character. As you yourself confess in your manuscript, you have often crucified frogs and young birds; what is the feeling that led you to do such things?

A. I took pleasure in them.

Q. You took a very considerable pleasure, since it is established that you nearly always carried nails or brads in your pockets in order to procure an enjoyment for which you were avid whenever you chanced to find one. It is even said that you spent hours on end contemplating your victims and laughing as you watched their torments?

A. It is true that I amused myself with that; it is possible that I laughed, yet I did not take any very great pleasure in it.

Q. Did you not one day threaten one of your brothers that

you would cut off his legs with a scythe you were carrying; it was your brother Jean, now dead?

A. I never intended to do him any harm; I do not remember the circumstance you speak of, but if it is true, it was only a joke of mine.

Q. It seems that you have a horror of cats and chickens?

A. Yes, I have long loathed cats and chickens and all animals in general and that out of a hatred of bestiality.

Q. You have always been of an extremely obstinate disposition; why did you try, some weeks before your crime, in spite of all urgings against it, to make your horse harnessed to a loaded cart mount a heap of dung, when there was no need and when it was obvious that you would hurt or kill your horse?

A. I was convinced that it was possible to get the cart up that heap of dung and the work would consequently go faster.

Q. At about the same period, when carting tree trunks which, when you had reached the top of a slope, had become so disarranged that they threatened to crush your horses, did you not insist on descending the slope without changing the loading of your cart in any way; did you not ill-treat your horses to make them go in spite of the advice of M. Hamel who saw the imminent danger that threatened your horses and had warned you about it?

A. That is not true; I stopped my cart of my own accord when I noticed that it was badly loaded.

Q. About two years ago, you were cruel enough, it seems, to kill a jay belonging to your brother Prosper to which the unfortunate child, who was then unwell, was greatly attached.

A. I had no part at all in the jay's death; I had fed it, the bird was too young to feed itself.

Q. You were then at least eighteen years old; why at that age did you do something which only children normally

36

do; accompanied by little children from the village, and
conducting a mock funeral ceremony, you went and
buried the jay and even composed an epitaph for it?

A. That is true, I amused myself by doing that.

Q. Will you tell me what the epitaph was?

A. It was in these words:

*"Here lies the body of Prosper's jay Charlot, native
of the lower part of the great Yos, died . . ."*

I had put on the other side of the paper:

*"A while since among the living he was numbered.
Of the care of a human being he was the sole object.
Hope said that one day for his language
All the peoples amazed would come to pay him homage.
And he is dead! . . ."*

Q. Did you not tell your father one day that you were
going to "scamper about" like the horned beasts?

A. Yes, sir, it was very hot, I told my father that and ran
off home to get a drink; it was a joke of mine.

Q. But it has been said that your father looked for you that
day for a long time and found you in the stable stark
naked?

A. That was another day; my clothes had been soaked
through by a thunderstorm and as the house door was
not open yet, for my parents had not yet come back, I
undressed in the stable.

Q. Why did you call an instrument of which you speak in
your manuscript, an instrument you intended for killing birds, a Calibene?

A. I imagined that word; I tried hard to find a name that
could not mean any other instrument.

Q. Why did you go and bury that instrument, followed
by the village children?

A. When I buried it I was alone; when I went to dig it
up again, I told the village children what I was going
to do and they followed me.

Q. But why did you bury it?

A. I had worked on it for a long time, I did not want to destroy it and, so as to keep it, I put it under the earth.

Q. Do you recognize the bill I am showing you?

A. Yes, sir, it is the instrument of my crime.

Q. How, you wretch, does not the sight of this instrument cause you to shed a tear?

A. I am resigned to death.

Q. Do you at least regret committing these fearful crimes, steeping yourself in the blood of part of your family? Do you truly feel some remorse?

A. Yes, sir, an hour after my crime my conscience told me that I had done evil and I would not have done it over again.

This interrogation having been read over to the said Rivière, he said that his replies are the truth, and he signed it together with us and the clerk; the investigation is herewith concluded.

4. APPLICATION TO PRE-TRIAL COURT FOR COMMITTAL

The District Prosecutor Royal at the civil court at Vire, having taken cognizance of the criminal proceedings instituted against Pierre Rivière, herein set forth:

On the third day of June last a serious crime was committed in the commune of Aunay. The officers of the law proceeded forthwith to the scene of the occurrence and found that Anne Victoire Brion, wife of Rivière, farmer at the village of la Faucterie in the commune of Aunay, Jules Rivière his son, and Victoire Rivière his daughter had been murdered in broad daylight in their house by means of a sharp instrument with a cutting edge. Every part of the body of the three victims was slashed in several directions with broad and deep wounds, the blows on the unfortunate woman Rivière had been struck with such force that bones and muscles appeared reduced to a pulp, the doctors proceeded to perform an autopsy of her body and found a female fetus which had reached about six and a half months of gestation.

The perpetrator of this crime was soon known, for the woman Marie Rivière whose dwelling neighbors that of Anne Brion, wife of Rivière, had seen the murderer holding his sister Victoire Rivière by the hair and striking her with a pruning bill several blows on the head which stretched her dead at his feet. She cried out: Oh wretched boy what are you about! but her cries could not arrest the crime, for it had been consummated in less than a minute.

At the same moment two neighbors named Jean Postel and Victoire Aimée Lerat, wife of Jean André, saw Pierre Rivière leave his house by the glazed door giving on to the local road; he was holding a bloodstained bill and told them: "I have just delivered my father from all his tribulations. I know that they will put me to death, but no matter."

The gendarmerie immediately set about seeking the murderer, but were not able to locate him. It was not until the second day of July that he was arrested in the district of Falaise by the sergeant of gendarmerie at Langannerie.

Questioned by the examining judge at Vire about the motive which had led him to murder his mother, his brother, and his sister, Pierre Rivière replied that God had appeared to him in the company of angels and had ordered him to justify his providence. But when questioned further Rivière abandoned this method of defense and stated that he had wished to deliver his father from an evil woman who was driving him to such despair that he was sometimes tempted to commit suicide. He added that he had killed his sister Victoire because she took his mother's part, and he gave as the motive for the murder of his brother the latter's love for his mother and his sister. He then gave in an orderly and methodical manner a very circumstantial account of the innumerable afflictions which, according to him, his father had suffered from his wife since the first days of his marriage. At a second interrogation Pierre Rivière persisted in this method of defense which he developed at great length in a memoir which has been placed among the exhibits in evidence.

The investigation has gone carefully into Rivière's past, and it has been found that from his earliest youth he had the cruellest propensities. He took pleasure in frightening children and torturing animals. He was accustomed to carry nails and brads in his pockets for the purpose of attaching the animals he tortured to trees, and lastly he admits that he had even invented an instrument of torture to kill birds.

Education was not able to correct Rivière's evil propensities, for he received none; he learned only to read and write, and no one took the trouble to set his mind on the right road. Gifted with a remarkable memory, he seems to have drawn from his reading only examples calculated to justify his deed and to cause it to be a title to fame in men's eyes. His intelligence has degenerated so grossly that he has raised murder to the level of a system and has made a logic of the practice of crime.

Rivière is not a religious monomaniac as he tried to make out at first; nor is he an idiot, as some witnesses seemed to suppose him to be; so that in the eyes of the law he can only be regarded as a cruel being who has followed the promptings of evil, because, like all heinous criminals, he stifled the voice of conscience and did not struggle hard enough to control the propensities of his evil character.

Wherefore the District Prosecutor Royal requests that it may so please the Court in chambers to issue, in accordance with articles 133 and 134 of the Code of Criminal Procedure and 296 and 299 of the Penal Code, an order for the detention of the aforesaid Pierre Rivière, it having been shown to satisfaction that he did on the third day of June kill and murder (1) Anne Brion, wife of Rivière, his mother, (2) Jules Rivière his brother, (3) Victoire Rivière his sister and to order that the documents in the case be transmitted to the Regional Prosecutor at the Royal Court at Caen.

Done at the District Prosecutor's Office this day, July 20, 1835

The District Prosecutor Royal

5. DECISION OF THE PRE-TRIAL COURT

The Royal Court at Caen (sitting as a pre-trial court) hereby issues the following decision:

Having considered the report addressed by the District Prosecutor Royal to the said Court on the proceedings against Pierre Rivière, aged twenty, farmer, residing at Aunay, by the examining judge at the court of first instance of the district of Vire relating to a homicide with malice aforethought,

Having duly considered all the documents in the case, which were read out by the clerk of court and which have been placed on the table together with a memoir produced by the accused,

The district prosecutor and the clerk of court having withdrawn,

Having likewise considered the arraignment signed on behalf of the district prosecutor by M. Lustigue, his assistant, which is attached to the documents in evidence,

And having consulted together,

Considering that the weight of the evidence shows sufficiently that Pierre Rivière may be accused, *primo*, that he did on the day of the third of June in the year one thousand eight hundred and thirty-five in the commune of Aunay then and there wilfully commit a homicide on and against the person of Victoire Brion, wife of Rivière, his mother,

that he did commit the said homicide of his malice aforethought,

secundo, that he did on the day aforesaid wilfully kill Jules Rivière his brother and Victoire Rivière his sister,

that he did commit the said homicides of his malice aforethought,

and that the acts are termed crimes in articles two hundred and eighty-five, two hundred and eighty-six, two hundred and eighty-seven, and two hundred and eighty-nine of the Penal Code within the competence of the courts of assize,

acceding to the request by the district prosecutor,

now therefore the Court hereby orders that the said Rivière be committed for trial and that he be transferred to the Court of Assize of the department of Calvados at its next session at Caen, for which purpose a bill of indictment shall be drawn up by the regional prosecutor,

likewise orders that all documents and writs be sent to the registry of the Royal Court at Caen and that the warrant for the apprehension of the said Rivière issued in chambers by the civil court of the district of Vire be promptly and duly executed,

the terms of the said warrant being given hereunder:

On the twentieth day of July in the year one thousand eight hundred and thirty-five the court of first instance of the district of Vire sitting in chambers issued the following order:

Having heard the report by the examining judge on the proceedings instituted by the District Prosecutor Royal against Pierre Rivière charged with the crimes hereinafter set forth:

On the third day of June last a number of horrible crimes spread terror and dismay in the commune of Aunay. A son had murdered his mother several months pregnant. A brother had murdered his brother and his sister. The culprit had been seen dispatching his unfortunate sister on the threshold of the door of the house in which his victims lived, though she was seeking to escape and uttering lamentable cries; somewhat further off, still holding the pruning bill he had just used to slaughter three of the members of his family, he said to one of the neighbors as he was passing: I have delivered my father from all his tribulations. I know that I am to die, but I have sacrificed my life for him.

This murderer, this parricide was Pierre Rivière, aged twenty, considered by all those who knew him as an idiot. He was commonly called "Rivière's idiot" or "Rivière's madman." Many characteristics were reported of him which, to judge from what his neighbors and the friends of his family have said, denoted a complete lack of intelligence or even aggravated mental derangement.

Be this opinion as it may, the accused has certainly given the lie to it by the many tokens of intelligence and sagacity he has evinced since his arrest; Rivière, though, to judge by appearances, he had originally resolved to give himself up to justice, though he had been to Vire several times while the gendarmerie patrols were very actively trying to find and apprehend him; Rivière, though, if he is to be believed, he went to meet gendarmes when he saw any of them on his way, was not arrested until the second day of July, even though he had traveled through most of the districts which constitute the department of Calvados for twenty-nine days without shelter and without bread, feeding on roots and shellfish, traveling on roads used by a great many people, almost without concealment and never being molested, and spending the nights in the woods; Rivière, having been brought to the jail at Vire on the seventh day of July, was interrogated on the ninth. At first he adopted the method of defense which would have probably secured his acquittal on the grounds of insanity if he had maintained it to the end, supported as it was by the reputation for idiocy and feeble-mindedness he had gained among the inhabitants of Aunay

43

by some extravagant but misunderstood actions. He claimed that he had received the command to kill his mother, his brother, and his sister directly from God and for the purpose of justifying His providence. It was objected to him that God never orders a crime, he replied with quotations from the Bible perfectly adapted to the position he was trying to adopt; for three hours he persevered in this method of defense which he developed with a logic surprising in a peasant boy who had received no education or at least had learned only to read and write. Finally, however, when pressed by questions, he admitted that he had hitherto been trying to deceive the law in order to give the impression that he was afflicted with mental derangement. He further stated that he had killed his mother because she was constantly tormenting his father, was ruining him, and was driving him to despair, his sister because she took her mother's part, his brother because he loved his sister and his mother. Later he stated that he had murdered his brother because he wished to draw his father's hatred upon himself and to relieve him beforehand of the very slightest regret at his loss.

During his interrogation, after he abandoned his claim that he had been urged to crime by divine inspiration, Rivière asked permission to set out, and did set out in an orderly and methodical manner of which he could certainly not have been supposed capable, the many quarrels which according to him had arisen between his father and his mother, she being ill-tempered, shrewish, vicious, and generally hated, he being a mild and peaceable man loved and esteemed by all.

At a second interrogation, on the nineteenth day of July, Rivière maintained his later admissions and the next day, the twentieth, he handed to the examining judge for inclusion with the documents of the case a written document of some fifty pages on which he had worked ever since he had entered the jail at Vire. This document is in two parts; in the first the very circumstantial details of his mother's continual harassment of his father; in the second a sketch of the character of the accused, a sketch drawn with a vigor which is simply astonishing and makes it most regrettable that Rivière has by an atrocious act rendered henceforth useless to Society the gifts so liberally imparted to him by nature without any assistance whatever from education; a remarkable memory, a great aptitude for the sciences, a lively and strong imagination coupled with an eagerness for instruction and the achievement of glory. In this latter part of his memoir Rivière states that he conceived the project of his crimes a month before he committed them and that for this purpose he had sharpened the bill he used. This bill was found in accordance with his directions and has been placed among the exhibits.

Thirteen witnesses were heard . . .

In these circumstances the documents in the case were transmitted to the district prosecutor's office on the twentieth day of July, and that office stated its conclusions on the same day and date.

Thereafter, the documents having been read out,

Whereas it appears that the evidence shows a sufficient presumption that on the third day of June Pierre Rivière did feloniously and wilfully and of his malice aforethought kill and murder Marie Anne Victoire Brion, wife of Rivière, his mother, Victoire Rivière his sister, and Jules Rivière his brother,

Whereas the facts constitute the crime defined in articles two hundred and eighty-five, two hundred and eighty-six, two hundred and eighty-seven, and two hundred and eighty-nine of the Penal Code,

Considering articles one hundred and thirty-three and one hundred and thirty-four of the Code of Criminal Procedure,

Now therefore this Court, in conformity with the conclusions of the office of the district prosecutor, hereby orders that the documents of the investigation shall be transmitted to the regional prosecutor at the Royal Court at Caen and that Pierre Rivière, aged twenty, farmer, born in the commune of Courvaudon, residing in the commune of Aunay, cantonal administrative center, district of Vire, department of Calvados, height one meter six hundred and twenty millimeters, hair and eyebrows black and scanty, forehead narrow, nose ordinary, eyes reddish-brown, face oval, mouth ordinary, chin round, beard light chestnut, complexion swarthy, gaze furtive, head aslant, be apprehended and taken into custody in the jail of this district until the Royal Court shall otherwise order.

Given at Vire in chambers of the Court aforesaid on the days aforesaid, Maîtres Legrain, examining judge, acting as president in the absence on leave of the regular judge; Hibert, judge; Ozanne, barrister-at-law and first assistant judge, sitting; M. Robert, Prosecutor Royal, attending, and assisted by Théodore Le Bouleux, assistant to the clerk of court,

And further orders that the said Rivière be taken to the prison situate at Caen in accordance with article two hundred and thirty-three of the Code of Procedure, that he be entered on the prison calendar of reception in the custody of the said prison and that a copy of these presents as likewise of the bill of indictment be served upon him.

Done at Caen, July 25, 1835

6. BILL OF INDICTMENT

THE REGIONAL PROSECUTOR
at the Royal Court of Caen

Hereby declares that in a decision delivered on July 25, 1835, this Court sitting as a pre-trial court declared that there are good and sufficient grounds for accusing one Pierre Rivière, aged twenty, born at Courvaudon, residing at Aunay, of acts termed crimes by the law and that the said Rivière was committed to the Assize Court of Calvados, which will hold its next session at Caen.

The Regional Prosecutor has re-examined the documents in the case in the light of this decision and hereby declares that the following facts emerge therefrom: Between eleven o'clock and noon on the third day of June of this year Victoire Brion, wife of Rivière, Jules Rivière, a child of eight, and Victoire Rivière, aged about eighteen, were cruelly murdered at their residence in the commune of Aunay. The last-named was slaughtered before the eyes of a woman neighbor, for she had dragged her murderer to the house door in her struggle with him. The perpetrator of this triple crime was none other than the son of one of the victims and the brother of the other two. Taking advantage of the moment of panic caused by the cries of the first witness of his crime, he went off calmly, apparently not even bent on flight, still armed with the bloodstained ax he had just used. He had disappeared before there was any thought of securing his person, and it was not known in what direction he had gone. The nearest authorities were immediately summoned, and with the aid of two doctors they recorded the state in which the three corpses had been found. The mother was stretched out near the hearth, and everything around her testified to the fact that she had been taken unawares while busied with her housework; her head lay in a pool of blood, the bones in it were smashed as were those of the face, which was horribly disfigured and bore the marks of deep wounds. The vertebrae of the neck were broken, and the head remained attached to the trunk only by the muscles on the left side and a few shreds of skin; everything, therefore, conspired to show the violence with which he had wielded a heavy instrument with a cutting edge against her. This unfortunate woman was nearly seven months pregnant. Near her was lying the corpse of her young son, and several deep wounds in the head, such as the near-severance of a part of the crown of the skull, likewise showed that he had succumbed to similar violent blows; several blows had also left their mark on the shoulders and the nape of the neck. Lastly, near these two corpses was that of the Rivière daughter; her lace bobbins overset and her clogs left near the window of the room showed that she had attempted to flee; the disorder of her clothing and some of her hair torn out and lying beside her testified to the struggle she had put up. Several blows from the same instrument had cut deep into the throat, and the face was also furrowed with broad slashes. There was no doubt, therefore, about the causes of death or the perpetrator of the crime, but what motives could have impelled the accused to such an atrocious deed? At first the impossibility of accounting for them helped to gain credence for the opinion that he had yielded to an access of raving madness. The bizarre behavior of a character universally considered to be sullen and unsociable and certain circumstances, which were little noticed when they seemed insignificant and were promptly distorted by imperfect recollection and by prejudice against him, soon rendered this opinion general. After wandering about for a month, Rivière was arrested in the commune of Langannerie; he himself had aroused suspicion by his manner; he made no resistance and did not try to conceal his identity. This apparent unconcern and his admission of his crime, with explanations which seemed to reveal mental derangement, appeared for a moment to support the general opinion of him. But the role of feigned madness was hard to sustain. There were already indications of his intelligence in everything that did not bear on the method of defense he had adopted, and the method itself smacked of calculation, so even at his first interrogation the accused gave up representing himself as a religious fanatic to whom God who had appeared and urged his crime and proceeded to the most circumstantial admissions. He had killed his mother to avenge his father for the wrongs she had long been doing him and so to ensure his tranquillity; his sister because she loved her mother and had always associated herself with the wrongs her mother had done her father; his brother because he loved both of them. These crimes he had meditated, calculated, and prepared, and his language authenticates his full and entire knowledge of what he did and of his situation; some observations on the character, propensities, and habits of the accused leave no doubt about this.

Pierre Rivière is twenty years old; from his childhood he gave signs of a savage character which to this day has led him to avoid young persons of his age and seek solitude. Serious and reserved, the expression of his physiognomy like his attitudes shows the habit of reflection; he speaks little—only when he is questioned—and his answers are brief and precise. Gifted with a memory on which everything is readily engraved and from which nothing fades, he attracted notice among his fellows by his aptitude for learning, equalled only by his avidity for instruction. He has always shown the utmost eagerness to take advantage of every opportunity to read books of every sort, and his taste for reading has often led him to devote his nights to it.

His predisposition to cruelty has at all times been revealed by his amusements; they customarily consisted in acts of barbarity to animals; he loved to subject them to tortures, the sight of which filled him with glee; certain facts which testify to a violent and coldly cruel disposition have also been established; furthermore he is so headstrong and obstinate in what he wills that no one at all, not even his father, has ever been able to sway him.

Such is the accused, taciturn and reflective, with an ardent, cruel, and violent imagination.

All his life he had witnessed his parents' domestic quarrels; and—here he concurs with local opinion—he attributed to his mother's conduct the tribulations that made his father's life a continuous misery; so he had taken the side of his father with whom he lived for a long time in a home apart from his mother's. These circumstances led the accused to harbor a hatred for her which repentance and remorse have not wholly stifled to this day. Daily witnessing his father's distresses and knowing their cause, the thought of putting an end to them occurred to him. Once it had taken hold of an imagination somber and accustomed to hold firmly to the object which took possession of it, this thought never left him; it became the subject of his constant preoccupation, his solitary meditations. Ceaselessly beset as he was by this lethal purpose, all the powers of his ill-organized brain, heightened by reading books which he misunderstood, were directed toward a purpose and its fulfillment, and his sanguinary instinct was to indicate to him the frightful means to accomplish it.

The death of his mother was thus resolved upon, as well as those of the other victims. For several days the lethal weapon had been prepared and at hand. Twice, however, as he himself narrates, his ferocious courage failed him; but at length, on the third of June, after watching all morning for the favorable opportunity, he consummated his crime, less extraordinary perhaps than its perpetrator's character and narrated by him as cold-bloodedly as it was conceived.

Rivière was visited and observed in prison by a qualified doctor. In this professional practitioner's opinion nothing about him reveals any sign of mental derangement, and even if his flight after his crime and this attempt of his to pass for a madman in order to evade the ends of justice did not evidence on his part his perfect understanding of what he was doing and of the consequences which must ensue, his rationality would yet be quite evident from a very detailed memoir written by him since his arrest. No doubt many of the thoughts expressed in it denote a deplorable aberration of ideas and judgment, but it is far from being the work of a madman, and its style is not the least surprising thing in this singular composition.

In consequence of these facts established by the documents in the case the said Pierre Rivière is hereby charged (1) that he did on the third day of June 1835, in the commune of Aunay, then and there feloniously and wilfully commit a homicide in and upon the person of Victoire Brion wife of Rivière, his mother,

That he did commit the homicide aforesaid of his malice aforethought

(2) That he did on the day and at the place aforesaid

kill and murder Jules Rivière, his brother, and Victoire Rivière, his sister.

That he did commit the homicides aforesaid of his malice aforethought.

> At the Regional Prosecutor's office
> at Caen, on this day July 28, 1835

7. NEWSPAPER ARTICLES

Le Pilote du Calvados, July 17, 1835

Pierre Rivière was transferred to Vire two or three days after his arrest at Langannerie. The investigation has nearly been completed and will shortly be sent to the criminal division of the Assize Court.

It is confidently stated by some that this murderer is a kind of religious maniac or is trying to pass as such. With very limited mental faculties and a somber character unsuited to his age, he claims that in consummating his triple crime he was merely obeying a divine command. It seems that this wretched youth eagerly read books of devotion and that it was from this reading that he derived the fanaticism that led him to crime for lack of sufficient discernment. It seems, too, that the guilty thinking which he has so fearfully put into execution was the result of a fixed idea, a species of monomania under which he had been laboring for some time.

In any event, the judicial investigation will bring out this young madman's background, the degree of his intelligence, and the fatal inspiration which impelled him to lay criminal hands on three members of his family.

P.S. We learn from the latest information from Vire about the Pierre Rivière case that after a long interrogation by the examining judge he has ceased to represent himself as a religious maniac and has confessed that he was motivated to crime by the idea of avenging his father for the conduct which, according to public opinion, Rivière's wife had long displayed.

Le Pilote du Calvados, July 29, 1835

It is said that Pierre Rivière, the author of a triple murder of the members of his family, has transmitted to the judges in charge of the proceedings instituted as a result of his crime a very remarkable memoir. This young man, it was at first confidently stated, was a kind of idiot who was presumed to have acted without properly understanding the nature of his ferocious act. If what is said of his memoir is to be believed, Rivière is probably far from devoid of intelligence, and the explanations he has given to the judges, not in order to exculpate himself (for it seems that he confesses both the crime and the intent) but in order to set out the reasons which led him to his criminal act, prove on the contrary that the man who appears so simple-minded was in reality far from it. It is stated that the memoir of which we are speaking is wholly rational and written in such a way that it is impossible to say which is the more astonishing, its author's memoir or his crime.

(Article reproduced in the *Gazette des Tribunaux* on August 1, 1835.)

3

The Memoir

TRANSLATOR'S NOTE

IN THE ORIGINAL FRENCH EDITION of this book, Pierre Rivière's "memoir" was transcribed with the capital letters and punctuation exactly as they are in the manuscript. A few changes were, however, made to facilitate reading.

The problems connected with transcription were commented upon in a footnote to the first section of the "Notes." This commentary may, however, be more pertinent at this point. It reads, in substance:

"An interesting question is why the original form of the manuscript, with its shaky orthography and punctuation and its vagueness in the use of capitals, was left as it stood when it was printed in 1835. Historians who have seen manuscripts of the late 18th or early 19th centuries, in particular manuscripts by doctors, who were after all persons of good education, know that their orthography is frequently very idiosyncratic. After all, too, the 'prescriptive and Republican schoolteacher' had not yet appeared on the scene to standardize the formal details of writing. But the printer's foreman had already begun to set type in accordance with his own uniform rules for spelling, punctuation, and the use of capitals when such manuscripts came to be printed. Why, then, were these rules not employed with Rivière's manuscript? Was the idea to show that it really was by a peasant, the parodic act of someone miming a discourse and making a muddle of it because it does not fall within the normal province of the written word? At all events, it is symptomatic that the version we have was so badly transcribed at the time that Pierre Rivière is constantly saddled with mistakes and incoherences which are belied by a comparison with the manuscript itself. Almost any sort of nonsensical errors could be ascribed to a peasant; hence the copyist or the printer's foreman constantly fabricated more of them than there really were. They made such a confusion of commas and periods (though they are legible enough in the manuscript) that the sentences become so inextricable as in fact to make up an *insensate* text. The problem was, therefore, to decide whether we should leave the text within the province of its own special status by accurately preserving its spontaneity or whether it, like the other materials in the dossier, should be entitled to be given a correct form. But would that not mean *correcting* it? In the end we decided (but we may well have been mistaken) that time itself had conferred upon this text a sovereignty so to speak empowering it to come forward in its own person without any lingering prejudice still attaching to it."

Particulars and explanation
of
the occurrence
on June 3 in Aunay at the village of la Faucterie
written by
the author of this deed

I, Pierre Rivière, having slaughtered my mother, my sister, and my brother, and wishing to make known the motives which led me to this deed, have written down the whole of the life which my father and my mother led together since their marriage. I was witness of the greater part of the facts, and they are written at the end of this history; as regards the beginning I heard it recounted by my father when he talked of it with his friends and with his mother, with me, and with those who had knowledge of it. I shall then tell how I resolved to commit this crime, what my thoughts were at the time, and what was my intention. I shall also say what went on in my mind after doing this deed, the life I led among people, and the places I was in after the crime up to my arrest and what were the resolutions I took. All this work will be very crudely styled, for I know only how to read and write; but all I ask is that what I mean shall be understood, and I have written it all down as best I can.

Summary of the tribulations and afflictions which my father suffered at the hands of my mother from 1813 to 1835

My father was the second of the three sons of Jean Rivière and Marianne Cordel, he was brought up in honesty and religion, he was always of a mild and peaceable disposition and affable toward all, and so was esteemed by all who knew him. He was due for the draft in 1813. At that time, as is known, all the lads went; after the quota had once been filled, some time later they looked over the numbers again and took the rest; but those who had married before this second call-up were exempted if they had done so. My uncle, my father's elder brother, was serving in the army, and it was feared that in spite of his high number my father might still be obliged to go, so it was decided that he should marry. An official who was a friend of his promised to warn him as soon as his quota was filled, but advised him in any case to take a betrothed in the meantime. Through his acquaintance with François le Comte at Courvaudon my father went and asked for Victoire Brion; their ages and fortunes more or less matched, she was promised him and my father visited her for six months. Then he was warned that it was time he married, but my mother's parents were no longer in favor of it, their sons were dead in the service and they feared being distressed yet again for their son-in-law. My father then objected that if they were going to call it off they should have done so before, for now they would leave him in straits. My mother agreed with what my father said and wept because her parents opposed their union. When my father saw her weeping he thought to himself: she loves me because she is weeping. Finally her parents made up their mind to it, and they went to sign the contract in the presence of Maître Le Bailly notary at Aunay. The clauses of this contract stipulated that husband and wife should have a joint estate comprising all movable property and immovable property present and future, that if one of the spouses predeceased the other and no children were living at that time, the survivor should enjoy the whole of the estate owned by the spouse during his lifetime, and if there were children, should enjoy his own properties only and the children the other half; that the father and the mother of the future wife shall contribute to the marriage settlement and that she herself shall contribute any movable and immovable property she may inherit from her father's and mother's estate; that the said properties shall be managed and administered by the husband in conformity with the law concerning the dowry system. The inalienability of these properties as specified in the civil code is also mentioned in the contract. It stipulated further that the husband's marriage portion was valued at 100 francs and the wife's portion consisted of linen and personal effects of several sorts, a cupboard with two doors, a bed, bed linen and several other articles mentioned, the whole valued at the sum of four hundred francs. That on the marriage day the said portion of the joint estate shall be deemed as constituting a receipt for the joint estate. That the said wife under the aforesaid authorization reserves the right to renounce the settlement in the form of joint estate at any time or in any manner should the dissolution of the said settlement occur and shall recover exempt from all debts and encumbrances her portion aforementioned as well as everything which she may inherit, of which she shall give a satisfactory inventory in evidence. That should such dissolution of the joint estate occur in the lifetime of the spouses, the survivor shall in no way be deprived of his rights aforementioned to enjoy the personal properties of the spouse during his lifetime. Such were the clauses of the contract. A few days later they were married by civil ceremony. And thereafter in church. At the time of these latter acts my mother was not of the same mind as formerly; they held no wedding banquet, and on their marriage night they did not bed together, because the recruiting board had not yet arrived, and my mother said: he has only to get me with child and then leave, and then what will become of me? As this was reasonable, my father did not compel her to bed with him. A few days later the board sat, my father produced his marriage certificate, and owing to some delay, he stayed in Caen three days longer than he expected. During this time my mother did not come to Aunay to see what was happening. On his return from Caen my father stopped at Courvaudon, and this was the first time he bedded with her. I will explain here how my family was composed, my father's and my mother's. In my father's house at Aunay there were my grandfather and my grandmother, an aunt of my father's, my uncle who was ten years younger than my father, five persons in all. At Courvaudon there were my maternal grandparents and my mother, three in all. My paternal grandfather owned about 6 acres of land and my father and my uncle worked this land as well as doing the other work and some trading they engaged in. They had a horse and lent to and were lent work horses by a man who also had one. My maternal grandfather owned about three acres of land which he worked by hiring laborers by the day. The village of le Bouillon where he lived is a league distant from the village of la Faucterie where my father lived. After the marriage my mother stayed on with her parents at Courvaudon, and my father went there to do what work there was to be done. In the early days of his union with my mother he often went to visit her, but she received him with a coldness which put him out of countenance; his father-in-law and mother-in-law gave him a warmer welcome. Because of this coldness my mother showed him he ceased visiting her as often as he had; his mother was surprised to see that he was not so warm as the newly-wed usually are. But, she used to say to him, are you not going to le Bouillon this evening?—oh, said he, where do you think I should be going? In the marriage contract it was stipulated that my mother had some good pieces of furniture. But it is only a matter of course that people put that in contracts; she had none, and since she needed a bed and there was one for sale in a village not far away, she told my father she wanted it. He asked her whether she would not rather have a new one, but she said no, and kept at him telling him that he would be too late getting there. My father then thought he would buy it no matter what the price, and he bought it for about what it was worth, but during the sale other women told my mother that they would not want secondhand rubbish, and she told my father that she did not want it and it was too dear; he answered her: but it is bought now, someone must use it. She said she did not want it, my father said: it is not worth so much fuss and took the bed away and had to resell it. At the beginning of 1815 my mother gave birth to me, and the birth made her very ill. My father took all proper care of her, he did not go to bed for six weeks, he said at the time he would go to bed later, he could not sleep, he was accustomed to lie awake. In this illness of my mother's her breasts went bad and my father sucked them to extract the poison, and then spat it out on the ground. During her illness my mother displayed contempt and harshness especially toward her mother, she maintained that she was not capable of doing anything for her; she then maintained that my paternal grandmother was the only one who was able to look after her. When she asked her why she did not want it to be her mother, she answered: oh because she is so stupid. The illness my mother was then suffering from might have excused her if her conduct had not continued the same ever after. In this illness she had the flux, she would not let anyone put her own linen under her, she insisted on her mother's. After six months she recovered. My father, as I have said, did what work had to be done at Courvaudon and throughout his entire marriage, except for the short time she came to live with him, of which I shall speak shortly, he only bedded with my mother when he went to till the land there or to do some other work such as preparing grain, felling wood, planting trees, making cider, etc. The following year, my mother being again with child, her parents decided to send her to her husband, and she let him know that she intended to live with him. My father was very glad, and a closet was fixed up to put her household things in. My father bought a cupboard and they brought over all the furniture my mother had at Courvaudon; she was to live with my father's parents, and all be together. This went well for two or three months until her confinement and she gave birth to a daughter named Victoire. Her illness was again serious and lasted three months, she was cared for as every sick person should be, my father and my paternal grandmother spent their nights at it, and she was given what the doctor ordered, they got the bread from the widow Michel-Guernier baker at Aunay. Despite all the care my father and my grandmother took of her, she heaped abuse and mortifying words on her, my paternal grandmother was no longer able to do anything with her, her mother came from Courvaudon to see her and she maintained that only she could look after her; she demanded dishes of roast pork, and several other indigestible things, and as my father and my paternal grandmother[1] opposed it, she said that they grudged it her, it was avarice, that they were letting her starve. My m-g-m came to see her and she said she must have some, she made her cook it, and at last to satisfy her they gave her what she wanted, and after she had partaken of all these things, she was again seized with convulsions, it may be said that this greatly retarded her recovery. When she began to get better, my m-g-m came to see her and said that she would like her to return to her, my m-g-f badly wanted to see her, she should be taken back in a cart. My mother too said she wanted to return to her place and that she would live at Aunay no longer. It was in vain that my father remonstrated that it would be shameful to him if she went back, she said she was absolutely set on it and if he did not take her back her furniture, she would send for it. She then returned to her parents, and my father took her back her furniture, he took some of it by night because people laughed at him. Now at that time my mother showed a great dislike for my father, she put it about in Courvaudon that she had returned only because they were letting her starve, she lacked everything, and during her illness they had milled two bushels of maslin without sifting it so that it should last longer. When my father went back there to work she displayed all her dislike to him; he tried to win her over, he said to her: since you were unwilling to stay with me would you like me to come and stay here with your parents? What would they do with you, she answered; he asked her what she wanted him to do, she wanted him

[1] I will not go on repeating the words paternal and maternal grandfather and grandmother, I will designate them by these signs: paternal grandfather p-g-f, paternal grandmother p-g-m, maternal grandfather m-g-f, maternal grandmother m-g-m.

to hire himself out as a servant and bring her the money from his wages every year for her to do as she pleased with. My father said that since he had work to do on his own land he would not hire out as a servant and then, seeing how she treated him, he resolved not to go back to see her any more. Several persons among others my p-g-m and the late Nicolle of Saint Agnan with whom he shared horses advised him to go back, and then he told his brother and Nicolle to go and work the field that was to be plowed at Courvaudon without telling anyone about it and to come back afterwards, but they were seen there and my m-g-m came and gave them something to eat. Some time later my father was there cutting clover, my mother brought him some soup, and he said to her: will you kiss me? It is too much trouble, she answered; ah well then said my father, eat your soup for I do not want it, and he scythed all the clover without eating and returned hungry to Aunay. At that time, I do not know how it came about, I was living with my father at Aunay. I was three or four years old, my mother came with her mother to fetch me, she found me in the meadow where they were haymaking, my p-g-m was holding me in her arms; then without saying a word to anyone she took me and carried me off. As I cried out my father ran after her, and said he would not let her carry me away crying out like that, he would take me to Cour-vaudon the next day on the horse; seeing which my mother said to her mother who was with her: hit him, hit him; my m-g-m was rather malicious, but nothing in comparison with my mother, she had a good heart and always wel-comed my father kindly, she took good care not to do what my mother then told her. My mother therefore seeing that my father did not want her to take me away that day, started screaming in the streets: I want my child back, I want my child back, and she went straight to the cantonal judge at Villers to ask him whether my father had the right to keep her child from her. My father as he had promised took me to Courvaudon next day and distressed by all these troubles did not go back there; he was advised to return, he again took the advice and continued to go to work there and my mother played him every conceivable nasty trick even taking away the pillow and feather cover from his side of the bed. At that time, my father and my uncle bought a thousand *écus'* worth of land and houses which adjoined their property on their own account. They borrowed half the money and my father is still paying the interest on it, as for the other half, they had some of it and they hoped to earn the rest, and my father had nearly paid it off in spite of my uncle's illness and death in 1825 when a lawsuit unexpectedly arose about my mother's properties of which I shall speak later. Although this may seem to have little bearing on the cause of this history I have nevertheless mentioned it, for my mother spread it about several times that my father was a wastrel and was letting his children starve. There were intervals when my mother did not display such a dislike of my father, without however showing him much kindness, nothing but mortifying words to my father and my uncle when they went to do the plowing or else to bring them wood when they needed some, for my mother's parents did not gather enough and my father gathered more than they did and brought them some when they needed it. My uncle was more prone to anger than my father, he could not bear all my mother said to him; when I hear her nagging like that, he said, she drives me too far, if she goes on I shall end by knocking her teeth in. Fearing lest he do that, my father told him not to go back there, so that it was mostly my father who afterwards went to work the land. In 1820 my mother gave birth to a daughter named Aimée and in 1822 to a boy named Prosper. I shall tell here of the life my mother led with her parents, every day she quarrelled with her mother, not a word she said to her that was not by way of mortifying her, they blamed each other constantly for fifty thousand things, as witness all who

have heard them talking to one another; it was no use my
father remonstrating with my mother and saying that she
should show more respect to her mother, it was in vain,
she paid no heed. I stayed at Courvaudon for my first six
years, I was witness of all these quarrels, I can say that I
was not greatly attached to my mother, I loved my grandfather and my g-m much more, especially my g-f; he told
me stories and I went walking with him, and he is generally
known as a good man, he carried on the occupation of a
carpenter, but at the time I am speaking of he no longer
went out to work by the day, his legs would not carry
him, he still worked in his shop, and there he was quiet,
it was far enough away for him not to hear the clacking
perpetually going on in the house. My sister Victoire had
gone to live for some time with my father at Aunay, she
was about three or four years old, and my p-g-m who had
once had a daughter whom she had lost at about that age
seemed to see in my sister the resurrection of that child.
My mother went to fetch her back, my father made the ob-
jection I have spoken of, but he would have done better
to say that she was dependent on him. I myself went to
live with my father when I was ten and since then have
always stayed with him. In 1824 my mother gave birth to
a boy named Jean, it was agreed that it would be my
p-g-m and I who should name him, my father being absent
at the time of the birth; my p-g-m went to Courvaudon,
and after seeing my mother who was lying in, she examined
the child, it was dressed in a few dirty rags, my p-g-m
then said: oh I suppose we shall not dress him in his other
clothes till tomorrow. Ah, said my mother, there is nothing
else, lucky to have that. My p-g-m then understood that
she had done that knowing that it would be she who would
name him. Filled with deep grief she returned to Aunay
and told my uncle, who was then sick, all about it; ah,
said he, is this to be more of the same, bring the poor little
child here, he will not get bad examples. My g-m went to

the market town and ordered a cap and what was needed for dressing the child, the seamstress spent the night making them, and the next day he was baptized; my father had returned and asked my mother if one of the children who were more than she could manage should not be taken away, but she said she wished only the one who had just been born to be taken; well, said my father, we shall take him and straight from the church, for it is on the way to Aunay; when my mother saw that they were about to leave, she said to my father: oh I see that you want to leave me to starve, and she was no longer willing that it should be taken away. At that time my m-g-f was wholly infirm, he still had some money which he wanted to give my father, preferring to entrust it to him rather than to his wife and daughter, and that was done. He died in 1826. At that time, my father wished to have some of his children with him; my sister Aimée had shown a desire to come there, moreover my mother demanded grain to feed them, and she sent the miller to get a sack of it; my father said there was bread for his children at his home, they could come and eat it, and he gave no grain. Seeing which my mother, knowing he was friendly with the curates of Aunay, dressed up as a beggar and came to Aunay, she went into my father's house, she accused him of being a wastrel and a lewd person, he kept harlots; you pretend to be devout, she told him, but you do not tell your confessor everything, I am going to see him and tell him about your life; then addressing my p-g-m she said to her: how wrong you were to bring him up in vice like that, how nasty and filthy that is. Hearing such words, my p-g-m replied: oh what are you saying, get out; well I am going, said my mother. My father had displayed only his usual mood at all these reproaches, always mild and seeking to justify himself by explaining the truth. My mother went straight to the late M. Grellay who was then curate at Aunay. She told him that her husband was letting her starve to death, she lacked everything, he had other women besides her, indeed everything she could think of to slander him; that surprises me, said the curate, I took Rivière for a respectable person. Finally he said to her, listen if you lived with him you would have what he has. In the course of the day he saw my father and spoke to him of this matter, my father defended himself as best he could and the curate did not put much faith in what my mother had said. At that period there was a house for sale beside my mother's houses at Courvaudon, she wanted it, but my father saw that they already had more houses than they needed, and was afraid of the result of a lawsuit which had just been brought concerning my mother's properties, and so was against buying this house, but my m-g-m bought it on her own account and they used the money they had for it. The lawsuit which had just been brought was about a piece of land which my m-g-f had bought from a man whose wife had by her marriage contract a dowry of twelve hundred francs encumbering it, and this mortgage had not been paid off, it became more serious than had at first been thought, my father and my mother went to consult several people who knew the law, and they were warned that they would certainly be worsted in the suit, it was generally agreed however that it was robbery.

This woman had never brought her husband any marriage portion, and as my mother wished to contest the suit, lawyers whom they consulted at Caen said that if they proved that this woman had not brought in anything she could not claim anything, so the suit was heard, but it was soon lost; my father as I have already said had friends, they all offered him money to put his affairs in order and to prevent this land being sold, and he agreed to a composition, he had to pay 850 francs in all in costs. My mother had an annuity whose redemption provided about 200 frs, my father paid the rest, he had to borrow it all, and he was in debt for it for two years. My p-g-m had an annuity of 90 francs which her brothers had given her for her marriage; they redeemed a third of it, which made up nearly the sum my father owed, so that it was my p-g-m's annuity which was used to pay off my mother's properties. During the whole of this suit my mother was very kind to my father, and from that time until two years ago there were no serious quarrels between them. The year after this suit, in 1828 my mother gave birth to a boy named Jule; my sister Aimée and my brother Prosper had come to live with my father. The following year my brother Jean also came to live with him; my sister Victoire and my brother Jule always lived with my mother. At this period I went with my father to do the plowing, and I saw that the quarrels between my g-m and my mother were still going on, but my mother got the upper hand over my g-m who was growing feeble, this poor good woman was completely miserable, not only did she suffer from the continual quarrels, but several persons report having seen my mother strike her and drag her by the hair. My father never struck my mother except for slapping her sometimes in the big quarrels with him she started, of which I shall speak; but he said that if he had been involved in quarrels like those he would have been unable to hold back from striking her; my mother furthermore ordered my sister Victoire never to obey my g-m so that they were leagued together and both persecuted her. She told my father several times that she wished to divide up the property and retire to one of the other houses near, but my father said to her: do I want to divide it up with you, is not everything for you? During their quarrels my g-m had several times accused my mother of being unfaithful to her husband and reproached her for taking lovers, but my father did not believe a word of it, he said that the troubles she was enduring made her imagine and say such things. He did everything in his power to try to secure peace and quiet with my mother, he bought her cows, and sold them when need be, and they made up the accounts *liard* by *liard*.* My mother had a clump of osier in her garden, she sold it; if my father needed some bundles of withies, he paid the price she asked of him; one day he

* A very small coin. (Translator's note.)

66

bought a quarter of thatching straw from her; he had to take a long way round and he had to say that someone had asked him for some thatching straw, and bought it at such-and-such a price, and my mother said he could have it free . . . but he paid her and took the straw; for if he had taken it without this precaution, she would always have said that he would not have paid what it was worth; of all the dealings he did for her she maintained that none of them was done properly; when he bought it was always too dear, when he sold it was always too cheap, she flared up in a rage at every trifle. One day when one of her neighbors had planted some stakes perhaps an inch or two inside her land, she told my father about it; unfortunately enough he said that no great harm was done, she set to abusing him and got into such a fury that she foamed at the mouth. I come to the last two years of the marriage, beginning in 1833; my m-g-m was then confined to bed with the illness she died of, my mother had a dress made for my sister Victoire, and as she passed by la Faucterie every Saturday on the way to sell her butter at Aunay, she said as she went by that my sister Aimée should also have a dress made for her; as my sister had enough dresses and my father had no money to spare, he answered that there was no need for the present. The following Saturday my mother speaking to my p-g-m asked whether it had not been decided to get a dress made, the answer was no. Ah, that is it, she said, people do not mind spending so much on others; and she went off saying that, my p-g-m understood that she was accusing my father again of debauchery and adultery; this proved to be so the following Saturday, my mother when passing by came to see my father at the barn where he was threshing with me, my father had just made a large shed and had finished painting the door as she arrived; ah, said she, you take far more trouble over your shed than your house, have you decided to give me some money to pay Bringon;[2] my father said: but it is not the custom for me to supply you

[2] A draper.

with money, give me, she said, what you owe me from the rest of the price of our calf; my father said you know that we have reckoned up and it came out about even. My father had in fact bought a cow from her, and they had made up the account to within thirty or forty *sous*,[3] and my father had also bought a cow for her which he had kept on his land; as it was sick, he had lost it and he did not reckon it against her. My mother said to him: oh yes you would like to rob me, when you have money on hand you keep it, you old villain, you clapped-out old beast, you old whoremaster you would rather support your goodwife, you starve your children to support hers,[4] you sow her land and plow it; but, said my father, I have to earn my living. My mother told him, all you want is your fun, she is a forward bitch, she has a damn good arse, Sulpice told me so, you ought to be ashamed of yourself, here you have had my children, but you must have your goodwife too, I want to come and look after them, I do not mean to let you starve them, I will put a stop to your debauches, and she went off. My father then told me with tears in his eyes, I am sorry I gave so much money for the Champ-Poulain, that was the name of the plot of land he had bought back from my mother.

In spite of everything she had said, she did not fail to come and see my father on her way back from the market town and tell him to go and kill her pig, for my father was good at killing and salting pigs, and he went there during the week, and when he got there he asked where he should put his horse, my mother said there was no place for it,

---

[3] It is shameful to speak of such matters, but the judges and the lawyers said afterwards that my mother was very badly treated, see the order by the president of the court obtained by my mother to secure a separation, the letter of the cantonal judge of Villers, several persons at Courvaudon also said that my mother was a very ill-used wife.

[4] She meant a woman in my father's village, who was left a widow with three children, she is a very good woman, she owns a few roods of land and paid my father to work them.

she could easily have found one if she had wished, but she
said that it would do quite as well outside, my father stabled
it with one of the neighbors, and then he prepared the pig,
it was the custom that he should take in a piece to taste,
this time he did not take any. My mother asked him why;
if I took any, he said, it would be on my way back to give
it to her who has a damn good arse, and thereupon my
mother said she thought the same, and my father went away
at once. My mother did not often go to confession, she had
not taken the Easter sacrament for several years, but since
my father was friendly with the priest at Courvaudon she
went to confession, and also spoke to him about my father,
accusing him of what I have already said she had reproached
him with, and she said that she wanted to come and take care
of her children whom he was starving to death. Some days
later my father saw the priest who told him he had seen
his wife and that she wished to come and live with him.
My father asked him did she not say some other things
too? Ah as to that, said the priest, we know you well, but
she wants to be with her children; my father said, I should
like that too, but now the position is very critical. You see
her mother is very sick and may perhaps die of it, it would
be better to wait till she is well again, or else if she is set
on coming, get someone else in to take care of her; the
priest thought that was right, and my m-g-m's illness
growing worse, she died a fortnight later. My father paid
what was needed for the funeral, and a few days later he
said to my mother, you wanted to come to me, now there is
nothing to keep you, you can come; however knowing her,
he made her this proposal: if you wish to stay here, he told
her, I will continue to come and do the plowing, and I will
do for you as before; no she said I am going to put a stop
to your almsgiving, my father said to her, you still hold
to your opinion, are you saying that to hurt me or do you
really believe it? But my mother still maintained it was so
and said that when he had come some time ago to make

cider, he had caused her to have to pay for a day more than need be for the press, she knew that before he arrived in the morning he had been to fetch his whore,[5] she also spoke of it in front of my sister Aimée; my sister vainly begged her in tears to desist from these ideas, and as to her saying that my father had been to fetch that woman that was not true, it was another man from the village Nativel, who had been to fetch her; my mother replied, if Nativel went to fetch her he did not do it for nothing, he paid for it, poor fool a whole lot of things go on, you do not notice them. My father told my mother that since she wished to come to him, they would have to let the land on lease; she did not intend to do that, she said that they would leave the two girls there, they would see to the housework and feed the animals; so that my mother was thinking she would come and go and would collect the money for the whole lot; she was not content with enjoying the control of her property all sown and tilled as it was, but she wanted to manage my father's too, and she would not let him have his way in anything at all, not even drink without her permission, a quart on Sundays with his friends; my father said that the girls would not be respectable if they stayed like that alone in a house, she should choose either to continue staying there as before or that the land should be let, he asked her whether she would rather it should be let as a whole or in plots, she said she would rather it was let to a single tenant. As my father had enough furniture at Aunay, he said to her that the furniture at Courvaudon might be sold, she said she did not wish her furniture to be sold, well, said my father, it will not be sold. Some days later I went there to break up some wood at midday, she mistook what I was doing, saying: oh he wanted to sell our furniture, it was doubtless his mother who advised him

[5] When my father went to work at Courvaudon he took all the tools in a cart so as to have time to set everything to rights and then had to travel a league, so that he did not get there till after daybreak.

to, to make a bit of money, truly that is ridiculous. I told her,
he would sell it if he wished, ah yes, said she, if he could;
if you were dealing with some people, I told her, they would
treat you otherwise, but he makes you another proposal,
stay on just as you were; ah yes, she said, *and then when he
has sold something, he will keep the money*, I will not stay
there. My sister Victoire appeared to be paying no heed to
the arguments I put forward, my father spread it around
that he wished to let the land, and then Pierre le Comte
his cousin came to ask him for it, he had land at le Bouillon
but no houses, he wished to set himself up and said that
that would suit him, my mother was quite willing, the
price was agreed in her presence, and she received the wine;
this man leased all the plowing land as well as the meadow,
with the main part of the premises in which my mother
lived, two rooms, a loft, and a byre, the whole from roof to
foundation, for 250 francs a year with 50 francs' worth of
wine which he supplied free, the lease was for nine years,
it stipulated that the tenant would fertilize the land in
accordance with local usage, that he would be responsible
for the upkeep of the houses, that he would replace any trees
which decayed with good ones, that he should have so
much straw on entering on occupation and that he would
leave the same amount, that he would have a felling of wood
two years before the end of the lease. There remained two
main houses for letting which could bring in 60 francs.
Within a fortnight my mother no longer approved, she said
it was too cheap, and whenever my father went to Courvaudon, for my mother was to stay there until Michaelmas
when the tenant was to take occupancy, she told him that
the contract must be cancelled, that her daughter was
continually weeping and did not want to leave; my father
asked my sister if that was true, she said no. Seeing that my
mother still wanted to cancel the contract, my father spoke
to the tenant, and they both went to see my mother and
took their leases to her, then my father said to her, you can

cancel the contract if you wish, here are the two deeds, but take warning that I shall not come back here again, you shall manage as best you please; my mother would not cancel the contracts, she said neither yes nor no, and my father went off with the tenant taking their deeds with them; but my mother persisted in saying that she would never leave her home. One day when I was there talking to my sister, I told her among other things that she would not be there a year hence, why will I not be here she said, we shall see whether Pierre le Comte will turn us out of our house; but, I said to her, he will certainly compel papa to turn you out. Ah, she said if papa did that to us, mama would always hold it against him she would do all she could to harm him; as I thought that the tenant would not compel my father, I answered my sister: but if you stay there how will you fare, your papa will not go there any more to work the land? Well, she said, we will hire hands, if he had not come back fifteen years ago all of us would have been happy, mama was in no hurry for it. My father hoped that the tenant would not compel him, and it was then the beginning of the harvest; seeing that my mother persisted in wanting to stay, when she came to him and asked whether he would not bring in the grain, if you wish to have it brought here, he said to her, I will go there; since that was not agreeable to her, she said several things and went away and my father said to her, away with you, you miserable old idiot; when she had gone, never, said he, have I said as much as that to her. About that time my father made a journey to la Delivrande and took with him my brother Prosper who had bad eyes; my sister Victoire had shown some intention of going there, my father went to let her know, oh, she said, we have no time to go running around, who will work our land. My mother hired hands to get her harvest in. But the tenant who had leased the land seemed disposed to want to hold to his contract, they talked with each other sometimes, my mother and the tenant, and she defied him saying that he was not able to put her out, that angered him and made him even more determined to hold to his contract, and as my mother was still afraid, she had several trees pruned in the month of August fearing that he might take advantage of this; he came and informed my father about it; but what could he do about it, he begged him to release him from the contract; but this tenant thought that my father and my mother were in agreement to withdraw from it; they are in agreement, he said, but they will not pull wool over my eyes. Michaelmas came, my father went to see this tenant. He offered him as much money as he wanted, several persons went with my father and also pleaded for him, at last he made up his mind to give up the contract, on condition that they drew up a deed stipulating that my father would not lease to others, but the following Sunday he came to say that he was going back on the arrangement, my father then said to him: you can do what you like to me, I shall not budge even if you ruin me. But what do you expect me to do then, he answered, hey cousin[6] have you no head on your shoulders, and he went off saying that he would see what to do about it and he registered his lease that week and showed it to my father who seeing that he was behaving like this decided to go and remove the furniture. Before that he went to see my mother and took with him François le Comte of Courvaudon who was an acquaintance of my mother's to try to bring her to reason. It was all in vain, she said that no one should put her out, that she would rather fight to the death. A few days later we left with the cart to go and fetch some pieces of furniture, there were three of us, my father, Fouchet with whom we shared horses and I; as he passed by, my father asked the assistant to the mayor of the commune to come with him to remonstrate with her, and he came, he said he would not show himself in case she said nothing; when we got there my father began by loading grain which was in sacks,

[6] That was what he customarily called him.

my mother said nothing and the assistant went away. My father asked for the key of a loft, and when she refused, he took a chest which was in the house, my mother objected; then he held her while I loaded it with the man who was with us. As he held her she set to scratching his face and bit him in several places, my little brother Jule coming up, she told him: bite him, bite that wretch, my father told me he got his fingers in his mouth but did not dare clench his teeth on them; but seeing that the child was worrying him, I caught hold of him and carried him into a neighboring house, we finished loading and went off. In the afternoon we went back, as we arrived the whole village came out of their doors, my mother set to arguing, and my father climbed in a window to get into a loft, then she seized him by the legs and pulled him down, broke his watch-chain and tore his clothes, he did not strike her at all, but he said he would shut her up in a house to keep her quiet, he caught hold of her to carry her away, but her hands were free and she scratched him again even worse than the first time, then he seized her hands to take her into that house and she fell down purposely; he did not drag her, as she said, but he tried to get her on her feet to take her there, my sister joined in to stop my father, and seeing that she was hindering him, I pulled her away and slapped her several times while my father took my mother off, she was shouting and so was my sister: vengeance, he is murdering me, he is killing me, vengeance my god vengeance. Once they were in the house, one of her cousins came and remonstrated with her, telling her that she would do far better to help us load and go with her husband than do all these things. And that calmed her down a little. My father was so exhausted when he got to his house that he was spitting blood. He returned to continue loading, my mother took away some other things he wanted to carry off, he took some others instead and we went off. I spoke to my sister, she said that I had mistreated and crushed her, I said to her, but why did you join in too, do you not know all the things she has invented against him? She answered me: she has not invented a thing; my father, with Fouchet, also spoke to her, he told her to advise my mother to come to him instead of holding her back and she replied that she continually advised her everyday to go with him but could make no impression on her. My father also asked the thresher who was there if he was owed anything, he answered no. The next day my mother came to take back her cow, my father objected, she uttered several bad words against him and went on to say: you carried off the chest, you thought you were carrying off the money but you shall not have it. Then addressing my g-m: you told him to come and rob me, it is your good virgin I am sure who advised you to do that. And she went off at once to see the cantonal judge of Villers, who believed her and sent my father a letter drawn up in these terms: your wife complains that you went with carts yesterday to the residence at which her late mother died whose sole and single heir she is, that you removed the grain, cows, and furniture of all kinds. It is my opinion that your wife was entitled to have an inventory made of the movable property in this estate and that you were not entitled to seize them without any legal formalities, the more so because you were on bad terms with her because you dragged her away by the arms and hands because she opposed your breaking and entering. It is certain that if she laid an information against you she would obtain legal redress for the injuries committed by you against her. In order to avoid unpleasantness which is always to be deplored between husband and wife I invite you to come to my office at Lande at nine o'clock in the morning on Sunday next to make an amicable settlement. Or else go to the cantonal judge of your commune who I believe is likely to summons you and bring you to reason.

My mother taking this letter showed it to the cantonal judge of Aunay, and thereafter came and gave it to my father, who was preparing to go and fetch the calf which was not sold, and he went to fetch it in the tip-cart, but when he got there and my mother made further objections, he returned without bringing anything with him, my mother went and sold it two days later at Villers with her thresher. The cantonal judge of Aunay who had seen the letter said when speaking to M. Rivière postmaster at Aunay and to his brother: what the devil, this surprises me, I did not take Rivière for a fellow like that; but they told him what the position was. Since it is a husband's duty to live with his wife, when my father told the priest of Aunay that the tenant refused to cancel the contract, he had said he was very glad to hear it. Then my father went to see the priest and showed him his face, ah, said the priest how I pity you my poor Rivière. He also showed him the letter he had received. The priest gave him a letter to go and consult a lawyer of his acquaintance at Condé, Maître Davou. My father took his contract to him, and because of a clause which appears in what I have said of it, he told him that it would be as well for him to draw up an inventory of the furniture. My father asked him how to do it, and he said: let your wife make the valuation herself. My father had not been able to explain his position to him, it may be judged by what I have already said of it whether this advice could be carried out. My father asked him how he could make her come to live with him, he told him: the national guard, if the mayor was willing, or else the gendarmerie would see to the formalities. My father did not have time to go and see the cantonal judge at Villers on the Sunday, he was busy setting up boundary stones with one of his neighbors. The wheat had to be got in and the harvest was at its height. My father had no time to go and dispute and wrangle; he made an inventory of the trees for the tenant, agreed that he might fell the wood in the last year of the lease for the trees which my mother had had cut, and gave him the manure for the straw which he had agreed, so this tenant entered into occupation and harvested the wheat, my father also harvested his, and when at last he did not have so much work to do he decided to hand over the houses. Before that he told the tenant that he should go and see the cantonal judge at Villers and ask him to summon both his wife and himself, but the judge replied that he had already written to the man and that he had not seen him, that he believed that his wife was in the right and she stated a good case. That since he had let his property, he could compel him to hand it over and demand compensation from him for what he had not enjoyed. This tenant replied that he did not want to put him to expense. Well, said the judge, then what are you asking for? And he left it at that. Some days later my father went with him to empty a house for him, and he said to my mother, would you like us, my father said to her, to put the furniture in your other houses which are not let, you shall retire to them and you shall receive the whole income from your property, but she said no and the furniture should be put out; what do you mean by out, said my father, and what will come of that. But she insisted that it should be put out; when it was done he said to her, do you want it taken into the other houses, no, she said; then my father shut up the house which had just been emptied, and went off with the tenant. But no sooner had they gone when my mother and my sister put all the furniture back inside, and my sister said as they put it in: no doubt they did that for fear we would not have enough work to do. During the week my father decided to take the mayor's assistant and some respectable persons with him and a locksmith, and to go and break the locks, empty the houses, shut them up, and take away all the furniture. On the night before the day on which he was to do all that, he wondered whether the tenant was still willing to make a settlement, for if he reimbursed him for all he had done and paid compensation besides he would still be better off than if he compelled her to come to live with him. In the morning

77

he told us what he intended and told me that he was still going through with it, and I should take the cart to the tenant's village, and if he made the settlement we should go no farther and the tenant consented to this. They reckoned up all he had done. The land he had sown, the wine he had given, the registration of the lease, that all added up to the sum of 119 francs and that much again for cancelling the contract, which made 238 francs; then the tenant cancelled the lease, and gave him a deed which the mayor's assistant wrote out, saying that he cancelled the contract. My poor father truly believed that he was quit, he did not have the money, he went and borrowed it from Hébert, one of his neighbors. I am tranquil now, however, he said, let all my children come and kiss me, let her remain on her property as long as she wishes. All I wanted was the poor little fellow[7] to stay on here, for as for the other she is at the age of discretion. About a month later, my mother came to see him and said to him: now that you have played all your stupid tricks, I have come to find out when you are really going to give me back what you have taken from me and let me have the management of my property; my father answered, you can be at rest now, your wheat is in, you still have a cow, you are not in need,[8] leave me in peace, you need no longer fear I shall return to you; my mother said, I want my land back, my father said I will give it back to you if you are also willing to return what I paid for you; but she said, and has always said since, that it was not true that my father had paid the tenant compensation, that they had agreed together to put her out, that my father made her get in the wheat, he had made her register the lease, and the deed they had made when he cancelled the contract with my father for so much money was nothing but a put-up job. She went to see the cantonal

[7] He meant my brother Jule.
[8] It is certain that my mother had plenty of money, it cost her nothing to get her work done, and she had always sold various things.

judge of Aunay and he summoned both of them to a reconciliation hearing, he remonstrated strongly with my
mother to no avail, she said she would think it over, she
went and consulted François le Comte at Courvaudon who
tried his best to bring her back to her duty, he told her
that she might set her mind at rest, her husband would leave
her to herself; she had seemed to have made up her mind,
but one day she said to him that her daughter told her that
he would still have the right to come and plunder her some
other time, and she wished to take out insurance; Le Comte
said to her: it will cost you money. Well, she said, if it puts
me to expense he will be put to expense too, and that week
she went to Vire, she returned with nothing done, but she
told those who inquired about her journey that it would
be time enough six months hence, and that she would eat up
all my father's property if she wanted. Then she set about
running up debts for him. She usually bought articles for
her own and my sister's dresses from Mme. Aod at Aunay.
She had always duly paid for them, now she no longer paid.
The thresher whom my father had asked whether there was
any money owed to him came to see him at this time and
told him that my mother refused to pay him twelve francs
she owed him, it was the same man who had pruned the
trees. My father was somewhat surprised at this, then he
said that it was not right that he should lose his money,
and he would go and see my mother with him and if she
would not pay him, he should take the cow and sell it to
get his pay; on the agreed day he went there and found
the thresher in the house, and my mother and my sister in
the byre one each side of the cow, thereupon he said a few
words to my mother, then he told the thresher to get his
payment how he would. This man summoned him to a
conciliation hearing before the cantonal judge, but my
mother went there too. The judge spoke only to her,[9] he

[9] This judge conversing one day with my father asked him whether
his wife was not an evil-liver and whether she did not love other men

remonstrated with her again and said that she would do far better to go and live with her husband, and she said that she would come to him, and my father paid the thresher. My mother complained at this hearing that my father neglected working her land so as to work other people's.[10]

The bystanders who heard these words turned them to ridicule. They understood them in two ways, and my father thus became the butt of the people's mockery. Marie Fortain said to him: oh I beg you do not appear before the cantonal judge again when she summons you, people mock at it so. My father went back to work at Courvaudon since my mother said that she would come to live with him. He asked her when she would come, oh soon, she said; thereupon my sister speaking up said to him: oh I shall go into service on Saint Claire's day I shall, and she did not venture to say what she meant, at last she said: oh do you think we shall go there under your orders; my father keeping his temper said to her,[11] you said it was not you who were holding back your mother but I see that you are as bad as she is; it is not me, she said, who made her come back fifteen years ago, it is you who should have left her in peace and stayed where you were at that time. My mother also said some words which revealed to my father that she had no intention of leaving. Some days later as she

---

than him. My father said: no, that I have not suspected her of. It surprises me, said the judge that you tell me that she has no religion, that the way she is she does not love you, and yet she is no evil-liver; my father said: I do not think so, but she does not say the same of me; ah, so that is it, said the judge, she is jealous.

[10] Some days before, when my mother was threatening to run up debts, my father had gone to le Bouillon, he had spoken to my sister who had told him that since he was leaving them like that my mother would run up an infinity of debts, she would borrow right and left and get everything she needed on credit. My father said to her: but why did she not come to me when I wanted her to, she answered she does not want to live with her mother-in-law, she wants to be in a separate house and to put all our things in it.

[11] Ask M. Fouchet.

passed by she asked him if he would come soon to get in the barley. He asked her if she thought he was stupid enough to go to so much trouble for someone who only sought to vex him; well, my mother told him, you do that but it will not be twelve francs this time you will find, you will find it is more than that, my father said to her, but if you run up debts for me I shall come back and fetch some pieces of furniture to pay them. Well, said she, we shall see. And she went off. Fearing lest she put her threats into practice, my father went to consult a lawyer at Caen Maître Beaucher, to ask whether he could not advertise that no one should give her anything on credit or they would lose it so far as he was concerned. This lawyer told him that that would be defamatory, he would do better to make her come and live with him. My father told him some of what the position was. It is very unfortunate, he replied, but go and fetch her furniture one day when you know she is not there. My father left and went to consult another lawyer Maître Pouillier; this lawyer told him he must do it in legal form and present a petition to the court to make her come and live with him, it was as much as to say he must have the devil to live with him, and my father left it at that, he only warned the laborer who asked him whether it would not vex him if he worked for her: work there as much as you like, my father told him, but do not count on me for your pay. He also warned Mme. Aod to whom she already owed 45 francs not to let her have anything more without getting paid for it; but my mother used more than one shop, and besides she bought from the drapers who passed through her village, she bought grain and resold it, she told a draper, Le Roux of Courvaudon from who she wished to buy three or four cotton caps: tell my husband that I owe you twelve francs and you shall give me the rest. This man would not let her have her caps, she said the same to a woman shopkeeper whose name I have forgotten. While she was doing all these things, my brother Jean fell sick in the month of July of a malady of the brain, he lasted only a fortnight.[12] Toward the end it was decided that his mother should be told nonetheless; it was a Monday, my mother went back home and came back on the Tuesday evening, during the night my brother was seized every quarter hour with convulsions which made him writhe horribly. This child had already shown more sociability to people than I or my brother Prosper. He already helped in all sorts of work and my father loved him. His sadness and dejection at this child's feet may be conceived. In the meantime my mother gave him two letters one from Mme. Aod and the other from the tax collector requiring her to pay her debts and she uttered the opinions I have reported above. Transfixed with grief my father cried out: how sad is my plight, ah Lord will you visit yet harsher tribulations upon me, yes my poor child you will be truly happy when you have quitted this world, you will go to heaven.[13] My g-m being present reproached him and then her blood mounted in her she became quite hoarse. The next day this child expired, the neighbors tried to move my father from beside him, no, he said, I will not leave him, and then seeing him dead: oh, he cried, my poor little Jean, and he said, no, mother, stay here, I am no longer as strong as you, oh I shall leave this place. Where will you go my poor son, my g-m said to him; then he flung himself on a bed and tore his hair; my sister Aimée flung herself into his arms; your daughter will never abandon you, the neigh-

[12] I forgot to say that some time before this, my sister came to Aunay to buy a dress for her second communion; fearing that Mme. Aod would not give her one she got it from Rabache, she took 29 francs' worth and she told him she was not going to pay for it, he asked her who she was, the seamstress who was with her said: it is Rivière of la Faucterie's daughter. Oh, very well, she said, take it. My father having come to know of this spoke to my sister as she went by and asked her who would pay for this dress: ah, she said, I will, but I must have some money. Then she added: if you had not taken what we had, we should have enough to buy fine dresses.

[13] Witness the neighbors.

bors told him. My mother went back to her house and did not fail to put it about everywhere that my father had starved her child to death, and she continued to run up debts, she warned the laborer that he should get paid as best he could. When the shopkeepers asked her for money she said: get it from him who has taken my property, do you want me to make out a note. Fearing lest my father might come and fetch something away she had her harvest threshed as soon as it was brought in, she had most of the wheat threshed too early so as to get it in faster, she sold at every market at Aunay and Evreci, she paid the tax collector only, for she was warned that he could distrain upon the furniture in her house, the other creditors demanded money from my father, who seeing that he would be ruined if he let all this continue resolved to go and fetch some pieces of furniture to see what that might lead to. My g-m was extremely afflicted by all these things: ah, she said to Marie Fortain, would I were in the graveyard, ah must I have lived such a life of toil[14] and be recompensed like this, why has the good God made me suffer so, why does he leave me so long on earth; Marie Fortain consoled her as best she could and we went off my father and I one market day to Evreci where we expected to find my mother and to take the calf and a pig we had. When we got there we met my sister, but my mother was also there not far away. My father said that he was going to take the cow, whereupon my sister set to crying: mama, mama, come quick he is trying to take our cow; she came up and tried to prevent it, my father caught her and shut himself up with her in the house, then she again scratched him and bit him in several places, then she set to reproaching him for the death of her child. Yes, said she, if I had known

[14] She spent her life in constant toil, her husband was bedridden for 20 years with an illness and was unable to walk; of four children she had raised, and loved, only one remained and she had to watch him being treated like this.

about it I would have had him trepanned, at least people would have seen your evil doings; he slapped her, she set to calling for vengeance once again. As I was trying to take the cow, my sister tried to prevent me by letting it loose, then I hit her several times with my whip handle, we took a sack of barley with the cow, my father told the thresher to go, and asked him how much was owing to him, he said he was owed 28 *sous*, and so we went off. My mother ran after us and caught up with us; my father then took her arm as if they were going to a wedding banquet, she dropped down purposely three times, and falling the third time, she slid her foot along her leg, all my father did to her was to say, faith you lie down and set yourself well enough for me to put you to rights but I am not in the mood. There were several persons who saw this scene. My mother made use of it later in demanding her separation. Some days later she came to see my father to get him to give her back what he had taken from her. Pay your debts, he said to her, but she wanted to make a settlement under which he would pay her debts, give her what he had taken from her, and pay her an annuity so that she could remain living on her land. Where do you expect me to get money from, he said to her; do as the others, said my mother, get it from the bank. She went to see Maître Foucaut at Vire to obtain a separation, but he summoned my father by letter to come and put matters in order, my father went to see him and took with him certificates of his conduct from the priests of the two communes, my mother was there and they agreed that she should come and live with him, but he would put her in a separate house with her furniture and effects and that my g-m should enter the house only with permission, or if she did enter it, my mother should return to her property at Courvaudon, and that this house should be ready within two or three weeks at latest. My father brought her back from Vire in the cart, and they agreed that he would go and thresh the buckwheat at

Courvaudon at the end of the week; my father went to advertise the land to be let, for Michaelmas was approaching; but my mother was not satisfied with this arrangement, she went back to Vire during the week and had the buckwheat threshed straight away without telling my father, she made arrangements for all the grain to be sold before he came to fetch her; he got the house ready as fast as he could, and he learned of my mother's intention to sell everything in the meantime. Then he took the cart and two persons from the village, and went to get the rest of the grain. He found the buckwheat still there, all the other grain was overthreshed, he also took a pig; while we were loading, he stayed with her in the house to keep her quiet, we made two journeys; when we made the second my mother was no longer there, she had gone to get her shoes mended; as we went away he tried to take some sheets and since my sister objected, he said that they might just as well be brought in a few days, no she would not go to him, she said, she was going to go off to put matters straight. And indeed she went back again to Vire, my father also went back to see Maître Foucaut to ask what to do about it, he asked him whether he had not seen her again, and told him that she had come back twice. I have not seen her, he answered, she must have gone to seek some other saint. The evening she came back from having her shoes mended my sister said to her: go if you want to, but as for me I will never go and live with a wretch like that who takes all our property from us. But my mother seeing that she would be obliged to come made several arrangements to continue to do mischief. The house being ready my father went to fetch her, accompanied by Quevillon who shared horses with us and Victor a servant at M. Grellai's, he found very few pieces of furniture, there was no cooking pot, and though my mother had run up all the debts which I have spoken about, he found very few clothes. My mother made fresh objections, she said he must pay her debts before she came to live with him. My father said he had already paid some of them and would pay the rest. But he had no inkling of a letter which my mother thought he had already received. My father asked two women to come to reason with her. And he went off with a cart, this time he took my brother Jule the whole way, and those who were with him could report about this, he took up this child from time to time and kissed him. Ah, my poor little Jule, he said, how happy I am, yes you are truly the dearest piece of furniture I wanted to fetch; at the second cartload, when the women advised my mother to go with him, she began weeping, for weeping was quite a custom of hers, she said: ah he should have made me go while my poor child was alive, he would not be dead; and they came my sister and she. That evening though there had not been time to get everything ready she insisted on going to bed with her two children in her house. My father had come back to see my g-m, she showed him a letter which had come in the post, and receiving it had put my g-m to great distress; she had rolled on the ground and had beaten her body on the earth. Because of all the ills it caused I shall reproduce it here.

Courvaudon, on . . . memorandum of debts incurred in the year 1833. 40 francs to a draper at Hamars, 30 frs to Goffé, 10 frs to Victor Bourse, 10 frs to a cobbler, 10 frs for masses, 17 frs to Sophie Rivière[15] 27 frs to Marianne le Comte and a sack 3 frs to Rose Leminée 40 sous to Charles le Bas 8 sous to M. le Riche 48 sous to Sophie le Coc[16] 70 sous to Pierre Bretoure. If these debts are not paid within eight days a writ will issue and the debts for the year 1834 will also have to be paid and they are much more serious. All these debts were unknown to my father, besides those I have spoken of he had paid 25 frs to the laborer whom he had told not to count on him. But this man

[15] The schoolmistress who had taught my sister Victoire.
[16] Their seamstress for lacemaking.

had trusted my mother and she had deceived him; he was afflicted afresh at the sight of these debts; this letter had been written by my sister Victoire. My father asked around about these debts; Victor Bourse, to whom 10 frs was put down, said she owed him about 30 *sous*, he thought it would be the same thing with the others, but except for the 30 frs to Goffe and the 17 frs to Sophie Rivière, he was obliged to pay the rest; I will say that this Goffe and le Comte brother of this Marianne who is mentioned, and also a mason at Hamars, all those people whom my mother went to consult were bachelors, and not over-scrupulous with regard to purity. Some days after her coming, my mother and my sister Victoire and my two brothers my father and I went to gather apples at Courvaudon, and at midday the quarrel broke out again, my father spoke of the letter, he had not yet spoken of it to my mother, he asked why she persecuted him so, why she wanted him to pay for things which had nothing to do with the case, what had he done to her then, but she jeered at him and answered that because he had not been willing to leave her in peace he would not gain as much as he thought. And she went off to her cousin's with my sister and my brother Jule; as my brother Jule was weeping, for though this child was rather on my mother's side, he also loved my father and was pleased when he saw them in agreement, my father tried to hold him back by caressing him, but he could not. Then he said to my brother Prosper: are you too going to leave me and go away with them? No, he said, and all three of us stayed together. My father also spoke to Jacques le Comte's wife who was there and said to her: but what does she want of me that she is trying to ruin me like this, after I have taken so much trouble to get together what I have for my children, I shall have to sell some land and after I have sold a piece that will still not be enough, if she goes on like this I shall have to sell some more pieces, there were tears in his eyes as he said this; this woman answered him that she could not but think that my mother had always had in mind gaining the management of it and getting herself a separate purse. In the evening my mother and the rest came back to la Faucterie. One Sunday my father went to Hamars to speak to the draper, the 40 frs was owed to him my father paid the next Saturday and received a receipt from this man saying that the debt was discharged and that he would never give my mother or my sister Victoire anything on credit. On the Sunday he had gone to see him he returned to Aunay at vespers, and overcome by all these things was taken sick, he had to leave the church, and went in to the widow Guernier's. My mother wanted the children my sister Victoire and my brother Jule to sleep in the same house where she was. My father objected that it would not be good to put so many beds in the house and that there was a closet and other places where they could be put to bed, my mother would not have it so and these two unfortunate children slept in the same bed with her. Some people said to my father: I would like to bed with her if only to put her in a rage. My father put another bed in the house, my sister slept in it, and he bedded with my mother, and as she would not send Jule to bed anywhere else, all three of them bedded together. Since their great quarrels my father had had no carnal intercourse with her. Nevertheless if only to enrage her he wanted to try on the first or second night. My sister Victoire heard. Then she said: oh my god my god what are you doing to her? Look you, he said to her, what business of yours is it, I am doing to her what men do to their wives; ah, she said, let her be since she does not want it. Yes, my father said to her, I am going to leave her alone too. He bedded with her several nights and then seeing that she did not leave him any feather cover on his side or feathers in the pillow, and she was doing all she could to cause mischief, he preferred to sleep in the other bed, and my sister and my brother ever after bedded with my mother, she did the cooking, all of us went to live with her, except my g-m who was forbidden to enter her house; this woman, who had given the redemption of her annuity to buy back my mother's property,[17] had therefore to eat alone, which distressed her very greatly. One day when her resentments were gnawing her, and she had just given a shirt to Prosper and me, we were bedded in a closet near by, and she said: ah yes I have taken so much trouble to look after all of them, and to bring them up as well as I could, and a fine reward I get for it. And then I heard her knock her head two or three times against the table or the ground, yes, she said, I feel like beating my body on the ground, ah must the good God leave me to suffer so long, if there was any water here I would drown myself in it. My sister Aimée who was with her said: lie down grandmother I beg you; and she lay down. My mother still went on making trouble, she said she had been brought there so that they could starve her to death, her daughter was daily pining away; she took hanks of thread and bundles of tow to the shops, saying that she had to sell them to eat, witness Mme. Le Gouix known as Leminée. My father was driven to despair by all these things, he got into the habit of talking to her at the top of his voice when she overwhelmed him with her arguments; then people saw him with a sad countenance talking to her, shouting loudly and speaking softly but to no avail, my mother paid no heed, she was delighted to see him so distressed. As he was quarrelling with her one Saturday when people were passing by, Hébert's wife came and told him to be silent. Everyone passing by, she said, is talking about it, I have heard some say: oh, she is not getting used to it I think, and others but she is not so much in the wrong as you think, people say he beats her like a hunk of beef. Some time later she made various preparations. She washed some linen and repaired

---

[17] At the period when this annuity was redeemed, my mother even said that my father was a wastrel, that he was leaving nothing to his children, and that he was selling her annuities to support his goodwives' arses.

some shoes, we were making cider; and she saw my father busy one morning and she went off saying nothing to anyone taking dresses and several things with her, my sister Victoire and my brother Jule followed her, my sister carried her lace bobbins, people told my father, who was at the press, and he ran after them. I went too to see what would happen, and I found him coming back with the little boy on his back, my mother was following him, my father's face and aspect were despairing, what he seemed to want to say was: I give it all up I abandon all I have, there is only this poor little boy whom they shall not take away from me, I want to keep him and always take him with me; on the road I said to him: let them go where they will and advertise that no one is to sell them anything. He did not answer me, he was wholly taken up with his grief; when we came to the village my mother said to Jule: do not be afraid I shall come back this evening and she went off. As we were supping my father said to Jule: do not go with her any more she is only staying here in order to harm you my poor little one. And he kissed him. My mother came back with my sister that evening, there was no knowing what they had been doing, but my mother went on squabbling with my father, and jeered at the sadness which overwhelmed him. The next day he was very busy at the press, and as he had to go and work for Quevillon next day, I asked him whether it would not be wise to send and tell him that it could not be done, but he said no, and he pondered, at last he said: well, I give up I am leaving everything, I shall throw myself down our well; he went off, I followed him, and as my g-m was there also, he did not do it, he drank a glass of water and went back to the press; he agreed to let me tell Quevillon that we could not go and work for him the next day; in the morning we drew off the *marc*,* there were three of us, my father, my g-m and I. We talked of these goings-on of my mother's, and my g-m and I advised my father to put up a notice fearing

* Residue, *in this case from the making of cider.* (*Translator's note.*)

that she would finally ruin him, my father said he would not do that; you let her do as she likes, we told him, you let her spread false complaints. Ah, he said, I will not let her put about false complaints much longer you may be sure that will soon be over. Ah, my g-m said to him, you threaten that do you, very well I will threaten her too; and she went off. My father then took off his cap and tore his hair, as though seized by a fit of rage and despair. Oh oh oh, he said; I flung myself on him, ah my poor father, I said to him endure it. A moment later my sister Aimée came up in tears, what is happening, she said, my mother is up there weeping and wailing what has happened then? I leaned over and whispered in her ear: go and fetch the priest, he means to kill himself. My sister went. And they came back my g-m and she a little later. My g-m said to my father: he told Aimée to go and fetch the priest, do you want me to go. But he was calmer. And no one went. But these notions took hold of him once more, I do not know if it was that day or some days later that he said these words: though I am not resolute enough to take the way out of all these persecutions, there are some who do it for far less reasons. Some time later this Marianne le Comte to whom my mother said she owed a sack of wheat came in to get her money for it. It was assuredly a trick which my mother and this woman had devised together, she may well have sold her a bushel, for when my father asked her how she had delivered it to her, she said she had delivered it bushel by bushel, that as to the first three bushels she had taken them away one at a time on her back in a large bag, and with the last she had the miller's horse, and she had delivered this bushel with a sack to carry it in, and she had taken it away with her. My father asked my sister whether she had not helped my mother go and fetch this grain, she said no but she had helped her eat it. My father told this woman, who is reputed in those parts to be a cheat, that he would not pay her. My mother told her to sue him and that she would swear black and blue if need be that she owed it to her. This woman summoned him to conciliation proceedings. My mother went with her. My father contended that she must have been seen carrying away the grain on her back and my sister must have helped her, the cantonal judge asked the woman whether she would affirm on her soul that it was lawfully owed to her. As she seemed unwilling to do that, my mother said: well, you are an innocent, if it were me I should be ready enough to affirm. The judge concluded by saying: I see that this woman is so scrupulous that she will not affirm so pay her and go in peace, and my father paid her. The thresher whom my father had forbidden to go and work there any more and had settled with him for 28 *sous* had been to work there since then and wanted the rest paid him, the judge again said he must pay and my father paid him.[18] Sometimes when my father was talking to the judge about my mother, the judge said: look you, your wife has her weaknesses, you ought to spare her. These awards encouraged my mother to flout my father and argue with him all the more. There is another cause for dispute that happened before this which I have omitted to mention. A man who was about to marry came during the period when my mother was living with my father and asked him to let him one of the houses to live in with his wife, this house was one of those which had not been let to the tenant of whom I have spoken, there is a garden attached to this house. My mother was not willing to let at all. And the land he had advertised was not let either because people did not care for it in view of the changes that kept happening, or because it was too late because Michaelmas had gone by, my father had plowed it that year. As to the house of which I am speaking which was a carpenter's shop and the cellar, it was let for ten

[18] It is probable that this judge finally came to take my mother's part to avoid her importunities. He was not in fact derelict in his duty in complying with the rules, so my unfortunate father was left to his fate and the mighty prevailed.

écus, and it was stipulated that the tenant should have all the vegetables in the garden, and that my father should have the use of the cellar until the first day of the new year. This contract did not suit my mother, no more than any other, she said that this man should not have the use of it and she would pull up all the vegetables in the garden. One day therefore when she had returned there and my father had gone to work, in the evening she told my sister to cull the cabbages, she obeyed. My father said to her: but what are you doing I forbid you to thin them out because they are let, my sister said: Oh my faith they grow much too thick; he made her stop. But my mother seeing that set to picking them herself and my father forbidding her she said: go on and talk, I am going to top them all, he slapped her, then she set to crying: vengeance my god he is killing me; my sister Victoire ran up, I too and I saw my father trying to push her out of the garden; she kicked and punched him even after she was out. Do I have to be so ill-used, she said, by a wretch who is being the death of me at night, but I shall come back and get our cabbages I shall get them when daylight comes. I came back with my father and Quevillon by one way, and my mother and sister went by another. When the last of the cider was being made, my mother refused to let them take a cask which was at Courvaudon, and seeing that they did take it she went to consult a mason at Hamars to see how she could obtain a separation, and thereafter she kept going to consult people here and there and spread it about that her husband was being the death of her and that he beat her every day; some time after the laundry had been done my mother asked for some sheets to wash; she must have some left. My father asked her what she had done with them. She said very little but my sister said: there were not so many as he said. It seems that my mother had taken all her best linen and had hidden it with her cousins at Courvaudon, for she knew that my father had to supply her with what she

93

needed and her cousins came by on Saturday and conversed with her, one of them had told some people when my mother was still at Courvaudon that she was running up debts and some people said that Rivière was such a kind man, but she said: I do not see that he is such a good man, why did he not leave his wife in peace without taking all she had, they had made her come and live with them, they could not bear her, he should continue to work her land as he did without harassing her, was she not as attached to her property as he to his. This cousin looked kindly on my father when she saw him, and she said in the town of Aunay that my mother was a wicked woman and tormented her husband. My father and I listened at a place in the flooring to what my mother and my sister were saying to each other. I went and listened most often but I could hear them only when they spoke loudly. One day when my father had said to my sister that my g-m was hardly able to work any more, that she must have help in caring for the cows and each in turn must go to get the provisions, my other sister and she; when my mother returned she said to her repeating my father's words in a mocking tone: oh he said we should go and get the provisions, that his mother is no longer able to work. When my mother did the cooking she did it as badly as she could, she put in the soup herbs she knew my father did not like and mixed them with others he liked. My father sometimes conversed with his neighbors about all his tribulations, he told them of the linen she had hidden away, and he said: no doubt they want to go back, let them go back where they will but do not let them take little Jule with them, I do not want him to follow them, I want him to stay with me, after all they cannot hate him. My mother went to consult Maître Blain at Beauquay, she poured out her calumnies against my father, she also told him she was pregnant. There were other persons at Maître Blain's, it was soon spread about in Aunay, and a man talking to one of our neighbors said: it seems that one of your neighbors must be ill-treating his wife strangely, for she says some fine things about it. My father knowing that she had said she was pregnant, could not believe it, for, he said, she knows well enough how it is with me, what she is thinking is that he cherishes his honor, but if he sees something like this, he will say: how can such things be, he will not be able to contain himself, he will beat me and I shall be able to obtain a separation. I am sure, he went on, that she is putting something on her belly to make her look big, I shall have to have a look at it; he held forth in this strain before a large number of persons among them Hébert and his wife, the widow Quesnel, Victor servant at M. Grellai's and a cousin of my mother's from Courvaudon, Guérin the rural guard, a knifegrinder at Aunay and the priest of Aunay; the priest told him not to take any notice. My father said too: she says that I was the death of the other, but I shall tell her that she will have to account to me for the one she has in her belly. But fearing that he might be wrong I resolved to clear up this matter for myself by listening; once I heard my mother and my sister reckoning up the time she would take for this confinement by counting up the time the others had lasted. My sister said too: you must not make any dress for him, at least until he is formed, and if he comes to ask for the cap and people are there you will say: my faith, there is none, have you given me any money to get one. That will be a fine joke, said my sister; then she imagined what my father might say and added mocking: ah, he will say to you, ah you have done this to shame me again, you are always the same, if it had been anything else you would have been sure to find something; my mother was being careful not to be overheard and told her: be silent. My sister said not so loudly: do not keep worrying about it. Another time my sister had been to Villers to take her lace, she came back without having been paid. My mother said: how wretched I am to be in this position, I hope we shall not stay here long my god. Then she added: did you notice whether the shopkeeper paid the others who brought him lace as you did. Perhaps he has forbidden him to pay you. I took care not to tell my father all the things I had heard because of the notions he had. Another time when my father had left on a journey, I heard my mother and my sister wondering whether he had perhaps gone to try out those with whom she had left her linen and the contracts for the tenure of her lands; he is at Julie's, they said, or else with the Pinote woman, he will ask them for the contracts or things like that, ah but they will not give him them, they would be great cowards if they did; though my mother was pregnant she thought she could nevertheless start to institute separation proceedings, then she refused to cook except for the two children who were still with her and refused to take bread from my g-m where it was delivered, and after going to take advice for three or four days, one day she went to her cousin's doubtless to fetch her money. And the next morning she left for Vire; I noticed that when she went, a man was with her, he was no doubt one of the local people who took her side; while she was away my sister Victoire and my brother Jule stayed in the house eating the bread she had bought for them; not wishing to come to us they went to live with my g-m after that. That evening my father asked my sister why she let the bread that was at her home go bad and went and got other bread, ah, she replied, because we have the means to buy it. Then, he said pay your debts to Rabache and elsewhere where you said you would pay when you had money. Why do you prevent your little brother from coming to eat with us? I am not preventing him she said; you lie, he said, you are preventing him. My mother came back with a summons from the president of the court to appear for conciliation proceedings. It was Maître le Valois writ-server at Saint-Georges who brought my father this summons. Everyone was distressed to see a man of irreproachable conduct so unhappy and persecuted so cruelly by his wife. On Sunday when he was intoning the Asperges, for my father sang at the mass, nearly fifty persons wept. During the week my father obtained certificates, one from the mayor of Aunay which stated particulars of his good conduct and the esteem he enjoyed; one from the mayor of Courvaudon which contained the same and further some particulars about my mother's conduct and another written by the priest and signed by several inhabitants of the commune setting forth my father's conduct toward his wife and various of the sacrifices he had made in order to live in peace with her. My father also took his marriage certificate, the settlement made before Maître Foucaut, which he lost on the way and which was found and returned to him, the lease he had cancelled, the letter with the debts which had been sent him, and he appeared on the day after Ascension. He found the judge predisposed in my mother's favor, almost no notice was taken of his certificates. The judge even said when he saw the certificate from Courvaudon: but it is against your wife that you had it made at Courvaudon. My father said that the mayor had made it out as he pleased. My mother again set to reproaching him for letting her child starve to death. In tears my father explained to the judge what the state of affairs was. He also produced the settlement made before Maître Foucaut. The judge asked my mother why she was not willing to keep to this settlement and told her that she had three choices. Either to keep to this settlement, or to return to her properties at Courvaudon, or to bring an action. My mother said that if she returned to her property she desired her husband to give back what he had taken from her, her furniture, her money, her cows, her casks and several other things she mentioned many of which she had never had. My father said: I will give them all back to you. They asked who would have the custody of the children. The judge said they should go where they would. My father said: but sir she says she is pregnant,[19] who will have the custody of this child? He replied: your wife rather than you, it is she who will be suckling it. But that did not suit my mother who as has been seen intended to have this child and not to do a finger's turn for it in any way whatsoever. My father said: Settle it as you like. She did not reply at all to what the judge said about it. This judge also said that if she wished to bring an action he would not refuse to authorize it but it would be a case which would cost a great deal of money. That was just what pleased my mother as she knew that my father would have to give her money to sue him. On the way to Vire M. Auguste Grellay had asked her why she wanted to ruin her husband. One has to pay money, she had answered him, to get profit from everybody. But she did not take out a writ that day. On the way back my father carried her behind him on the horse from Cadeholle to Aunay. When she returned her disposition did not seem any better. When my father spoke to her about the journey, a fine sight you were, she told him, you looked like a convict from the hulks. And she went on going to hold further consultations on the days following and getting bread from the bakers, when she got it the baker asked her whether her husband had none. Yes, she said, but when you go to fetch a loaf, there is an old woman there who makes a long face at you. I did not eat with my mother or with my sister Victoire since the day my mother started separation proceedings.

[19] My father no longer maintained the arguments I have mentioned above, he said to those to whom he had spoken about it that it was possible she might be pregnant and that it might be by him. But he was never convinced that she really was; when he saw that her pregnancy continued he said that since she often made journeys, she might perhaps try to say that she had given birth during her travels and present him with another child, that if she gave birth away from his house he would have her visited. He also said that why she was doing that was to carry off effects without being seen and hide them with her gossips: when she came back from Vire he said: that is the end of it, she was not so big at Vire as she is every day.

My brother Jule did not seek the company of my father or mine or my brother Prosper's so much, he did not like going on horseback so much as before.[20] But he nevertheless came back with me, he came to my g-m's house several times to eat with all five of us, and he was friendly enough to us, but he preferred my mother to my father. On the Saturday after we returned from Vire my sister Victoire opened the cupboard and gave her cousin who was passing by some more parcels to take away. After vespers on Sunday my father had visitors, several persons from Aunay came and had supper at my g-m's house. Then some of them left; and others stayed. There came a joiner of Courvaudon who lives in the village of le Bouillon where my mother used to live, he first went into her place and set to kissing her and petting her[21] then he went into the other house and drank with my father and the others who were there, they spoke of the carpenter's tools my mother had given him, my father said that she had said she had asked him for them and he had not been willing to give them to her, and they both went to look for them. But she said the same as the joiner, and my father was so dismayed that he set to shouting at her somewhat loudly. Meanwhile the other people with whom I had stayed behind said: my faith he is not safe with all these lads she runs around with everywhere. Then Hébert said to me straight out: never leave your father lad, he will not leave you in the lurch. Alas I had quite different ideas. My father came back and the joiner too. The people had gone out into the yard to take the air, the joiner said: oh I have fallen out with Rivière; my mother and my sister were peering out of the door, it looked as if they were just laughing at my father's distress. The joiner sat down and drank, then he said he would sing a song, well, said François Senecal, tell

[20] This poor child, now I come to think back on it, already did harrowing all by himself.

[21] This joiner had come and done the same several times since my mother had come to live with my father.

us what it is about in a couple of words, the joiner began and sang a song which amounted to mocking my father and laughing at his duplicity [*sic*]. The first couplet ended: let everything come in and nothing go out; in the second couplet it said: Lise was tired of always letting people in by the same door, after nine months someone simply had to come out. My father then said: let us go in we are more in a state for weeping than singing. The joiner went in with us, he began to talk about the tools again and said: I helped your wife bring in her grain and she said to me: well joiner you shall take the tools and then we shall be quits. François Senecal said to him: what are you pestering us about now; and after staying a while longer he went off. Some women who were there spoke to my father and my g-m of their troubles and they saw that they were truly distraught; these people, they said as they left, are certainly having their purgatory on earth. The next morning my father left for Tessel, my g-m expected him back in the afternoon; but he did not come back till about three o'clock in the morning of Tuesday; oh, she said, what have you been doing all this time I have been waiting for you and how worried I am; he said that having left intending to return about six that evening, he had rested a little on the way, he had gone to sleep, and when he woke up he had gone the wrong way, he had walked nearly a league before he recognized where he was and had come back. And that day he fell sick. My g-m told one of her neighbors about this and this woman said to her: it is all his tribulations that are tormenting and distressing him so much. He did not feel fit to work, he lay down and rested, and he was still distressed, distrait and thoughtful; several persons said: if he should fall sick he will not recover.

the end of the summary of my father's afflictions.

Having promised to explain my character and the thoughts I had before and after this deed, I shall make as it were a summary of my private life and the thoughts that have busied me to this day.

In my early childhood, that is to say when I was about 7 or 8, I was very devout. I retired aside to pray to God and I refused the quarter-of-an-hour's refreshments during the Rogation processions. I thought I would be a priest and my father said that he would see to it that I should be able to become one. I learned sermons and I preached before several persons, among them Nicolas Rivière of our village and at the house of his brother the innkeeper at Aunay before some gentlemen who were stopping there. I did this for two or three years. What I had already read inspired me to do this. Later my ideas changed and I thought I should be as other men. Nevertheless I displayed singularities. My schoolmates noticed this and laughed at me. I ascribed their contempt to some acts of stupidity which I had done since the beginnings and which, as I thought, had discredited me for ever. I amused myself all by myself, I walked in our garden and since I had read some things about armies, I imagined our cabbages drawn up in battle array, I appointed leaders, and then I broke down some of the cabbages to show they were dead or wounded. My g-m said, it is astonishing, he loves the cabbages and he breaks them down. I amused myself with this for a long time, though I did not break down many of them. Rivière's eldest son known as Cadet saw me as he passed by, and almost every time he saw me afterwards, he asked me are you still fighting your cabbages? I was good at learning to read and do arithmetic, but I did not get on so well with writing. After I had stopped going to school I worked the land with my father; but that did not suit my inclination at all, I had ideas of glory, I took great pleasure in reading. At school they read the Royaumont Bible, I read in Numbers and Deuteronomy, in the Gospel and the rest of the New Testament, I read in almanacs and geography, I read in the Family Museum and a clergy calendar, some histories, that of Bonaparte, Roman history, a history of shipwrecks, the Practical Morals and several other things. If I found even a scrap of newspaper to be used to wipe one's behind I read it, I also read in the Good Sense of the Curé Melier, in Feller's philosophical catechism and the Montpellier Catechism. What I read about astronomy and some other things which I had examined made me irreligious after three years. At that time and before that I was consumed by ideas of greatness and immortality, I esteemed myself far better than others, and I have been ashamed to say so until now, I thought I would raise myself above my condition. At this time carnal passion troubled me: I believed that it was unworthy of me ever to think of indulging it. Above all I had a horror of incest which caused me to shun approaching the women of my family. When I thought I had come too close to them, I made signs with my hand as if to repair the harm I believed I had done. My father and my g-m were very much' distressed by these things which lasted for the space of a year. My father said perhaps he has scruples[22] but it is astonishing for he no longer has any religion. When they asked me why I made these signs, I tried to evade the questions by saying that I was trying to drive away the devil. They said too that I had a horror of other women, for sometimes when they were beside my g-m and my sister, I withdrew elsewhere. One day when Marianne Renaut who was then a servant in our house opened the garden door, I promptly thrust my hand to my breech, though I was very far away. Oh yes, she said, go on, hold your trousers tight; but it was not her I was afraid I would see when she opened the door, I was afraid it would be my g-m or my sister. These ideas faded away. But I was always preoccupied with my excellence, and on my solitary walks I made up stories in which

[22] Before my incredulity I had had other scruples, I feared distractions in my prayers, so that I repeated the words an infinite number of times and made absurd gestures and contortions.

I imagined myself playing a role, I was forever filling my head with personages I imagined. I saw quite well however how people looked upon me, most of them laughed at me. I applied myself diligently to find out what I should do to stop this and live in society, but I did not have tact enough to do that, I could not find the words to say, and I could not appear sociable with the young people of my own age, it was above all when I met girls in company that I lacked words to address them, so some of them by way of jest ran after me to kiss me. I was unwilling to go and see my relations, that is to say cousins, or my father's friends for fear of the compliments that must be exchanged. Finding that I could not manage to do such things, I got over it. And I despised in my heart those who despised me. I wished to revenge myself on Nicolas Margrie's daughter who had managed to kiss me by making a song about her honor which I had resolved to scatter along the roads; I then thought I could revenge myself on my other mockers by making up songs about all of them. I told Fortain, one of my friends, that I could revenge myself on all those people by making writings about all of them, I could put them to scorn and have them driven out of the district. Later I was several times tempted to call out someone in a duel. I also resolved to distinguish myself by making completely new instruments, I wanted them to be created in my imagination. I resolved first to make a tool to kill birds such as had never before been seen, I named it "calibene," I worked on it for a long time on Sundays and in the evening, and finding that it did not succeed as I had expected, I went and buried it in a meadow and later I dug it up again and it is still on the floor in one of the houses. I had also resolved to make an instrument to churn butter all by itself and a carriage to go all by itself with springs, which I wanted to produce only in my imagination. I told these things to my friend Fortain and to Jean Buot who worked with us. I was more at ease with children of nine or ten than with people of my own age, I made them bows which I called albalesters, and I busied myself in trying to get one to go off. I was arrested with one and though I said I had made it in order to pass for mad, yet it was not exactly that. At our home I made some go off but I took care to hide myself as well as I could. In myself I found that this was not a necessity, I had read that it was formerly used for hunting and even for fighting in war. Some time ago I broke a pane of Nativel's window by shooting one off, I was ashamed in case they said it was me; my two brothers were there. They were asked who had broken it. They said they knew nothing about it, and they never said that it was me. As it was soon suspected who it had been, my father asked Jule if it was not me. This child always maintained that it was not. I crucified frogs and birds, I had also invented another torture to put them to death. It was to attach them to a tree with three sharp nails through the belly. I called that enceepharating them, I took the children with me to do it and sometimes I did it all by myself. Two years ago I went to Sainte-Honorine all alone on Saint Claire's day to observe the talk which the masters and servants held together and to learn from it and do as much myself if I had the chance. I observed several persons, M. Viel of Guiberville among others, I saw him speak to several servants and hire one; I watched the people without speaking to them, without knowing them and without their knowing me. I often took a stroll through assemblages and markets all by myself without companions. I always had ideas about learning things and bettering myself. I thought that if ever I came to have some money I would buy some books and Abbé Gaultier's complete course[23] of reading, writing, arithmetic, geometry, geography, history, music, the French, Latin and Italian languages, etc., the whole costing 60 frs. I thought I would better myself. Despite these ideas of glory I cherished, I loved my father very much, his tribulations affected me sorely. The distress in which I saw him

[23] I had seen it mentioned in his geography book.

immersed in these latter days, his duplicity [*sic*], the tribulations he continually endured, all this affected me very
deeply. All my ideas were directed toward these things and
settled upon them. I conceived the fearful design which I
executed, I was meditating it for about a month before. I
wholly forgot the principles which should have made me
respect my mother and my sister and my brother, I regarded
my father as being in the power of mad dogs or barbarians
against whom I must take up arms, religion forbade such
things, but I disregarded its rules, it even seemed to me that
God had destined me for this and that I would be executing
his justice. I knew the rules of man and the rules of ordered
society, but I deemed myself wiser than they, I regarded
them as ignoble and shameful. I had read in Roman history,
and I had found that the Romans' laws gave the husband the
right of life and death over his wife and his children. I
wished to defy the laws, it seemed to me that it would be a
glory to me, that I should immortalize myself by dying for
my father. I conjured up the warriors who died for their
king and country, the valor of the students of the Poly-
thecnic [*sic*] college at the taking of Paris in 1814, and I
said to myself: these people died to uphold the cause of a
man whom they did not know and who did not know them
either, who had never given them a thought; and I, I would
be dying to deliver a man who loves and cherishes me. The
example of Chatillon who alone held unto death the passage
through a street through which the enemy was swarming to
seize his king; the courage of Eleazar one of the Maccabees
brothers who slew an elephant where he believed the enemy
king to be, although he knew that he would be crushed
beneath the animal's weight; the example of a Roman
general whose name I do not remember who laid down his
life in the war against the Latins to uphold his cause. All
these things passed through my mind and invited me to
do my deed. The example of Henri de la Roquejacquelain
which I read recently seemed to me to have a great bearing

on my concerns. He was one of the leaders of the Vendeans, he died in the twenty-first year of his age to uphold the king's cause. I pondered his harangue to his soldiers as the battle began: if I advance, he said, follow me, if I retreat kill me, if I die avenge me. The latest book I read was a history of shipwrecks lent to me by Lerot. I found in it that when the sailors lacked victuals, they sacrificed one of their number and ate him to save the rest of the crew. I thought to myself: I too will sacrifice myself for my father, everything seemed to invite me to this deed. Even with the mystery of the redemption, I thought that it was easier to understand, I said: our Lord Jesus Christ died on the cross to save mankind, to redeem him from the slavery of the devil, from sin and from eternal damnation, he was God, it was for him to punish the men who had offended him; he could therefore have pardoned them without suffering these things; but as for me, I can deliver my father only by dying for him. When I heard that nearly fifty persons had wept when my father had intoned the Asperges, I said in my heart: if strangers who have nothing to do with it weep, what should I not do, I who am his son. I therefore took this fearful resolution, I determined to kill all three of them, the first two because they were leagued to make my father suffer, as to the little boy I had two reasons, one because he loved my mother and my sister, the other because I feared that if I only killed the other two, my father though greatly horrified by it might yet regret me when he knew that I was dying for him, I knew that he loved that child who was very intelligent, I thought to myself he will hold me in such abhorrence that he will rejoice[24] in my death, and so he will live happier being free from regrets. Having therefore taken these fatal resolutions I resolved to put them into

[24] In conversations when people were speaking of robbers who were up for judgment like Lemaire for example, some people had said: perhaps he will not be put to death, because of his family and so forth. My father had said: as for me, if I had a robber in my family, I should be very glad if they put him to death.

execution. I intended at first to write down the whole life of my father and my mother practically as it is written here,[25] to put an announcement of the deed at the beginning and my reasons for committing it at the end, and the way I intended to flout the law, that I was defying it, that I was immortalizing myself and so forth; then to commit my deed, to take my letter to the post, and then to take a gun I would hide beforehand and kill myself; I had got up for several nights to read the Montpellier Catechism; on the pretext of doing the same I got up and began to write the announcement of the beginning, but the next day my sister found out, I then told her that I was writing the life of my father and my mother to present it to the judges or to a lawyer whom my father would go and consult to show the manner in which he was treated by my mother or else even that it would only be read to those of our acquaintance. My sister, it was Aimée, wanted to see what there was that had already been written, I took great care not to show her, for it was the announcement of the beginning. She came back a little while later with my father and Quevillon, I hid it, she asked: is it impossible to see it then? I said that she must wait till there was more written. But fearing that someone might read this announcement I burned it and I thought I would write the life without hiding from anyone and that I would secretly put in the reasons of the end and the beginning after this life was written. So I got up to write a night or two but I almost always went to sleep and I could only write a little. Then I took another decision, I gave up writing, and I thought that after the murder I would come to Vire and give myself up to the district prosecutor or the police inspector; then I would make my declarations that I would die for my father, that no matter how much they were in favor

---

[25] As I intended to write this history before the crime and had considered most of the words that I would put in it, it will not be surprising to find harsh expressions in it which would seem to show that I still harbored hatred toward my hapless victims.

of women they would not triumph, and my father would be quiet and happy thenceforth; I thought I would also say: in former times one saw Jaels against Siseras, Judiths against Holoferneses, Charlotte Cordays against Marats; now it must be men who employ this mania, it is the women who are in command now in this fine age which calls itself the age of enlightenment, this nation which seems to be so avid for liberty and glory obeys women, the Romans were far more civilized, the Hurons and the Hottentots, the Algonquins, these peoples who are said to be idiots are even more civilized, never have they debased strength, it has always been the stronger in body who have laid down the law among themselves. I thought it would be a great glory to me to have thoughts opposed to all my judges, to dispute against the whole world, I conjured up Bonaparte in 1815. I also said to myself: that man sent thousands to their death to satisfy mere caprices, it is not right therefore that I should let a woman live who is disturbing my father's peace and happiness, I thought that an opportunity had come for me to raise myself, that my name would make some noise in the world, that by my death I should cover myself with glory, and that in time to come my ideas would be adopted and I should be vindicated. Thus I took this fatal decision. However I feared lest my father, who as I thought did not have ideas as sublime as mine, might kill himself at the sight of it; but I thought I would do it when he was away and I would warn people to keep him away and once he had withstood the first shock, there would be no danger afterwards. I also thought that since I would have to appear before the judges to defend my opinions, I must do this deed in my Sunday clothes so that I could leave for Vire as soon as it was consummated. I went to have my pruning bill sharpened on Sunday May 24 at Gabin the Blacksmith's smithy at Aunay, who was accustomed to work for us; that day I did nothing, I thought I would do it during the week and I would put on my Sunday clothes before doing it; on the Saturday when I saw that my father and my g-m had left for the town of Aunay and the three I had resolved to kill were together in the house, I at once dressed in my Sunday clothes, but when I was ready, I saw that my mother and my brother had gone to the town; since I thought they would come back, and since my sister Aimée asked me why I was dressed like that, I said I was going to the town, and I went to pass the time until my mother returned; having seen her on the road coming back, I simply went to the town and came back, on my return I found all three of them in the house, but I could not make up my mind to kill them; I then said to myself: I am no coward yet I will never be able to do anything, I went into the garden; and I saw my father coming back; then I went and changed my clothes; my father and my g-m asked me why I was dressed up like that to go to the town, it would have been better only to put my smock on over my other clothes; I said that my other clothes, particularly my trousers, were too ragged; they asked me no other questions; I thought that I would do this deed the next day at my leisure; but no opportunity arose or if it arose I did not take it; in the evening I was going to do it while there were visitors with my father, for I thought that all those people would prevent him from doing himself harm. When he saw that, I did not go and sup with them, but went and wandered about in the gardens busying myself with my ideas; I had an opportunity, I said to myself, but I was held back by what I then called my cowardice. As I could not make up my mind to it then, therefore, and saw that it could no longer be done that day, I went with my father and those who were still with him, the joiner and the others of whom I have spoken. I thought I would do this deed during the week and that I would hide to dress in my Sunday clothes, I knew that it could not be done the next day, we had to go and plow for Quevillon, it was I who went; but he was to come and plow for us the day after, and it was ordinarily my father who

went to fetch him when he plowed for us, I thought I would
execute this project while my father was away plowing; so
I went on the Monday to plow for Quevillon, he said he
was not sure he could come and plow for us the next day, because he had to borrow a horse to go to a meadow where
three were needed on the Wednesday, he could if we could
finish working the meadow where we were and go and har-
row the meadow in the afternoon so that it would be quite
ready; that he would come and plow for us on the Tuesday,
but otherwise he would not be able to come. When I heard
this I worked the horses as fast as I could, and we finished
the field we were in, and in the afternoon we went and
harrowed as he had said. Next day he came to plow for
us, but as my father had returned sick after spending the
night in the open, he could not go with him, and I had to
go. At midday my father felt somewhat better and asked me
whether I would rather dig the garden or go back to plow, I
would dig; when I was in the yard after dinner, I said to my
sister Aimée: sing us the canticle happy day, holy joy; why?
she asked me; to learn the tune, I answered; and why, she
said, do you want to learn the tune? I said: I should be very
glad to know it, and then she set to singing, and Quevillon
said: oh that will do us all good I think, and he joked with
my sister; then he went off with my father to plow. But
again I did nothing that day, no great opportunity occurred,
and then I took another resolution, I had to go and work for
Quevillon the next day, I thought I would feign sickness
that morning so that my father should go. When it was time
to get up that morning I therefore pretended to vomit, my
g-m came. I told her I was not feeling well and I was not
going to be able to go plowing and my father went though
he too was somewhat ill; about an hour later I got up and
said I was a little better, I said I was going to work in the
garden, then I secretly got hold of my Sunday clothes and
took them into one of the other houses called Clinot's house,
then I dressed in my Sunday clothes; at that moment all

three of them were in the house, but when I was dressed, I
saw that my brother Jule had just gone to school; then I
decide to put it off to another time; I was in the garden and
I was about to go back into the house I mentioned and I put
on my old clothes again when my sister Aimée saw me; and
since she saw me I went off, I went over toward Beauquay
and I resolved not to return until noon when they would all
three be together. But that was too long to wait, I returned
to the house resolved to put on my old clothes again and to
do the deed without dressing in others. I thought to myself:
what does it matter whether I am dressed well or ill, I shall
explain myself quite as well without wearing good clothes,
then I came back to the house; the widow Quesnel was in
the yard; oh, she said to my g-m, here is Pierre back again;
I went and looked in the house where I had left my old
clothes, I found they had been taken away. I went into my
g-m's house and found her weeping; where do you want to go
to, she said to me, if you do not think you are earning enough
with your father and want to go elsewhere, say so, without
going off like that and saying nothing to anyone, and what
is more you have no money, what do you intend to do, you
want to abandon your father, yet you see how he is. Ah, said
the widow Quesnel, you are being the death of your poor
g-m who loves you so much, fall on her neck and kiss her.
My g-m went on to say to me: why do you do it, your father
offered you all the advantages he could, when you were little
he said he would sacrifice part of his property to make you
a priest, he offered to have you taught a trade if you wished,
if you want to leave him, he still will not let you go without money; the widow Quesnel said: ah he is not backward
in helping you do your work, he can be happy with all of
you if he wants to. My g-m said: ah he would have done
better to go this morning instead of his father who is sick,
he sees his position, if he leaves him, that will be yet another
forceful argument his mother will have against his father in
her suit, she will tell the judges: he is so bad that his children

will not stay with him; yet if he wishes to go, his father will not hold him back; let him tell us and we shall not be worried about where he is.

I evaded all my g-m's questions by saying it was nothing, they were making much ado about very little, and I went off to the closet where I put on all my old clothes again, then I went to dig in the garden till noon. My g-m came too to work a bed of peas, she asked me some more questions, to which I kept answering that it was nothing and she should not worry about it. Yes it is though, she said, it is something, when your father comes back I shall want you to explain it; well, I answered, I will explain to him this evening. My g-m ceased questioning me. Noon came and she went off to milk the cows with my sister Aimée. My brother Jule had come back from school. Taking advantage of this opportunity I seized the bill, I went into my mother's house and I committed that fearful crime, beginning with my mother, then my sister and my little brother, after that I struck them again and again; Marie, Nativel's mother-in-law came in, ah what are you doing, she said to me, go away, I said to her, or I shall do as much to you. Then I went out into the yard and speaking to Nativel I said: Miché go and make sure that my g-m does not do herself any harm, she can be happy now, I die to restore her peace and quiet, I also spoke to Aimée Lerot and to Potel, Lerot's servant, see to it, I said, that my father and my g-m do not do themselves a mischief, I die to restore them peace and quiet. Then I set off to go to Vire; as I wished to have the glory of being the first to announce this news there I did not want to go to the town of Aunay, for fear I might be arrested there. I resolved to go by the woods of Aunay by a road on which I had been several times which passes near a place called les Vergées, and to reach the road to Vire above the village at the foot of the wood of Aunay; I therefore took that road and I threw away my bill into a wheatfield near la Faucterie and went off. As I went I felt this courage and this idea of glory that inspired me weaken, and when I had gone farther and came into the woods I regained my full senses, ah, can it be so, I asked myself, monster that I am! Hapless victims! can I possibly have done that, no it is but a dream! ah but it is all too true! chasms gape beneath my feet, earth swallow me; I wept, I fell to the ground, I lay there, I gazed at the scene, the woods, I had been there before. Alas, I said to myself, little did I think I would one day be in this plight; poor mother, poor sister, guilty maybe in some sort, but never did they have ideas so unworthy as mine, poor unhappy child, who came plowing with me, who led the horse, who already harrowed all by himself, they are annihilated forever these hapless ones. Nevermore will they be seen on earth! Ah heaven, why have you granted me existence, why do you preserve me any longer. I did not stay long in that place, I could not stay at this spot, my regrets faded somewhat as I walked on. It is not hard to understand that I was no longer resolved to come to Vire to maintain the ideas I have set forth above. My ideas changed more than once in the month that passed between the crime and my arrest, I will report them with the places where I went. As I said I first went into the woods of Aunay where aching with regret I went on not knowing whither I went, when I reached the top of the wood of Aunay, I went as I think toward Danvou; but I do not know whether I was far from it when I passed; that evening I was in a small wood near Cadehol, I lay down and gave myself over to my despairing thoughts, I rose, and I went to reach the highroad, I passed through Cadehol and a little farther on I left the highroad on the right, I went by side roads, I rested under a hedge, and on Thursday I went by places I do not know all of them, I had not dined on the Wednesday, I ate various sorts of plants, such as cuckoo bread and wild sorrel, I also gathered mushrooms, I had no money but fourteen *sous* which happened to be in my pocket at the time I left, I came to Tourneur where I bought a pound of bread, I followed the local road. As I was passing through a town, which I was told was Saint-Pierre, I heard a woman saying to another; have you heard of the sad event which has happened at Aunay? Yes, replied the other, but I do not know if it is really true; ah yes, said the first, it is only too true. That evening as I was in the fields near the main road between le Mesnil au Souf and Cadehol, I resolved to kill myself, the vision of my crime was not to be borne. Fearing that they might perhaps accuse my father of complicity, of hiding me, or getting me away by one means or another, I thought to myself that it is necessary that my body be found, and as I ordinarily carried string and had some with me, I resolved to hang myself on a tree, I examined some which might serve my purpose, but when I went to do it, the fear of the judgments of God restrained me, I spent all day Friday in this agitation, at last I resolved to abide by my condition since the evil was irremediable, I resolved to live on plants and roots until whatever events might come; until the strawberries, blueberries and blackberries were ripe, I resolved to go to the seashore, and live there on crabs, mussels and oysters, I went off on the Friday evening, on Saturday morning I went a little way off the highroad, and I spent the day in the woods near le Mesnil au Souf on the left as one goes from Vire to Caen, I traveled the following nights except Tuesday when I walked by day, and I came to Port. That day near the wood of Juvigni, on Monday morning I had met a man who had asked me where I was going and if I had papers, I had answered that I was going to Fontenay, and he had asked me nothing further; I was at Port on Tuesday afternoon as I said; I ate some crabs, and I could see that that would not do, I resolved to go back to roots and wild saffron bulbs in the woods where I had been near le Mesnil au Souf, I went back through Bayeux on Tuesday evening and I slept in a ditch near Cremel, I no longer cared greatly whether they arrested me or not, and on Wednesday I traveled by day, I asked for two *liards'* worth of radishes on the bridge at Juvigni, they had none, I went off. Marianne Beauvais who was a servant

in our house for a year and is now at Dupont's the innkeeper at Juvigni noticed me as I was passing, and no doubt
she told these who were with her, for I heard people shouting behind me: ah ah, here he is call the gendarmes; as I did
not turn round, she shouted two or three times, Pierre, oh
Pierre; I came to the bend in the highroad and I met the
same man who had questioned me on the Monday, there
were no more shouts behind me, he said nothing to me, I
drank and ate a little cress at a stream where there is a
bridge near Juvigni and went on my way. I passed through
Villers by night and on Thursday I was back in the woods at
le Mesnil au Souf; I thought I could not go on in this fashion,
and feeling that it could only have been an aberration that
had brought me to commit this crime, I resolved to come and
give myself up to the law and be arrested at Vire, but I was
afraid to tell the exact truth; my first intention was however
to say that I repented but I had the idea of saying that I had
been brought to it by visions, that absorbed as I was by all
my father's tribulations, I had seen spirits and angels who
had told me to do it by God's order, I had been destined to
it from all time, and they would carry me up to heaven after
I had done this deed, that I had done it with these ideas;
but that immediately afterward I had come to my senses and
had repented, as it had in fact happened with the other things
I have spoken of. So during the night of Friday to Saturday
I left the woods at le Mesnil au Souf, by night, for I did
not wish to be arrested anywhere but at Vire, and I arrived
on Saturday morning, I could not bring myself to denounce
myself, I would have preferred that someone should ask for
my papers. When I got there I lay down in a ditch, and
seeing that no one said anything to me, I went to the upper
part of the rue du Calvados, I walked around a little, and
seeing that they did not arrest me, I asked the way to Cher-
bourg, I had read that a soldier had swum for two leagues
at sea to carry orders from Thoiras to Cardinal Richelieu,
and I thought that I could also swim to some of the islands

belonging to the English such as the isles of Jersai, Genesai, Aurigni and Vig* which I had seen in the geography book and on the maps not far off the mainland of France, or I should perish swimming, I must take the risk, so I went back to la Papillonnière and went a little way along the road I had been shown. But seeing that what I was thinking of was impossible and that even if I managed it I should not be saved after all, I resolved to return to Vire, it was in the morning that I had reached it, I came back in the afternoon. I sat down at the top of the rue du Calvados where there were several gendarmes and several gentlemen and I asked a woman for the residence of the inspector of police, she said to me: I suppose it is the lord and master's house you want? She told me the street he lived in, a gentleman who was there also told me where it was. I went to where they had told me; but as I did not know the house, and then feeling loth to do it, I sat down on some logs there near a church which is on the height; then I resolved to declare myself to a gendarme I went back to where they were; I sat down in front of them again, and seeing them still take no notice of me, I resolved to return to the woods and go on living the life I had led till then; I always slept out, and I only asked for alms at three houses near la Papillonnière and at one house on the way back from Bayeux, and they all refused me. I went back from Vire where I was on Saturday to a small wood beyond the chapel of the Ave Maria, where I spent the day of Sunday, I ate saffron bulbs there and the next night I returned to the woods at le Mesnil au Souf, there I ate more plants and roots, I still tried to distract my mind from my misfortunes, reciting my prayers passed the time, and furthermore I contemplated nature, I examined the stars, I thought I should see Hallay's comet, I spent some days in these woods, and then finding anew that I would not be able to go on like that I resolved to be taken by the law. But I resolved to disguise the truth even more than I had disguised it the first time and I conceived the design of

* *Jersey, Guernsey, Alderney, Sark. (Translator's note.)*

playing the role which I played at the beginning of my imprisonment. I thought: there were madwomen, and I have seen it in the Family Museum, madwomen who said that they were, one the queen of France, another the queen of all places, another Pope Joan and claiming to be inspired by God to preach to the whole earth. I thought therefore that I must not say that I represented myself, I must say that I was inspired by God, I was his instrument and was obeying his orders; that I had seen him and his angels too. I embraced this method of defense with great regret, but I thought it would serve my purpose. I left the woods and returned to Vire resolved to make gestures on the roads. However as I apprehended the result that might come of it, I resolved first to use the little money I had, until then, except for a pound of bread and two *liards'* worth of walnuts, I had saved it for fear I might need it for something even more necessary than food; my belly was so empty that I bound it with my neckerchief so that I might walk more easily, I passed through Vire this second time on a Thursday morning and as I passed by I bought two pounds of bread and a roll, I followed the highroad to Condé, I did not know it, but it turned out that it was the right one. On Friday I passed through Vassi, I lay down on the edge of a wheatfield near Vassi to see if they would arrest me, some people came and saw me and were astonished, but they did not arrest me; I arrived at Condé in the evening, and I bought two rolls from a baker, I slept in a ditch and the next day I took the road to Fler, I met a shopkeeper from Aunay whom I recognized from having seen him, he recognized me also and said to me: here you are lad, where are you going like that, you will get yourself arrested, you have done something bad, my son, a very bad thing indeed, I pretended not to take any notice of what he said and went off, I had no more money and I set to eating saffron bulbs again, the next day Sunday morning I met Laurent Grellay, known as Ficet, near Fler driving some oxen and he said to me: Oh Rivière you are going to get yourself arrested; I thought to

myself, that is what I want, and without answering him I
went on my way, I came to Fler, I crossed the market place
and came to the other side of the town near the last houses,
I lay down in the sun by the side of the road, I went farther,
and in the afternoon I returned to the same place where I
had lain down that morning. And in order to attract people's
attention, as well as to get something to eat I set to digging
for saffron bulbs in a ditch which runs beside the highroad,
all those who passed by looked at me and were astonished,
but no one sought to arrest me, in the end two men came up
and one said to the other: there is a man who has been
here since this morning. The other came up to me as well
as the man with him, he asked me what I was doing there;
thereupon I answered him according to the system I had
adopted, that I was from everywhere, in the end I told him
that I had started from Aunay, but this man had no suspicion
of what I might be, he told me to come to his house and he
would give me something to eat, he had to ask me more
than once, at last I went there and he gave me some bread
and cider, then I left him, I went back through the town,
and I resolved to return to Vire and make more gestures on
the road, I went back through Condé that evening as the
people were taking a stroll, and I slept near a limekiln a
little above Condé, in the morning I left and I found 50
sous remaining from a roll of *sous* near a small town which
is on a height, and in view of this I resolved to wait some
more before deliberately getting myself taken, I went back
through Vassi, and I stopped at an inn a little farther on, the
same one where the gendarmes stopped when they were taking me to Vire, I ordered bread and eggs and cider, I spent
14 *sous* there and in the evening I went back through Vire,
I bought 3 *sous'* worth of walnuts and I went to a baker's
where I bought six rolls, this baker told me, as the woman
selling walnuts had told me, to come and see him if I needed
any another time, I went that night into the woods at le
Mesnil au Souf, where I spent three days; during the night
of Thursday to Friday I left and went from le Mesnil au

Souf by side roads and across the fields and I came in the morning to between le Plessis and les forges Viret, I spent the day on the banks of a river and I sheltered under the rocks for it was raining, the next night I followed the local road, I passed through les forges Viret, I went straight ahead and I came to the highroad which as I believe goes from Condé to Halcour, I walked all day Saturday, I kept thinking they would arrest me, meanwhile as I had hardly any more money, I resolved to make a bow to kill birds and feed on them, or to amuse myself trying to kill some, and if they should arrest me with it, it might rather serve than harm the role I would be playing; but since I would have to cook any I could kill, as I passed through Halcour I bought a watch glass which cost me 4 *sous* to light a fire by the sun, thinking it would have the same effect as spectacles, but having tried it and seeing that it was no use I broke it. I had taken the road from Halcour to Caen, I came to a town, I went into a shop, I bought two *liards'* worth of tinder, a *sou's* worth of sulphur, I had flints which I had gathered on the road and with my knife I could strike a spark, I had some pages from a breviary and an almanac, which I happened to have on me when I left, I could use them for matches. I also bought a *sou's* worth of walnuts, I went into a baker's and bought two pounds of griddle-cake, in the afternoon I rested in the meadows by the hedges, and I caught a young lark, I put the bird in my pocket and went on my way, I had only four *sous* left, I spent them that evening on a quart of cider and a small butter griddle-cake, and I spent the night in a wheatfield; in the morning I passed through Caen, I took the road to Falaise and went into the woods near Langannerie, I gathered some sticks of dry wood, I lighted a fire at the foot of a tree which prevented the wind from putting it out, and I roasted the lark; it will perhaps be said that I also caught chickens and ducks and other things and took faggots from woodpiles; but the remains can still be found in the wood where I lit my fire and a few sticks piled up, or if they are no longer there consult those who removed them, all that is to be found is I say only a few dry sticks gathered in the wood and only the feathers from the lark. I came therefore to these woods on Sunday; after eating the lark, I made a bow and several arrows. I had found a long nail on the road; by dint of filing it with the less good of my knives I managed to break its head off, and I put it on the end of one of the arrows (the other arrows are still there if they have not been removed they are in the tree near which I made the fire) then I used this weapon to try and kill birds, but I could not manage this; if I had found any frogs too, I would have cut off their legs and roasted them, but I did not find any. I spent four days in these woods, they are three small woods not very far from each other, in one of which many strawberries grow, I ate them, and I thought to myself, either I shall be arrested, or I shall live in this way, or I shall die. Seeing some more woods, further along the road, I resolved to go and see if there was anything to eat in them until other fruits were ripe in the woods where I was; and I thought that until they arrested me, I would come and go from one wood to another to get my food. So I left on the Thursday morning, and I came to the town of Langannerie with my bow under my arm, as I was passing someone said: oh look, there is a fellow carrying a bow. I had soon passed through the town and was at the last houses, when a gendarme who was not in uniform, passing near me, surveyed me, and asked me: where are you from my friend? I replied in accordance with my system, I am from everywhere.—Have you any papers—No—What are you doing here—God is conducting me, and I adore him—Ho, I believe I have some business with you, where are you from —I started from Aunay—What is your name—Rivière.— Ah yes come with me I have something to say to you— What do you want of me—Come on come on I will tell you. And then speaking to a woman who was I think from his household, oh, he said, it is the fellow from Aunay. He took me into a room searched me and took charge of everything I had. When he was about to put me in the cells, are you, he asked, the fellow who killed your mother? Yes, I answered him, God inspired me, he ordered me to do it, I obeyed his orders, and he is protecting me. Ah yes so that is it, he said, opening the door of the cell, go on my lad, get in there. I afterwards maintained this method of defense at Falaise and at Condé, it was very painful for me to maintain such things and to say that I did not repent; when I came to Vire I thought I would declare the truth, but when I appeared before the Prosecutor Royal, I maintained the same thing. When they had left me by myself, I resolved afresh to tell the truth, and I confessed to the jailer who came and talked to me, and I told him that I intended to declare everything before my judges; but when I went to my first interrogation before the examining judge, I could not yet make up my mind to it and I maintained the system of which I have spoken until the jailer told what I had said to him. I was very glad at his statement, it relieved me of a great weight which was crushing me. Then without disguising anything, I declared everything which had brought me to this crime. They told me to put all these things down in writing, I have written them down; now that I have made known all my monstrosity, and that all the explanations of my crime are done, I await the fate which is destined for me, I know the article of the penal code concerning parricide, I accept it in expiation of my faults; alas if only I could see the hapless victims of my cruelty alive once more, even if for that I must suffer the utmost torments; but no it is vain, I can only follow them; so I therefore await the penalty I deserve, and the day which shall put an end to all my resentments.

THE END

This manuscript begun on July 10, 1835 in the jail at Vire, and finished at the same place on the 21st of the same month.

Pierre Rivière

4

Medico-legal Opinions

1. CERTIFICATE BY DR. BOUCHARD

I THE UNDERSIGNED, Doctor of Medicine, corresponding member of the Royal Academy of Medicine and the Athénée de médecine, Paris, hereby certify that I have examined with the greatest care and on several occasions the man Pierre Rivière of the commune of Aunay charged with the murder of his mother, his sister, and his brother. The results of my observations are as follows:

Pierre Rivière is twenty years of age; his constitution is good, he is of medium height, of sallow complexion, his general aspect calm but gloomy, he will not look people straight in the face. He shows every sign of a bilious-melancholic temperament.

His health is ordinarily excellent, he eats and sleeps very well. He has never had any skin diseases or hemorrhages recurring at regular intervals. Since he has never had any ailment of the blood, he has not contracted the habit of being bled. His bowels habitually function very well. He has never fallen on his head; he does not recall ever having been hit on it. In short, despite thorough questioning, I have not been able to detect any malady which may have acted on the brain in a way likely to have impaired its functions.

Like all persons of a bilious and melancholic temperament, Rivière is chary of speech. When asked questions, he answers clearly, but briefly. The most surprising thing about him is his concentration, from which it is hard to distract him. After I had spoken to him at some length and had asked him a great many questions, he immediately took up his pen again and continued writing his memoir as if he had not been interrupted. Nothing in his answers indicates any derangement of the mental faculties. When reminded of his crime, he speaks of it with a sort of tranquillity which is truly shocking.

I made no phrenological examinations, for this science has not yet made much progress, and I must admit that my acquaintance with it is too imperfect for me to venture to apply it in so serious a case.

But if I had to give an opinion on the cause of the crime, it would be as follows. Endowed with a bilious and melancholic temperament, a frequent witness of his parents' quarrels, Rivière was deeply affected by his father's misfortunes. Shunning society as he did, he was beset by the darkest ideas. They obsessed him and thereafter left him no peace of mind. From that time on, Rivière wanted one thing only, to deliver his father, and in order to achieve his purpose he had to murder his mother. This obsession pursued him at all times; twice, it is true, his courage failed him at the very moment when he was on the point of committing the most heinous of crimes, but he still did not relinquish his fatal project. It was in solitude that he had conceived the idea of the crime; it was in solitude that he went to steep himself once more before laying homicidal hands upon his mother.

To sum up:

In Rivière's case no malady can have damaged the functions of his brain, and during my many visits to him after he was brought to Vire I observed no sign of mental derangement. The triple murder of which he was guilty can be ascribed, I believe, only to a state of momentary over-excitement brought on by his father's tribulations.

Vire, July 21, 1835
(signed)

2. MEDICAL OPINION BY DR. VASTEL

On the third of June, a young man about twenty years of age killed his mother, his sister, and his brother with premeditation and in cold blood. Then he calmly left the scene of this ghastly crime, showed himself to his neighbors, and, drenched with blood, ax in hand, he announced to them that he had just delivered his father, recommended him to their care, walked slowly away, and disappeared.

A month later he was arrested on the highroad and taken to the jail at Vire. There, questioned by the District Prosecutor Royal and the examining judge, he made a full confession, entered into every detail and explained the motives on which he acted. At the request of these officers of the court, he himself wrote out a long memoir in which he depicts himself with great truth. Finally, he was transferred to the prison at Caen and brought before the Calvados assize court.

A young barrister, reputed no less for his humanity and probity than his knowledge of the law and his talent, consented to undertake Rivière's defense, for the wretched man's father protests that his son is mad and has been known to be so ever since his childhood and has furnished evidence of this to the young counsel for the defense, who, after long and mature consideration, has come to share his conviction. Before undertaking the defense in court, however, he wishes to have the opinion of a doctor whom he considers to be more fitted than anyone else to give him the benefit of his advice since he is attached to one of the largest mental hospitals in France.

It is to this circumstance that I owe the honor of a consultation by Maître Bertauld, who expounded the matter in detail to me and communicated to me the documents in the case as well as the memoir written by Rivière and took me to visit his client in prison for observation and interrogation. The question he had asked me was soon clarified to my satisfaction in the light of the documents and of my own observations, and I became deeply and fully convinced that Rivière was not sane and that the act which the prosecution considered to be an atrocious crime was simply the deplorable result of true mental alienation.

The reasons which led to my conviction and formed the basis for my judgment derive from Rivière's external appearance, his behavior as a whole, his origins and family, the state of his mental faculties since childhood, the very nature of the act committed by him and its attendant circumstances and, lastly, from all that has happened between the occurrence and the present.

1. *Rivière's external appearance and habitual behavior*

The subject is twenty years of age, of medium height, rounded forms, phlegmatic constitution, inexpressive features; he habitually keeps his head, which is of average size, lowered; the forehead is low and narrow, the eyebrows knitted, the gaze ill-assured, timid, and furtive, his speech has something childish and unmanly about it; his answers are slow, he often smiles vacantly, his poise is awkward, his gait strange and jerky. To anyone observing him attentively and without preconceived notions it will soon be evident that the subject is organized differently from others, that he is an aberration from the ordinary condition and that he resembles, I would not say the absolute idiots, but those semi-imbeciles whose faculties are very limited and who reveal their mental deficiency in their entire external appearance. Now, though no more importance than is due is to be attached to a man's physical constitution, I believe nonetheless that the light it throws on the state of his intelligence should not be neglected, especially when the presumptions arising from it are corroborated by a large number of more weighty facts, as we shall see is the case with Rivière as we proceed with this examination.

2. *Origin and family*

Rivière comes from a family in which mental deficiency is hereditary. His mother's brother died insane after displaying during his lifetime several of the same traits of madness which we shall mention shortly with regard to his nephew, including his abhorrence of women. Two of his first cousins manifested numerous and habitual symptoms of madness. His mother's disposition was so irritable, her will was so obstinate and simultaneously so unstable, she was so continually ill-natured and so extravagant that her husband could not, despite all the torments she heaped upon him, hold them against her, for he had long realized that her brain was deranged and that she was not capable of controlling her actions. Lastly, Rivière's brother is almost wholly an idiot, so much so that his parish priest has no hope of being able to let him make his communion because he is totally unable to get him to grasp the simplest truths of religion. The youth is, however, fifteen to eighteen years old, and his emotional faculties are no more developed than his intellectual faculties, since, as Maître Bertauld has observed, the disaster which he witnessed elicited from him not a sigh nor a tear.

Let us not, then, be surprised if we find, as we shall shortly see, Rivière acting in the most aberrant manner and if we observe in him the external stamp of madness, since his origin and his consanguinity with so many madmen certainly account for the presence in him of this cruel

malady. Indeed, heredity is one of the most potent causes
in the production of madness; this is emphasized by all the
authors whose specialist studies have given them an opportunity to appreciate its morbid influence; and if I had
to support this truth which they have so often stated by
the findings from my own experience, I should say that,
having studied nearly eleven thousand madmen in the
course of thirteen years and spending as I do several hours
each day amid three hundred of these unfortunate beings,
I have found heredity to be the most active and perhaps
the most frequent cause in the production of mental
alienation. It is not necessary, therefore, to seek elsewhere
the cause of the originally defective organization of
Rivière's brain.

3. *Condition of his mental faculties since his childhood. Numerous signs of insanity.*

Born as he was with this unfortunate predisposition, it
was not long before he confirmed what could be predicted
of him. Until the age of four, the witnesses state, he was
like other children of his age, but from that time on he
was always held to be an idiot or imbecile. Thus he soon
became the butt and laughingstock of the other children,
and this, by making him even more timid and diffident,
undoubtedly hampered the natural development of his
emotional faculties; for it is noteworthy that not only was
he cold and unfeeling toward his parents, but he never
even had any playmate and lived in an isolation from affection most calculated to aggravate his mental and moral
inferiority. Instinctively seeking out the most extreme solitude, he spent entire days in the depths of disused quarries
or in the remotest corner of the loft, and there, meditating
on the few subjects of his reading and gifted with a highly
developed imagination coupled with a distorted judgment,
he grew attached to everything that smacked of the miracu-
lous, neglected the positive, and bent his mind in a direction

the more vicious in that, since he never confided in anyone, no one could correct his errors; thus he soon became alienated in the truest sense. He was often overheard talking to himself and conversing with invisible interlocutors, or laughing loudly, or uttering plaintive cries. At times he was seen rolling on the ground, at others making the most bizarre gestures. Religious ideas passed through his head, he sacrificed and tortured small animals to reproduce the scenes of Christ's passion. Did the narration of some battle strike his imagination, then in a species of frenzy he flung himself upon the vegetables in the garden and smashed them, uttering loud cries as he did so. Did he entertain some notion of power and superiority, then he sought to put it into effect by frightening unfortunate children. At times he threatened to cut them with his scythe, at others he seized them and, holding them over a well, threatened to drop them in; and on other occasions he was for feeding them to his horse, and when he had sufficiently terrified them, satisfied with the notion of his power he believed he had given them, he let them go, expressing his glee in peals of immoderate laughter.

The devil and the fairies held an important place in his diseased brain, and by dint of thinking of them he came to believe that he saw and heard them. He held conversations and made pacts with them, and, terrified by his own visions, he often fled in terror crying out: alas! the devil, the devil! Ever preoccupied as he was with bizarre ideas, he paid only distracted attention to the ordinary acts of life; he had to be called several times over and pretty loudly at that before he answered, and such was his obstinacy that incredible efforts were required to make him relinquish a piece of work once he had started on it. Incapable as he was of appraising the consequences of many of his actions, he often very nearly put his own and his horses' lives in danger by trying to perform work beyond their capability.

Lastly, just as if he had to represent in himself alone an

example of every sort of delusion, he imagined that a fecundating fluid incessantly flowed from his person and could thus, in his own despite, render him guilty of crimes of incest and of others yet more revolting. So he lived amid perpetual fears, he approached women only with great reserve, and often recoiled with horror from the proximity of his mother, his grandmother, or his sister when he thought he had come somewhat too near them. In order to repair the harm he thought he had done and to prevent incest, he indulged in ridiculous motions in order to draw back into himself the supposed fecundating fluid which so greatly perturbed him. The neighborhood of a female animal infinitely disturbed him for the same reason, and everyone who knew him was struck by the sort of alarm, even terror, he evinced whenever a hen or she-cat approached him.

Is anything more required to show a characteristic case of madness and do I need to cite any more facts? Which of us knowing the facts described above would not have considered Rivière insane and would not have concurred in the general opinion that designated him a madman?

4. The murder committed by Rivière and attendant circumstances

The Rivière family was not a united one. His mother, with her self-willed, imperious, and shrewish disposition, for years on end made his father's life a burden to him. Constantly harassed and almost never getting any rest, the father became so violently distressed that he even thought of trying to commit suicide and thus rid himself of the continual torments to which he could foresee no ending. His son's imagination was so vivid that it could not fail to be struck by these things; they made a strong impression upon him, excited him, and distorted the few sound ideas he still had. He conjured up the human race bowed beneath the yoke of women, suffering their shameful domination, enslaved to their caprices, He thought that it would be a noble and glorious thing to deliver it from their sway, that all that was needed was a generous example; that in all ages and during great crises men had come forward and had dedicated themselves, and their names had been handed down to posterity. His memory furnished him with several instances of voluntary self-dedication in the Old Testament, the very mystery of the Redemption presented itself as a confirmation of his ideas; if God himself had sacrificed himself for men, all the more reason ought he to have to sacrifice himself for his fellow men; the gallantry of Larochejaquelin, the example of Charlotte Corday came to mind; he believed that he was inspired by God and was acting in His name, and, resolved to give his life to deliver men in general and his father in particular, he decided on his mother's death. Soon, too, his sister was included in this lethal decision, for she had always lived with her mother and had always taken her side; should she remain alive, she would continue to exercise a disastrous ascendancy over her father, so he must be delivered from her too, the sacrifice must be complete. It is hardly conceivable that delusion could be carried to greater lengths, yet Rivière went further. He imagined that no matter how tranquil his father might be after these murders, he would nevertheless not enjoy complete happiness; delivered by his son, he would mourn him when his head had fallen to the law. This regret he must prevent, his father's happiness must be whole and entire, and he must even rejoice at his liberator's death. Did we not know it, we would never have imagined the means which Rivière, still wrapped in his delusions, resolved to employ to this end: it was to kill his young brother too, the brother whom he tenderly loved and who was loved tenderly by their unhappy father. When I have committed this crime, said Rivière, my father will conceive such an abhorrence of it that he will no longer regret me and will even wish for my death. Thus, proceeding from delusion to delusion, the madman decided on the bereavement of his whole family while wishing to procure its happiness.

This resolution in itself, in my opinion, bears so pronounced a stamp of madness that it alone would suffice to declare Rivière mad. Never was distorted judgment carried to greater lengths; never was the fanaticism of an unsound mind more marked. For a long time, however, the wretched man's courage flinched, he could not make up his mind, and he vainly reproached himself for his cowardice. But at last the fatal day came, he donned his holiday clothes, had his sister sing a canticle beginning: "O happy day! holy joy!" and, his mind wholly deranged, his weapon, an ax, in hand, he executed his mother, his sister, and his young brother.

This fearful disaster, this human butchery, all this shed blood and the fact that he was drenched in it troubled him not a whit; he went out calmly, peaceably announced that he had just delivered his father, and, the murderous steel still in his hand, calmly took the road to Vire, vaunting his intention of himself declaring to his judges the great deed he had just performed.

Truly, I have never seen a more manifest case of insanity among the hundreds of monomaniacs I have treated; so manifest indeed that one's heart feels pity far rather than horror for this wretched being.

I venture to think that no doubt in this respect would ever have arisen had Rivière kept to his original project and immediately presented himself to the legal authorities. But no sooner had the wretched man walked on for some time than the contrast between the aspect of the heavens and the calm of the woods he was traversing with the act he had just committed restored a ray of light to his clouded intellect; he came to a halt as if in terror at his own self, wondered whether it had not all been a horrible dream, but, convinced in a moment or two that it was indeed the fearful reality, he gave way to the most violent fit of despair. A glimmer of reason had returned and, the exaltation of fanaticism dispelled, nature had resumed her sway, and the parricide recognized himself for what he was.

5. Rivière's behavior and feelings from the murder to the present

In this regard, there occurred in Rivière a mental phenomenon so important that it merits dwelling upon. For a whole month he thought about the act he had just committed, pondered it, prepared for it, and worked out the means for putting it into execution, and yet he never saw it in its true light. The more he thought of it, indeed, and the more tenaciously he grasped his project, the more fanatical did he become. But no sooner had he done the deed than the scales fell from his eyes, and all of a sudden he became saner than he had ever been before. This can be seen as none other than the effect of a powerful shock to his entire nervous system, and since we daily witness the loss of sanity resulting from a powerful mental impact, we ought not to be surprised to find its recovery in similar circumstances. Indeed, this is by no means the first case in point; all the authors who have written on the subject of madness record analogous cases, and I could quote several examples, did I not fear that this might extend this opinion to too great a length. "It often happens," M. Orfila states in his *Treatise on Forensic Medicine*, "that fits of madness terminate abruptly after a grave mental disturbance and that a state of calm re-ensues when patients have successfully put into execution projects to which they attach great importance." Hoffbauer, one of the most celebrated forensic doctors in Germany, states that "the recovery of sanity is often the sequel to the execution of the project." I emphasize this fact because, from this moment on, Rivière, though not yet perfectly sane, is nevertheless a totally different person.

I, Pierre Rivière . . .

It is quite intelligible that once he contemplated the atrocious and insane act he had just committed in its true light, he should no longer have harbored the determination to go and boast of it to the legal authorities. Utterly crushed by the weight of remorse, he wished that the earth would swallow him. Life became a burden to him, he resolved to rid himself of it, and he was making preparations to hang himself when the idea of divine justice restrained him. From that moment to the time of his arrest (exactly a month), he led a wandering life. At times, yielding to the instinct of self-preservation, he hid in the depths of the woods; at others, on the contrary, weary of existence, he longed for death and sought arrest, but nevertheless did not have the courage to denounce himself of his own accord. Anyone who compares this weakening, this hesitation, this lack of resolution with Rivière's character at the moment he committed his parricide will be convinced that his entire firmness of purpose, his grim determination were a transient and morbid mental state and that when it passed, it left the wretched being as he really is, incapable of strength of mind, timid, and irresolute.

The parricide he had committed constantly returned to disturb his mind, and it appeared to him at length as what it actually was, an act of madness. He then recalled other tales of madmen he had read, decided to express the feelings which really guided him as if he still felt them, in order to pass for insane if he was finally arrested, and when he was, he indeed attempted this and sustained this role for several days before the examining judge. But he could not make up his mind to go on with it for long; he came to see it as a culpable pretense, confessed all his real feelings and, at the judge's request, wrote a long memoir, which I must now proceed to examine.

I must first point out that the shift employed by Rivière in no way contradicts the previous fact of his insanity nor does it necessarily support the presumption that he enjoys very developed mental faculties. He did not invent the role of a madman in order to play it, he merely concealed the horror with which his parricide inspired him, and he declared to the judge the motives which truly led him to act, but whose extravagance he fully realized only afterward. Is there anything surprising in the fact that the idea of the supreme penalty and an ignominious punishment should cause him a momentary tremor when he had recovered his sanity, though it did not restrain him at the time and he held them in contempt while his intellect was obnubilated. "One can imagine," M. Orfila states, "that in such cases the fear of punishments, nonexistent at the time of the state of agitation, may very well succeed it." And just as if that celebrated authority on forensic medicine had divined Rivière's behavior, he goes on to say: "This is no bar to most of such patients' making a full confession later and not shunning the legal consequences; they say they are truly deserving of punishment for the atrocious acts they have committed." This is precisely the language now employed by the wretched man with whom we are concerned.

If we now proceed to examine Rivière's written memoirs, we shall find that, no matter how sane they are, they do not give grounds for ascribing to him as many faculties as might be thought at first sight; indeed, since the first part contains only an accurate narration of fact, they hardly called for the exercise of more than one highly developed faculty, to wit memory. Indeed, he recalls the very slightest circumstances of facts which occurred several years ago, and nothing escapes his memory. But, besides the fact that a prodigious memory is very commonly met with in the case of persons whose other faculties are very unevenly distributed, memory is also found brilliantly manifested in a large number of madmen. Nor is a complete relation of Rivière's feelings and actions to be sought in the second part of this narrative. There are many of them which he has passed over in silence, and they are precisely those which best establish his previous state of insanity. Lastly, even if these memoirs were a masterpiece, as some people are pleased to claim, still no positive conclusion could be drawn from them with respect to their author's unimpaired intelligence, since they were written only after the parricide and since, moreover, it is a daily occurrence for the most irrational mental defectives to write letters of the most rational sort.

The subject therefore seems to me to be still in such a mental state at present that, despite the moral shock which has rid him of some of his manias, he is likely to be subject to further fits of madness whose results might perhaps be as deplorable as the earlier ones. Society is therefore entitled to demand, not the punishment of this wretched man, since there can be no culpability in the absence of mental freedom, but his restraint and confinement by administrative process as the only means of having an easy mind about what this madman may do in the future.

To sum up:

Rivière has suffered from mental deficiency since his early childhood.

The cause of this deficiency resides in Rivière's own family, in which madness is hereditary.

The circumstances amid which he lived aggravated this initial defect still further.

The madness was manifest in a large number of acts previous to, and without connection with, the crime with which he is charged; there are many acts of this sort which have been reported by a large number of witnesses and had caused Rivière to be generally reputed a madman and imbecile.

His insanity could not be more evident than it is in the manner in which he conceived his horrible project and in the motives which determined him to execute his young brother.

It is further manifest to the full in the calm manner in which he put it into execution and in the way in which he spoke of it immediately afterward.

The greater sanity he appears to evince since then is accounted for by the powerful moral shock administered by the blood he shed.

The writing of his memoirs does not in any way rule out the existence of insanity prior to the parricide.

Lastly, Rivière's return to saner ideas may not last long, and if not guilty, he is at least dangerous and should be confined in his own interest and above all in the interest of society.

L. Vastel

Caen, October 25, 1835
(A third report by medico-legal experts, that by the Paris doctors, has been placed, for convenience of presentation, in the section relating to the reprieve, pp. 163–6.)

5

The Trial

A. THE ASSIZE COURT

1. INTERROGATION OF PIERRE RIVIÈRE BY THE PRESIDING JUDGE OF THE ASSIZE COURT

August 4, 1835

THE PRESIDING JUDGE, Armand de Gournay, informs Rivière of the peremptory refusal by Maître Aimé Bardou, member of the bar at Caen, chosen by the defendant, to undertake his defense.

Pierre Rivière not having chosen any other counsel ("no, I have not chosen any and I do not think I should"), Maître Berthauld, barrister at Caen, is appointed counsel ex officio.

2. THE MEMBERS OF THE JURY

The jury was composed of four persons described as property owners, two doctors, two members of the Conseil général, a solicitor, a wine merchant, a merchant, and a barrister.

3. WITNESSES AND CERTIFICATE FROM CERTAIN INHABITANTS OF AUNAY

(a) Thirteen witnesses were called for the prosecution.

(b) Nine witnesses were called for the defense.

(c) *Certificate Transmitted to Rivière*

We, municipal councilors and property owners of the commune of Aunay undersigned, hereby attest that to our definite knowledge Pierre Rivière now charged with a triple homicide has consistently shown signs of a disposition so gloomy, strange, and unforthcoming ever since the age of about twelve or thirteen that everyone who saw him as he passed by (for he had no personal relations with anyone at all) could not but say: There goes Pierre Rivière's imbecile. We likewise attest that since the murders were committed everybody has expressed pity for the father after his own fashion and we have all said among ourselves: Instead of one imbecile the poor father has two, for the murderer's brother, Prosper Rivière, aged about fourteen, has an extremely defective intelligence bordering even on idiocy.

(Fifty-two signatures authenticated by the mayor, November 4, 1835)

4. NEWSPAPER REPORTS OF THE TRIAL

(a) *Gazette des Tribunaux*, Monday and Tuesday, November 16 and 17, 1835

[*This report recapitulates in substance a report published in the* Pilote du Calvados *on November 12, 1835.*]

Sessions of the Assize Court at Caen

(From our special correspondent)
M. Daigrement—Saint Mauvrieux [or Saint-Manvieux] presiding

I, Pierre Rivière . . .

Hearings in court on November 11 and 12, 1835
Charge of parricide and fratricide
Prisoner's astounding method of defense

Pierre Rivière is a young man barely twenty-one years old; he seems dejected, but his features yet inspire some interest despite the heinousness of the crimes with which he is charged. The court is crowded with spectators. We note on the bench the First President of the Assize Court and the Regional Prosecutor; several doctors and teachers from the local secondary school are among the spectators. It is known beforehand that the question of the material facts will be virtually eclipsed by the even more serious question of the prisoner's discernment and rationality. The indictment is read out by the clerk of court; it is to the effect that on the third of June this year in the town of Aunay he did kill and murder with a pruning bill his mother, his sister, and his brother. In a memoir written by himself Rivière confessed and explained his crime with all its attendant circumstances. He alleges that he believed that he was performing a praiseworthy action, though one apparently condemned by the laws of God and man, because he was willing to die for his father to whom he wished to restore peace and quiet. Rivière the father was distressed by his wife's conduct; the husband and wife lived apart. The mother lived with her eighteen-year-old daughter Victoire and her eight-year-old son Jules. Pierre Rivière remained with his father, a sister named Aimée, and another brother named Prosper. Rivière the father had a great affection for little Jules; he was greatly distressed too, according to the accused, on account of his domestic troubles.

[*Here follow extracts from the memoir describing Rivière's meditations, the commission of the crime, and his subsequent repentance in the woods (see pp. 104–13), considerably condensed. The same extracts were published in the* Pilote du Calvados, *November 12, 1835.*]

The hearings merely confirmed the facts set out in the indictment. Pierre Rivière barely replies to the questions he is asked and seems absorbed in the most gloomy thoughts. When he is shown the bill still stained with his victims' blood, he averts his gaze and he is heard to utter a long and dismal groan, and to say: I am in haste to die. He maintains his confessions entire. The defense is based on the prisoner's state of insanity at the moment of committing the act; and examination brought out some facts which, if they do not prove the complete derangement of his faculties, at least testify to a notable enfeeblement of his intelligence. Pierre Rivière had received virtually no primary schooling; he was regarded as a sort of "idiot" or "innocent"; he was commonly called "Rivière's beast." Nevertheless, M. Bouchard, a doctor who visited him frequently at the jail at Vire, stated that he had not observed any symptom of madness in the strict sense of the term; nor had he noted any homicidal monomania in the murderer.

A very brisk and most interesting exchange on this topic took place between M. Vastel, physician at the Bon Sauveur lunatic asylum at Caen, as a witness for the defense, and Drs. Trouvé and Lebidois, called by the Presiding Judge in the exercise of his full authority to call for additional information.

The prosecution's case was forcefully put by M. Loisel, the assistant regional prosecutor. Since the facts were conceded by both parties, he was primarily concerned to establish by means of the whole tenor of the preliminary investigation and the hearings in court, and in particular by means of the prisoner's own memoir, that he was perfectly capable of knowledge of good and evil, that he had fully comprehended his crime and that he was not afflicted with pronounced madness or homicidal monomania.

The defense entrusted to Maître Berthauld, a young barrister of the Caen bar, was urged with great talent, and his efforts would have succeeded, had success been feasible.

The jury was out for three hours; no doubt they wished to read and assess the prisoner's memoir, which very probably furnished a singular contrast to the line of defense. At a quarter to two o'clock in the morning they brought in a verdict of guilty and, amid general stupefaction, the court sentenced Pierre Rivière to the penalty for parricides.

(b) *Annales d'hygiène publique* (1836, p. 201)

M. Bouchard, being called to testify and being questioned as to whether Pierre Rivière was mentally defective, replied: Pierre Rivière is not mentally defective, for two reasons: (1) because a study of his physical constitution does not show any cause which might have damaged the functions of his brain; (2) because his mental state cannot be classified in any of the categories accepted by the relevant authorities. "Thus," M. Bouchard said, "Pierre Rivière is not a monomaniac, because he does not harbor delusions on one and only one subject; he is not a maniac, because he is not in an habitual state of agitation; he is not an idiot, because he has written a wholly sane memoir; he is not in a state of continuing insanity, as may readily be seen. *Therefore Pierre Rivière is not insane.*" Four doctors attended the trial and were called. Two of them shared M. Vastel's conviction; two supported that of M. Bouchard.

Despite M. Berthauld's eloquent and sincere address for the defense, the jury found Pierre Rivière guilty; and in consequence, the unfortunate man was sentenced to the penalty for parricides. Nevertheless, alarmed perhaps by the excessive severity of the punishment inflicted on a man who, by their own admission, *had never been in full possession of his reason*, the jurymen met and drew up a petition for the commutation of the penalty.

5. REPORT BY THE PRESIDING JUDGE OF THE ASSIZE COURT TO THE DIRECTOR OF CRIMINAL AFFAIRS

Wednesday 11. Jean Pierre Rivière, aged twenty, farmer, born at Courvaudon, resident at Aunay

being charged that he did feloniously, wilfully, and of his malice aforethought kill and murder Victoire Brion wife of Rivière, his mother, his sister, and Jules Rivière, his brother

was sentenced to the penalty for parricides.

[*Here are described the bodies as found and the circumstances attendant on the murders. See pp. 38–9 and 43–5.*]

In a very long memoir, the whole written by Rivière over a period of two weeks, he gave a very detailed account of his mother's culpable behavior toward his father, the feelings to which this behavior prompted him, the reflections which led him to frame the design of killing his mother to ensure his father's peace, his hesitations, the efforts he had to make to steel himself to put it into execution, his repentance, the remorse which racked him, the manner in which he lived until his arrest, the thoughts which incessantly agitated him and his desire for the ending of a life which had become intolerable to him.

After admissions of this nature all that remained was to discover whether Rivière was in possession of his reason at the time of committing the act, and it was toward this end that the preliminary investigation and the hearings in court were directed.

There is nothing noteworthy about Rivière's physiognomy; it would seem to indicate gentleness rather than any propensity to cruelty. During the hearings in court it remained as impassive as his demeanor; his mind appeared calm and seemed not to be agitated by any feeling; however, he averted his gaze at the sight of the bill still stained with blood, saying: I am in haste to die. His answers were invariably clear and exact, and he heard his sentence with the greatest unconcern; it required reiterated urgings by his father, his confessor, and his counsel to induce him to sign his appeal.

It was established conclusively that Rivière had had no illness and had received no injuries that might have occasioned any damage to his mental faculties.

In his childhood Rivière's intelligence appeared defective; he had difficulty in learning to read and write. But his parish priest, a person of outstanding ability, very soon detected in him considerable aptitudes, especially for the exact sciences. He had a remarkably retentive memory, read all the books he could lay hands on with the utmost avidity, and forgot nothing of what he had read. He was extremely devout to begin with, later wholly gave up the practice of religion, but later again returned to his original sentiments. He has explained his conduct as follows: the religious instruction I had received and the books of devotion had at first persuaded me of the truth of religion, a book entitled *The Good Sense of the Curé Meslier* had caused me to doubt; the Montpellier Catechism and my own reflections dispelled my doubts; and I acted in accordance with the feelings I experienced.

All the local inhabitants who were most fitted by their education, their social position, and their relations with Pierre Rivière to give accurate information depicted him as of a gloomy and melancholic disposition, avoiding all society; he sometimes left his father's house to spend all night in the woods. He was regarded as an idiot, but no one ever observed any vicious propensities in him. Reliable witnesses have reported facts which seemed to them to testify to his mental derangement. As a child Rivière nailed birds and frogs to a plank and gave way to imbecile laughter as he watched them die; Rivière himself says he imagined Jesus Christ's passion like this. He was seen several times beside himself and greatly agitated because he believed he was seeing the Devil and he also said that he conversed with the fairies on his nocturnal walks; he did so, he replied under examination in court, to mock at those who believe in such absurdities. On several occasions he was seen knocking off heads of cabbage in the garden with a stick, shouting: right, left; he was imagining himself, he said, an army general. For two years he worked in his loft constructing an instrument to kill birds, which he had named "Calibine"; later he went and buried it in a field followed by the village children. At the same period he buried a jay which had belonged to his brother, carrying out a mock religious ceremony; he was then eighteen years of age. Several other facts of this nature denoting bizarre behavior or extravagance were related in court.

It has been established conclusively that Rivière had a great aversion to women and all female animals; he was particularly afraid of the sight of his female relations, and when he was asked the reason, he answered that from his reading of the Holy Scriptures he had conceived the greatest horror of incest and bestiality and that he feared there was an invisible fluid which, despite himself, might bring him into contact with women or female animals when he was in their presence.

Two relations fairly closely akin to Rivière's father's wife died insane; one of them had been certified; they had a similar aversion to women. One of Rivière's brothers aged thirteen or fourteen is considered completely idiotic.

The hearings in court disclosed nothing to raise any presumption that Rivière was animated by any feeling of hatred, revenge, jealousy, or greed toward his mother, his brother, or his sister. The dissensions between Rivière's father and his wife were common knowledge, and everyone thought that she was in the wrong; Rivière was pitied for having to consort with such an ill-tempered woman.

Pierre Rivière nourished the most tender affection for his father, and the constant sight of the annoyances to which he was subjected and the miseries which assailed him seems to be the sole cause that, by overexciting his gloomy and melancholy imagination, caused him to conceive the horrible project which he put into execution on June 3.

Rivière's memoir is written with order, clarity, and precision; all his mother's wrongs to his father are narrated in the most scrupulous detail. It can be seen that Rivière was tormented by an immoderate longing for glory and fame and that a chain of false reasonings supported by examples drawn from history led him to suppose that he would be performing a meritorious deed and would immortalize himself by sacrificing his life to ensure his father's happiness. This memoir indicates the simultaneous existence of very great intelligence and the greatest possible aberration of judgment; though Rivière received only a village education, the style is tolerably correct, and it contains passages of remarkable eloquence.

In this memoir Rivière gives an explanation of the motive which led him to kill his young brother which differs from that which he gave in his earlier interrogations; he states that he killed his brother to make himself more odious to his father and to ensure that his execution would cause him no grief.

Toward the close of the hearings several doctors were called to give their opinion on Rivière's mental state; three of them considered that he was not sane when he acted, three took the opposite view and, while acknowledging the bizarre aspects of his behavior and the aberration of his judgment, stated that they believed that he had sufficient command of his reason to discern the morality of his actions and to be responsible for them. The two doctors in charge of the Bon Sauveur lunatic asylum at Caen took a different view.

The jury, some of whose members were persons of outstanding education and intelligence, unanimously declared Rivière guilty, but six jurymen considered that extenuating circumstances should be admitted. A reading of the memoir seems to have had a considerable effect on this opinion.

The project framed beforehand by Rivière to kill his mother, his sister, and his brother, the horror with which the deed he was going to commit inspired him, his hesitations, his repentance, his fits of remorse, and his confessions are evidence that he comprehended the full atrocity of his act, that he was aware of it, and that consequently he must be declared guilty and convicted. Nevertheless, is Rivière to be considered as a person to be treated on the same footing as the murderer who is motivated by the guilty passions which ordinarily impel men to crime? He was not led to act by personal interest, his motive was the misconceived desire to procure his father's happiness; if at the moment he acted he was in possession of his reason, his crime must be punished with the full rigor of the law, regardless of any aberration of judgment. But did not the very heinousness of the crime and the lack of rational motive, coupled with the bizarre features of his character and the extravagance of some of his actions, give rise to doubts about his mental state? Opinions were divided among the doctors, all equally trustworthy, and among the members of the jury. The public which followed the hearings of this case with the liveliest interest is also divided on this point, and *grave doubts would have arisen in the minds of the members of the Court if they had been called upon to hand down a decision*. Since Rivière has been so diversely judged by conscientious and enlightened persons, there is reason to believe that there is something about him which ought to preclude his being regarded in the same way as other men guilty of equally atrocious actions; and if there are degrees of derangement of the mental faculties, may his crime not be ascribed to a state of momentary overexcitement induced by his father's misfortunes, a state which no doubt is not madness, but which nevertheless does not imply the full possession of reason, especially in the case of someone whose actions had at times appeared acts of aberration?

In the eyes of those who believe that Rivière is guilty in the fully accepted sense of the term, and this opinion is supported by the jury's verdict, his execution is an example peremptorily demanded by the interest of society; but this example can be salutary only insofar as no doubt arises about Rivière's full guilt, otherwise the effect it will produce will only be undesirable.

Should His Majesty deign to exercise the royal prerogative of mercy in favor of Rivière, Rivière's mental state would be the sole ground; and should it be so exercised, I consider that his sentence should be commuted in such manner that he be placed under restraint for the rest of his natural life.

6. NEWSPAPER ARTICLES AND CORRESPONDENCE RELATING TO THE TRIAL

(a) *Journal de Rouen et du Département de la Seine-Inférieure*, Sunday, November 15, 1835

Calvados Assize Court
Lacenaire and Rivière

Our columns, like those of the newspapers of the capital, have been filled for the past three days with lengthy disquisitions on a horrible case providing at once an abundant harvest for curiosity and matter calculated to instil into the mind the most harrowing reflections on mankind in general and on the present state of our morality. The chief protagonist in the sordid drama supplies us with the spectacle of the most hideously criminal existence that could possibly be conceived. It is crime personified in all its cynicism, in its stark simplicity, so to speak, devoid of remorse, repentance or hope; it is Robert Macaire transformed into frightful reality, strutting in his bespattered cloak, swaggering in the braggadocio of his legend of outrage, as he tells us the whole tale of his murders with the shameless assurance and verbose complacence of a writer of medieval romances conducting us through the labyrinths of a gothic castle, a Nero of corruption aspiring to be the keystone of the empire of evil, who, from his hover on the heights of Pandemonium, looked down in scorn on his accomplices, mere plebeian killers unendowed with genius like his own to show themselves worthy of the dignity of the scaffold; yet his judges confine themselves to a mere audit of his frauds, his puerile cogging, like doctors devoting all their skills to eradicating the corns from the foot of a gangrenous leg already ripe for amputation.

True, our contemporary frenetic literature has gone to some lengths these days in the extravagance of satanic inventions, but it has not advanced any further than the infernal figure posturing at this moment in the Assize Court of the Seine. Shall it be said that the influence of our contemporary literature has engendered a unique monster? Or has this literature been merely the learned study of an impure race suddenly bursting into full bloom under the afflatus of the sinister clime we are traversing? Both of these questions give rise to terrifying reflections when we plumb their depths.

The Calvados Assize has taken it upon itself to present us with a counterpart to the horrid melodrama which has just drawn to its close before the Assize Court of the Seine. Young Rivière, who has lately been tried at Caen—we borrow an account of it from the *Pilote du Calvados*—had killed his mother, his sister, and his small brother. What motive impelled him to this triple murder? He himself informs us in the fragment of a memoir which we reproduce: it was with the sole intention, wholly spontaneous and wholly disinterested, of rendering his father a service.

Of deliberate purpose and at no one's instigation, he sought to rid his father of a wife, his own mother, whose irregular conduct was an object of opprobrium to the entire family; he coupled it with the murder of his sister because she sympathized with her mother and showed herself deserving of following in her steps; he supplemented it with the murder of his brother because he, conversely, merited all his father's affection; and in determining to incur the penalty of the scaffold, simply out of a desire to be of service to one of his parents, he wished to place him in a position, by virtue of a diabolical compensation, whereby he would be relieved from any form of gratitude toward his memory.

All this, it must be allowed, smacks of the delusion, the madness, the morbid exaltation of an unhinged brain. Yet the prosecution cited Rivière's memoir, in which the conception and logical deduction reproduced elsewhere in these columns are set out in detail, as a proof of the prisoner's *sanity*; and the Calvados jury, accepting the prosecution's arguments, brought in a verdict which led to Rivière's sentencing to death.

The jury found on their honor and on their conscience, and it is not for us to censure the result of a legally constituted verdict. But if we accept the fact that Rivière could have acted with discernment in perpetrating his threefold crime, what then is the moral condition of a society which engenders characters so depraved as those of Rivière and Lacenaire? The latter representing *egoism* in its most abject nudity, the former devotion in its most monstrous aberration; both culminating in sheer nihilism, one by the denial of all law, all moral belief, the other by an epileptic over-stimulation of the organs of sensibility!

Those who still dream of a return to the past will not fail to invoke such lessons, which they will view as the consequences of the latest victories of philosophy over the Christian religion, and will redouble their efforts to restore Throne and Altar. And yet it is quite wrong to suppose that such cases furnish a justification for anathematizing philosophy. Philosophy is not to be judged by its relative fragments, but by its operation as a whole, in the one aspect destructive, creative in the other. What there was to destroy in the old order had to be destroyed if a new edifice was to be erected. The victory of philosophy over the Catholic faith has produced within the moral order a disturbance of mind and a breach to which must perhaps be ascribed all the ills with which our society is at present afflicted. But these are wholly transient conditions, whose ill-effects will be remedied by the advent of new beliefs, not by the revival of beliefs now extinct. De Maistre, the author who has paid the most eloquent testimony to the political and moral potency of Catholicism in this age, whom the most devout will certainly not accuse of impiety and materialism, has put on record in the *Soirées de Saint Pétersbourg* these memorable words, which confirm our own appraisal: "We must be prepared for an event in the divine ordering toward which we are moving ever more rapidly, one which must needs strike all observers. The earth is devoid of religion, but the human race can no longer remain in this plight . . . But wait until the natural affinity of religion with science combines the two in the brain of a single man of genius. It will not be long before a man of this sort appears, indeed he may perhaps already be here . . . There is every sign of I know not what great unity toward which we are making great strides."

We have merely to look around us to perceive that we are living in times similar to those which preceded the establishment of Christianity. This is the world's second experience of a society given over to every sort of unbridled material appetite. Our age once again bears the impress of all the infamies which sullied the Roman Empire in its decline, but let us not forget that the Empire's decline by its operation prepared the way for the great Catholic unity, which has itself moved aside to make room, in accord with de Maistre's prophetic intuition, for a new, still greater, and still finer unity.

(b) *Pilote du Calvados,* November 15, 1835

A reader sends us the following reflections on the sentence recently passed by the assize court with a request for publication. Although the moral considerations set out in this letter diverge from our own views on this topic, we have thought it proper to lend the hospitality of our columns to these remarks as at least one of the elements in the solution of a problem which has for some time been exercising the most distinguished moral philosophers of our age.

Yet another capital sentence

"At a quarter past one in the morning today, after a lengthy hearing and despite all efforts, more especially the eloquently expressed conviction of his young counsel, Pierre Rivière, of the commune of Aunay, convicted as charged of the triple murder of his mother, his brother and his sister, was sentenced by the Calvados assize court to the penalty for parricides.

"Pierre Rivière is a young man who has not yet come of age, belonging by birth and education to the poorest and most numerous class of society; his external appearance, his answers, and even his smile are marked by every sign of idiocy; his aspect at first glance, moreover, is consistent with everything that the witnesses who were acquainted with him testified about his past and with everything that could be presumed from the circumstances of his crime.

"But Rivière's misfortune was that his mental constitution was impaired and disorganized in a way that differed from that of most of the madmen, maniacs, and monomaniacs whose custody the family hearth, the courts, and the asylums dispute and so often virtually tear from each other's grasp. Rivière did not harbor an obsession, one single obdurate idea, but was possessed by a number of strange ideas simultaneously and was dominated by them; he did not appear to be afflicted with a complete and persistent disability of mind; he was not deprived of all the mental faculties, for some of them were, on the contrary, exuberant and marvelously well developed; he possessed memory and imagination to an extraordinary degree; the one he applied solely to remembering his mother's vices and crimes, the other he expended lavishly on insensate reveries and absurd or ferocious projects, all of them, however, devoid of rationality or foresight, all of them groundless and fruitless.

"What was impaired and diseased was the faculty of perceiving relationships and deducing their consequences, in other words his judgment. He was endowed at birth with a false and erroneous judgment; nothing had remedied this deviation of the intellect; no one had tried to cure, or at any rate had succeeded in curing, this morbid mental state, in stifling the seed of death nurtured within him. Ever since his childhood he shunned the human society which alone could have modified and corrected it; he deliberately doomed himself to solitude, where his strange aversions and his blind passions burgeoned in the shadows. The books he avidly consumed haphazard held out to his vivid and unregulated imagination vast prospects perpetually clouded by a horde of contradictions. His intelligence wearied or dashed itself to pieces on chimerical illusions; his sensitivity expanded into insane but vivid hatreds and into an exclusive and profound love, into that excessive and fatal love which was shortly to make of him, as he himself believed, a *martyr* —or, as his judges decided, a *monster*.

"No, Pierre Rivière was no more a monster than he was a martyr; he was a wretched, a diseased, an unfinished being; he was an actor who was not fully aware of his actions and consequently ought not to bear full responsibility for them. Some doctors regarded him as an ordinary madman, others were not able to recognize in his organization the traits of an insanity which had been already observed. And because his species of insanity was unknown and novel, because there was no word in the language to express this imperfection of nature and this deplorable singularity, he was classified as a monster, a monster with ferocious instincts from whom society must imperatively be delivered— without any reflection that an organization of this sort could not be truly comprehended by different, and indeed contrary, organizations and without any awareness that unknown and exceptional facts were being rejected only so that general and commonplace facts might be accepted and appraised; without thought, indeed, that more than mere hesitation was called for when, by way of cutting through the tangle of such questions, they would be cutting off a man's head.

"Who knows, either, whether Pierre Rivière's fearful act was not based fundamentally on one of those fanaticisms of a powerful imagination which when aberrant become potent only for evil: fanaticisms in religion, in reasoning, in filial love? Has anyone sounded the depths of his heart and mind? Has any penetrating gaze succeeded in discerning beneath the wrappings of idiocy and total prostration in which the prisoner was enveloped in court a normal reason and an enlightened intellect? Could his judges acquire, after a couple of hours of examination conducted at a distance and amid the multifarious distractions of court proceedings, any revelation of this vital and ill-starred mystery and any certainty that was the prerequisite for assuming public responsibility for a capital sentence which counsel for the defense had, perhaps too rashly, stigmatized in advance as *judicial murder?*

"We will, of course, not go as far as that; we shall confine ourselves simply to throwing our scruples into the judge's scales, leaving it to each to weigh his own sense of duty and the satisfaction of his conscience. But we deplore from the depths of our heart the fact that once again we have had to resort to the *executioner* to cure the maladies, in some cases the hereditary maladies, of persons and societies.

"Blood should answer for blood, it is said; it is no longer public vengeance that requires it, but the example, the 'salutary' example, as if lessons of this sort had ever trained anything but murderers. Well, the fatal sentence has been delivered; the blood will flow if it is not arrested in time; this will, simply though tardily, fulfill the piteous wish expressed yesterday by the wretched man: 'I am in haste to die!' But may we be permitted to lodge our own appeal beside the legal appeal which will certainly be lodged on his behalf; may we be permitted to associate the expression of our conscience with the expression of emotion by counsel for the defense and to cry to the judges before whom Rivière will have again to appear or to the Sovereign who may be called upon to exercise his prerogative of mercy: pity for him, pity, but not infamy; and, above all, not the scaffold!"

Caen, November 12, 1835.

(c) *Pilote du Calvados*, November 21, 1835

A doctor at Caen who attended the hearings has sent the *Pilote du Calvados* a letter, the main passages from which we reprint below:

"Sir,

"When the matter at issue is saving from the scaffold a man whom one believes not to be guilty, I am sure that your columns will always be open to any ideas which may tend to that result. The sole question with which I shall deal is: Was Rivière in that state of mental disorder which is peculiarly apt to lead to murder?

"The testimony of all his neighbors concurs in the fact that he customarily engaged in the kind of actions which Dr. Esquirol, the most learned physician in France, has called *melancholy* (*Dictionnaire des sciences médicales*, vol. 32, p. 155). 'Madmen of this sort,' says the learned author, 'shun the world, and seek solitude; they believe that there exists in them a fluid which will put them in contact with persons even at a distance who can imprison them and do them infinite harm.'

"Rivière indeed believed he had a fluid such as that of which Dr. Esquirol speaks, which put him in 'carnal' (his own adjective) contact with his grandmother, his sisters, all women, and even female animals; and accordingly he scrupulously shunned all females.

"To the prosecution the memoir which he wrote in jail was the main argument to prove that Rivière was sane, and this observation may perhaps have been what determined the jury to declare him guilty. The jury were probably unable to believe that the mind of someone who evidenced a prodigious memory in narrating his father's misfortunes and his own ideas with such astonishing exactitude and sound reasoning was insane. But it is precisely Rivière's highly developed memory and sound reasoning, so inconsistent with all his usual habits, that a jury composed entirely of medical men would have taken as the confirmation of his state of mental disorder. To quote Dr. Esquirol again: 'In melancholic delusion, which involves partial impairment of the understanding, there are defective sensations and exaggerated ideas about the object of passion, whereas on every other subject the patient reasons and acts perfectly rationally.'

"Thus, Rivière took as his starting point fallacious and exaggerated ideas in deciding on his family's murder. But a capacious memory, all the more highly developed in that it daily called to his mind the facts which impelled him to his fatal design, must have presided over the narration of all these facts with the soundness of judgment which this disease permits. But the *melancholic insanity* is most manifest in the reasonings which decided Rivière to carry out his fatal project. His love for his father was excited to the highest degree; his every thought was directed toward freeing him from the ever-recurring tribulations inflicted upon him by an evil-minded wife. The exaggeration of filial love imperatively demanded that he sacrifice his own life on the scaffold. Esquirol goes on to say in this connection: 'The moral sentiments not only retain their energy, but are raised to the highest degree; filial devotion and gratitude are carried to excess, such madmen seem to devote their whole intelligence to strengthening their concentration upon the object of their delusion; the strength and subtlety of their reasonings in concentrating upon this object pass all conception. They combine certain distorted ideas and thereafter take them for truths, and on their basis they reason soundly and draw rational conclusions from them.'

"Is this not the living image of Rivière?

"Exaggerated filial love leads him to give birth to the distorted and extravagant idea of making his father happy by killing his mother; he knows that this premeditated murder will entail his own death; but suddenly the examples of Jesus Christ, Judith, Charlotte Corday, etc., who dedicated themselves to death for mankind or their country, spring to his mind. He loves his father as he loves his country; and so he supposes that his action will be no less praiseworthy than those whose example inspires him.

"Who but a madman could make such a comparison? But what reveals the ultimate degree of insanity in his act is the sacrifice of his brother Jules, tenderly loved by his father, with the idea that the father will be outraged by this heinous crime and so will not mourn for its perpetrator; is this not the maddest, the most aberrant reasoning that a lunatic could devise? Would not anyone whom he told of it have said: This man is mad? Yet this is the reasoning which impelled Rivière to his frightful deed and would seem to qualify him for the lunatic asylum, not the cells.

"Most of the doctors who attended the hearings concur in these ideas. Three out of six who were called to give an opinion stated that it was a case of insanity; I am acquainted with the views of five other doctors who were present in court, all of whom also recognized it as a case of insanity and are prepared so to certify."

F. (M.D.)

156

(d) *Gazette des Tribunaux*, November 25, 1835

The proceedings in the Rivière case reported in the *Pilote du Calvados* have aroused such widespread concern throughout the country that we have felt that we should again offer the hospitality of our columns to the following additional reflections on this sad case, all the more so because of our contributor's personal standing:

"Sir,

"If I had been called upon to pass upon Rivière, I would not have acquitted him; I would not have stood with the majority of the jury, but would have brought in a verdict of guilty with extenuating circumstances, leaving it to the royal prerogative of mercy to spare him the stigma of the scaffold or the brand of the convict prison.

"This view I held at the outset, nor have I changed it; moreover, the matter is so serious and is engrossing the public mind to such a degree that there may be some merit in each of us stating his opinion on it.

"From reading Rivière's interrogations and his replies in court I came to the conclusion that the man is rational. To my mind, his childhood and the circumstances of his crime showed that at times he was so inflamed by them that he reached a state of insanity; and while I saw some tokens of genius in the strange composition on which the prosecution relied as a weapon for use against him, I equally saw some element of delusion. In the earlier part he recounts his father's misfortunes, and this is the rational part of it; in the latter part, where he comes to his crime, he is no longer in control of himself. He is an enthusiast, a fanatic, an unhappy creature demanding martyrdom as the reward for the blood he has shed.

" 'I knew well,' he says, 'that in killing my mother, my sister, and my brother I was infringing the laws of man and the laws of morality, but I knew too that my blood would flow to requite the vengeance of society and I thought that when it was shed on the scaffold, it would consecrate my filial devotion.'

"That thought is the whole essence of Rivière; he felt that the act was an evil one, but at the same time he felt for his father's misfortune. It was because he was dominated by the fever of his ardent and imperfect intelligence that he plunged into a blood bath, not for the pleasure of seeing the blood flow, not because he had any interest in shedding it, but because he believed that he would thus secure his father's happiness. So much so that I venture to assert with the utmost conviction that such facts constitute, to my mind, extenuating circumstances.

"While I appreciate the view that Rivière should be given back to his family and then placed in some institution, I feel that those who hold that the interests of society require the unhappy man's confinement fail to take into consideration the fact that this measure is not feasible in Rivière's case; for if a man is to be confined in an asylum, he must be certified as a lunatic. But if he is to be certified, he must be of age and in a *habitual* state of imbecility and insanity.

"Even supposing that Rivière were of age, would it really be possible to find any court that would dare to decide that he is in a *habitual* state of imbecility or insanity or would declare him to be in a *habitual* state of frenzy? It would be impossible; all the more impossible because Rivière, certified and declared incompetent today, might well be relieved of his incapacitation and be readmitted to society, only to sacrifice further victims.

"Indeed, the hearings in court did not, and could not, come up to my expectations. I had thought that there would be a careful examination into the question whether Rivière did in fact love his father deeply, whether aside from his father's domestic misfortunes, the prisoner had at any time displayed a hatred of his mother, and whether he in fact loved his young brother. On all these points the preliminary investigation was totally silent, yet their appraisal seemed to me absolutely essential for obtaining a correct notion of Rivière's behavior.

"I thought, too, that in so grave a case a careful study would have been made of the prisoner, and I expected to see several men of science and with special knowledge come forward to aid the jury in their decision with a wealth of observation tested by prior examination and cross-examination. Yet only one person was in personal contact with Rivière long enough to enable him to give an opinion on the prisoner, and this doctor, having found or having detected no physical cause, stated that no malady existed. I give M. Bouchard full credit for his talent and conscientiousness; but, to my mind, Rivière is too inarticulate to possibly be judged by his conversation, invariably confined as it is to brief and terse answers to the questions asked him.

"I believe that what would really have been needed was to scrutinize him in his every slightest action, to observe him closely in solitude, his postures, his gestures, and even his sleep; but that would have required time and more than one observer.

"In the interest of truth I would most strongly urge far more thorough hearings than those which resulted in Rivière's conviction; and if that is not to be, I hope that a very full report on this case will be presented to His Majesty and that he will find in his clemency some means to reconcile the claims of humanity with the interests of society.

"I am all the more anxious for this outcome, should no other be feasible, in that I have come to know as a matter of observation that books and isolation had already effected an appreciable improvement in Rivière's heart and mind. Who knows but that this unfortunate man, corrected by good education, may not some day repay the preservation of his life by some great service to mankind?

One of your subscribers"

(e) *Pilote du Calvados*, November 15, 1835

After constantly manifesting his desire for a speedy ending ever since his conviction and in consequence obdurately refusing to appeal for his sentence to the penalty for parricides to be set aside, Pierre Rivière has yielded to the solicitations of his father, his confessor, and his counsel and has signed his appeal.

(Reproduced in the *Gazette des Tribunaux* of November 18.)

B. THE APPEAL TO THE COURT OF CASSATION AND THE REPRIEVE

1. NEWS ITEM

Pilote du Calvados, November 22, 1835

Following an attempted suicide by Pierre Rivière, recently convicted by the Calvados assize court, precautions have had to be taken, it is reported, to prevent its recurrence. He has therefore been placed in an observation cell. The wretched man seems wholly obsessed with the idea of the ignominy involved in mounting the scaffold before the eyes of a mass of beholders. He is wholly taken up with thoughts of religion.

2. EXTRACT FROM THE RECORD OF THE COURT OF CASSATION

[*The substance of the grounds of appeal on points of law only and the considerations on which the Court rejected them are summarized in the newspaper articles reproduced below.*]

3. ARTICLES RELATING TO THE REJECTION OF THE APPEAL

(a) *Gazette des Tribunaux*, January 17, 1836

The Court of Cassation (Criminal Division) had before it at its public hearings yesterday and today the appeal lodged by Rivière, sentenced by the Calvados Assize Court to the penalty for parricides. It will be recalled that this wretch determined to kill his mother and his brother because, as he believed, they stood in the way of his father's happiness; after perpetrating this twofold crime Rivière was struck by a no less deplorable thought: "I have killed," said he to himself, "they will kill me and my father will be distressed by my death; I must spare him this grief by depriving him of a cherished daughter [*sic*]." And Rivière murders his sister [*sic*] so that he will become odious to his father and so that on the day he is punished he will not have to mourn him who had deprived him of all that he held dearest on earth. Several doctors were called and attested to the disorder of Rivière's intellect. But in view of this triple murder the court passed the death sentence.

After Judge Mérilhou had produced the documents attesting Rivière's insanity and the Court had scrutinized them, Maître Adolphe Chauveau addressed the Court on behalf of the appellant. "The Court will of course appreciate," he said, "that I shall not advance before this Court grounds arising from the unfortunate Rivière's insanity; unfortunate indeed, for what greater misfortune can there be than to be deprived of reason? . . . But though the Counsel General for the Crown told you in court not long ago that a prisoner's impudent boasting strengthened the presumption of guilt, I shall be permitted to invoke the unanimous testimony of all that is most enlightened in science to interest you in a family which has already been so cruelly afflicted."

Maître Adolphe Chauveau then put forward several grounds for setting aside the conviction and in particular that the doctors called by virtue of the judge's full authority in court to give their opinion and proceed with what amounted to giving medical testimony had not taken the oath required in such circumstances. He drew a distinction between witnesses called to testify by virtue of the judge's full authority and witnesses called to enlighten the court by means of their expert knowledge; the former are not required to take the oath, whereas the latter appear before the assize court in the same circumstances as they appear during the preliminary investigation and so fall under the terms of article 44 of the Code of Criminal Procedure, which requires the oath; for when the presiding judge calls an expert, he proceeds to a further element in the investigation and in this particular case he is no more competent than the examining judge to exempt the expert from the oath he orders administered.

The Deputy Counsel General for the Crown rebutted these arguments; and the Court did not accept them. The Court disallowed the appeal and decided that witnesses and even experts called by virtue of the judge's full authority are not required to take the oath.

(b) *Pilote du Calvados*, January 20, 1836
   [*Reproduces the latter part of the report in the* Gazette des Tribunaux *above and continues:*]

The rejection of this appeal in no way prejudices the question of the petition of mercy on behalf of the condemned man which was drawn up at the same time. The petition seems, indeed, to have been strongly reinforced by the report prepared by a considerable number of leading Paris medical experts, expressing the view that Pierre Rivière is not in full possession of his mental faculties.

4. REPORT BY A CONFERENCE OF DOCTORS IN PARIS ON THE MENTAL CONDITION OF PIERRE RIVIÈRE

The undersigned, Esquirol, Head Physician at Charenton, Orfila, Dean of the Faculty of Medicine at Paris, Marc, Court Physician to His Majesty, Pariset, permanent secretary to the Royal Academy of Medicine, Rostan, professor in the Faculty of Medicine at Paris, Mitivié, doctor at la Salpêtrière, and Leuret, doctor of medicine.

Being called upon to state their opinion on the mental condition of Pierre Rivière before, during, and after the homicides by him committed for which he was recently sentenced to death by the Assize Court at Caen, have read and examined with the greatest care the documents to them communicated, consisting in: (1) an extract from the information laid against Pierre Rivière and containing the official report of his arrest, the medical certificate concerning the examination of the bodies of his victims, information on his previous life compiled by the District Prosecutor Royal at the civil court at Vire, the depositions of the witnesses heard at the inquiry and a certificate by M. Bouchard, doctor at Vire; (2) "the detail and explanation of the occurrence on June 3 at Aunay, village of la Faucterie, written by the author of this deed"; (3) the medical opinion by Dr. Vastel, doctor at Caen;

Considering that Pierre Rivière always sought solitude,

that he was often seen talking to himself and conversing with invisible interlocutors, roaring with laughter for no reasonable motive, hurling himself on cabbages and cutting off their heads as if he had been fighting against men, saying that he saw the devil and conversed with him, not daring to approach any woman, even one of his own family, for fear of polluting her with the emanations he believed flowed from his body, torturing animals in all sorts of ways and carrying a hammer and nails in his pocket for the purpose of crucifying them, and having engaged in so many aberrant actions from the age of four to the time when he put his mother, his brother, and his sister to death that he was known throughout his district as Rivière's imbecile, madman, or beast;

Considering that the aforesaid Rivière comes from a family which numbers several lunatics among its members (one of his uncles died insane after manifesting symptoms similar to those with which he himself was affected; two of his first cousins showed habitual symptoms of madness; his mother's character was extravagant and excessive to the last degree; one of his brother is almost wholly an idiot);

Considering that the motives which impelled Pierre Rivière to kill his mother, his sister, and his brother, such as to deliver his father from his domestic tribulations, to free the world from the yoke of women, to win immortality by some brilliant feat, by imitating the example of Châtillon, Eleazar, or Laroche-Jacquelin or by sacrificing himself like Jesus Christ for man's salvation, show a total deficiency of judgment;

Considering that the narrative of his life written by Pierre Rivière demonstrates a profound and consistent aberration of his intellectual faculties and moral feelings, that the soundness of memory and the sequence in the ideas displayed in this narration do not rule out mental deficiency since it frequently occurs in the narratives of maniacs or monomaniacs writing out the history of their malady;

Far from concurring in the opinion of M. Bouchard in declaring Pierre Rivière sane because he is unable to classify his abnormal condition in any of the main categories of madness, as if the categories established by nosographers were anything more than a method of classifying facts and thereby facilitating their study and that they do not have the slightest pretension to impose immutable boundaries on nature;

Taking into consideration the change which took place in Pierre Rivière's mental state shortly after the homicides, his despair, his agonizing reflections, his hesitation about going to denounce himself instead of proclaiming his triumph as he had purposed, his desire to take advantage of the reputation for madness he had acquired in order to be exonerated and his inability to sustain a role which was far beyond his strength;

Comparing this change with the change observed in many mental defectives, especially homicidal monomaniacs and suicidal madmen who sometimes become calm and even rational again after accomplishing the act toward which they were impelled;

Approving the conclusions set out in M. Vastel's report,

Have reached complete agreement and hereby declare:

1. That Pierre Rivière consistently showed signs of mental deficiency since the age of four;

2. That this mental deficiency persisted, though to a less intense degree, after the homicides he committed;

3. That the homicides are due solely and exclusively to delusion.

Done at Paris, December 25, 1835

Signed: Esquirol, Orfila, Marc, Pariset, Rostan, Mitivié, and Leuret

Note. Suppose a visitor to a lunatic asylum is shown a man of whom it could be truly said: "This patient often talks to himself, converses with the devil, fears that he may pollute any woman he comes near with emanations given off by his body; when at liberty, he was seen cutting off the heads of cabbages in the belief that he was cutting off men's heads; he often carried a hammer and nails in his pocket to crucify frogs or other animals; one day he tied a child's legs to the pothook and would have burned him if someone had not intervened in time; he was nicknamed throughout his district the madman, the imbecile, the beast; moreover, he knows when he is doing wrong and has even written out the history of his life very coherently," the visitor, no matter who he was, will not dream for a moment of stating that this man is in possession of his reason; and no judge or legal official would for a moment consider ordering his release. And if the patient concerned became homicidal inside the asylum, no one would dream of sending him to the scaffold. Yet the facts would be the same and only the places different. Pierre Rivière ought to have been placed in confinement; the young man was too ill to be left at large.

L[euret]

5. REPORT TO HIS MAJESTY THE KING BY THE MINISTER OF JUSTICE

Your Majesty,

I have the honor to submit to Your Majesty the report on the proceedings concerning Pierre RIVIÈRE, aged twenty-one.

[*The report recapitulates the substance of the report by the Presiding Judge of the Assize Court to the Director of Criminal Affairs, as far as the jury's verdict, with six jurymen suggesting that extenuating circumstances might be accepted; see pp. 142–6 above.*]

After sentence was passed, ten of the jurymen signed a recommendation of mercy on November 19, a passage from which reads: "We realize that all the ills he suffered in the person of his father, whom he cherished to the extent of sacrificing himself for him, must have powerfully contributed to the disturbance and derangement of his mental faculties, which were never wholly sound."

The Caen doctors drew up a memorandum in favor of Rivière presenting him as a prey to the singular monomania already mentioned above, namely, *aversion to women and female animals*. "Rivière," they wrote, "is of a gloomy and taciturn disposition . . . the only time he brightens is when a death sentence is hung over his head, and then it is only to smile with self-satisfaction, repeating four ill-made lines of verse which he had composed for the funeral of a jay." The doctors signing this memorandum consider that "Rivière has never been in possession of the full mental faculties which constitute a rational being; the convicted man is a taciturn and reserved madman, a prey to obsessions, wholly lacking in judgment, fearfully dangerous, yet deserving of the royal clemency which they venture to petition may light upon his disordered head."

In a recent medical opinion on Rivière, Drs. Orfila, Marc, Rostan, Metivié, and Leuret state that the convicted man is suffering from mental delusion.

The Presiding Judge of the Assize Court states in requesting a commutation of the penalty for Rivière: "The public which followed the hearings in court with lively interest is also divided in its opinions, and grave doubts would have arisen in the minds of the members of the Court if they had been called upon to hand down a decision."

"If I were compelled to give my views," the Counsel General for the Crown states, "I believe that the *doubt* (about Rivière's mental faculties) should be construed in his favor and I should be inclined to remit the death penalty for Rivière."

Nevertheless, there are grave circumstances which appear to establish that Rivière was aware of the full significance of his crime and ought in consequence to bear the responsibility for it. The hesitations of his conscience, his calculation to ensure that not one of his victims should escape death, his flight, the role of madman that he played at first and later abandoned, his very resignation and remorse all tell against him: "I repented so deeply after my crime," he said during examination in court, "that I would not have done it over again." Doubtless there were instincts of ferocity, tastes for strange cruelty, and misanthropic whims in the hidden depths of his unhappy and gloomy disposition, but could he not have overcome his horrid resolution if he had wrestled with himself awhile? On the contrary, Rivière seems to have collected his mental faculties in an effort to justify in his own eyes the crime to which he was about to abandon himself.

On the other hand, Rivière cannot be classified in the categories of ordinary criminals. He was not impelled by any of the motives which usually lead to crime; he harbored no personal grudge against any of his victims. Rivière felt a deep affection for his father; the sight of that father's misfortunes had inflamed his disordered imagination to the utmost degree. If Rivière failed to see that his action would merely aggravate the unhappy situation of the very person he wished to deliver from his ills, it could only be because the young man's judgment was indeed not wholly sound. The murder of his brother, no more than a mere child, and the reasoning which led Rivière to commit this murder appear to be characteristic only of a person of unsound mind.

In view of the doctors' conflicting reports and the various material facts, some of which disclose a considerable power of reasoning and calculation, whereas others appear to establish the perversion not only of his moral faculties but also of the functions of his discernment, I myself feel such grave doubts about the convicted man's mental state that I am wholly unable to conclude either that the sentence should be carried out or that he should be excused from all punishment. In these circumstances I believe it my duty to propose to Your Majesty that the penalty inflicted on Rivière be commuted to one of penal servitude for the term of his natural life, without exposure on a public place.

I am, Sire, with very great Respect,
    Your Majesty's most humble and most faithful Servant,
        the Keeper of the Seals, Ministerial Secretary
        of State for the Department of Justice and
        Ecclesiastical Affairs
Approved
February 10, 1836
By the King:
Louis Philippe

6. ARTICLES RELATING TO
THE REPRIEVE

(a) *Gazette des Tribunaux*, February 19, 1836
    It is reliably reported that the petition of mercy by Pierre Rivière, who killed his mother and sister in consequence of religious hallucinations, has been accepted and that the King has commuted the death penalty to which he was sentenced to one of life imprisonment.

(b) *Gazette des Tribunaux*, February 21, 1836
    On the seventeenth of this month in solemn session the Royal Court at Caen confirmed the reprieve and commutation of penalty granted to Pierre Rivière. The condemned man replied calmly to the questions put to him by the First President of the Court and showed the same unconcern as he had at the court hearings.

6

Prison and Death

1. MÉMORIAL DU CALVADOS,
MARCH 9, 1836

PIERRE RIVIÈRE, sentenced to death for the crime of parricide, which penalty was commuted by the King's prerogative to life imprisonment without exposure on a public place, was recently transferred to the Central Prison at Beaulieu.

The Memoir composed by Rivière in prison is on sale at Mancel's, bookseller at Caen, rue Saint Jean, 75 c.

2. BODY RECEIPT BY THE HEAD WARDEN OF THE CENTRAL PRISON

This day and date, March 7, 1836, one Le Blanc gendarme from the Caen barracks appeared at the registry of the Central House of Detention at Beaulieu bearing an order issued by the Prefect of Calvados dated the fourth day of this month whereunder he delivered to me the body of one Jean Pierre Rivière sentenced to imprisonment for life on November 12, 1835, as certified in the writ of sentence which has been produced to me in extract, the transcript being hereto attached.

The said Jean Pierre Rivière having been placed in my custody to serve his sentence, I have drawn up this entry in the calendar of reception and the said Le Blanc has signed together with me constituting the receipt.

(signed) Le Blanc, Lhomedé

Reasons and date of termination of detention
Jean Pierre Rivière deceased at half past one o'clock on the morning of October 20, 1840.

Lhomedé, Head Warden
p.p. the Governor

3. PILOTE DU CALVADOS,
OCTOBER 22, 1840

Rivière, who was condemned to death a few years ago as a parricide and fratricide but whose sentence was commuted to life imprisonment because his crime bore every sign of insanity, has just hanged himself in Beaulieu prison.

He had been showing unmistakable signs of madness for some little time. Rivière believed himself to be dead and refused to take any sort of care of his body; he said he wanted his head cut off, which would not hurt him at all because he was dead; and if they would not comply with this wish, he threatened to kill everybody. Because of this threat he had to be isolated from all the other prisoners, and he took advantage of this isolation to commit suicide.

Since the press may have had some favorable effect on the commutation of the penalty by the discussions it published at the time of the wretched man's sentencing, it is making a point of reporting a death of this sort because it completely confirms its opinion of Rivière's mental condition.

II

Notes

1

The Animal, the Madman, and Death

ONCE THIS DOSSIER is closed, harsh and bleak as it is, it might be wiser for persons of discourse such as we are (and, indeed, such as the judges and the doctors were) to respect the seal this life affixed to it itself and to keep silent. Yet ought we to leave without an echo, a speech whose resonance in us has lasted to this day and which in consequence generates words by virtue of the passage of time? We have not discharged our debt to these corpses.

If the peasants had a Plutarch, Pierre Rivière would have his chapter in the *Illustrious Lives*. And not he alone. His whole family falls into a rank of exemplary victims, a challenge, so to speak, to the galleries of storied urns and animated busts in the lofty ancestral mansions. But what Plutarch could conceive that exemplary lives could ever grow from the furrows tended by the stooping rustics? The humble earn only the meed of silence. So it is only right that one among those who stifle in their narrow confines should come to utter that insensate laughter which expresses the meaning even while it freezes and harrows the hearer, the prolonged peal of Pierre Rivière's laughter in the years leading up to the murder, a laughter which speaks of the intolerable. The purport of the speech engendered by the deed and the text is wholly that of ill-hap. The enclosed horizon of the hedgerows was from time immemorial a profusion of lives devoid of all future, deprived of all prospects. Enduring the unlivable, day in and day out.

Should one of them perceive it even for a moment, his whole world falls apart and everything around him. Everything falls apart. For the mute horror of the daily round, for the predicament of dumb beast and dupe he has substituted a more flagrant horror, protest by hecatomb. And thereby he assumes the right to break the silence and speak at last. To speak the heart of the matter like one returned from the dead, one who has long known that the lives of all of them were a long cohabitation with the uninhabitable.

Only a comfortable person, the very opposite of a native, a doctor, could be astonished, dismayed, and put out of countenance by Pierre Rivière because "when reminded of his crime, he speaks of it with a sort of tranquillity which is truly shocking."[1] The fact is that the horrible is the quotidian. In the countryside it has been everyone's lot since time immemorial; one of them laughs at it with a laughter which might well be held to be an idiot's laugh; another speaks of it tranquilly; and both are one. It is everyone's lot, but this family is exemplary in that it so lived as to yell furiously that everything hurts, all the time, and to this one becomes as accustomed as to everything else.

The weight of the impossible, too, hangs like a leaden cloak. But it is undoubtedly against this that this dumb beast measured himself, head down, throwing out every sort of challenge, climbing the dangerous tree, and seeking his ill-hap in the most diverse fashions.[2] The laboring folk, clinging to their land, reduced to their stifling dimension, Rivière's father who made an illusion of his work and never a success of it, these are they whom Pierre Rivière, in the metaphor of the driven horses, whipped up and pushed to their utmost limit and risked in his desperate wagers.[3] Something had, for once at least, to go beyond

[1] Certificate by Bouchard, p. 123.
[2] Statement by Hamel, p. 33.
[3] Statements by Marguerite Colleville, p. 29; Hamel, p. 33. It is worth noting the role of horses in Pierre Rivière's mind and actions. They are a force, but a fettered force. Mild, powerful, at once impotent

the possible, to transgress these limits. To his father he said: Go further, go higher, for once at least. To his horses: Do what no one has ever done. But, whether horse or peasant, the jobbing laborer can do everything except the impossible. Rivière alone could surmount the barrier and win a bitter victory, only he could simply die, or, in other words, kill. An explosion into a purple ceremony. By it and in it and after it he would be able to speak the truth and, as a monster, display in their monstrous light the rule of lies and the foul machine at whose whim his fellows, the disinherited of the earth, are and have always been crushed, each day, each life. So much patience and so much suffering armed one of them with the sudden trenchant lightning-gleam of the pruning bill: the divine impatience. By the weight of the sacrifice of his committed life and of three more suffering lives doubly victims beneath his blows, the just and the unjust were to change places and at length be re-established by Pierre Rivière where they first stood, on the day on which his own death began, a death that will go on and on and may well "put an end to all [his] resentments."[4]

MONSTERS AND EQUALS

He might well harbor resentments, this avenger. The French countryside had for ages suffered under the three-fold taxation of the lord of the manor, the Church, and the king. The peasants were drained to husks shivering in the slightest breeze. Mortality, with its train of hunger, cold, and epidemics, held sway over the countryside. The cus-

---

and dramatic. It is Rivière who mentions that Mourelle, the old mare, whom he loves and of whom he often speaks, grinds her teeth (statement by the widow Quesnel, p. 30). And he frightens a child and himself too with an ogre-horse (statement by Victor Marie, p. 31).

[4] The closing words of Rivière's memoir.

tomary result of peasant risings was to adorn the trees with bunches of the hanged for the police to harvest.

On the one side extortion; on the other the immediacy and weight of power. The contracts imposed by the over-lord or the Church were not a guarantee, but a snare. No matter whether, long ago, by promising some other thing, they made them serfs or, more recently, sharecroppers, they annulled the human being. The peasantry is a nothing. Michelet described this despair well enough, from the Middle Ages to more recent times.[5] Many of these things still existed at the close of the 18th century.

True, by this time the plague had disappeared and so had the great famines. Some advances in scientific farming had led to a greater productivity of foodstuffs; but a larger number of landowners (nobles, judges and lawyers, and the middle class) reaped all the benefits. So that dearth, even though it was little mentioned, was endemic, and hence undernourishment and malnutrition. But the point that concerns us is this:

For the first time doctors, men of the Enlightenment, visited the villages and the farms. The loss of workers' lives meant an inroad on capital, so that it was more profitable to care for them; Turgot projected a state health service. These doctors were appalled to find the universal poverty in the countryside. They complained and they acted. But the nature of the people they attended surprised them. In them the known diseases assumed very bizarre forms, re-vealed arborescent ramifications. Their bodies, their scabs, their ashen skin, the granulations and nodes of bones and flesh, as reported by the doctors, proclaimed that these men were not yet human and were still part of the animal, vegetable, or mineral. Squatting in the mud of their farms they were toads, and sheep in their credulous stupidity; and

[5] Jules Michelet, *La Sorcière*, bk. IV, chap. 2: "Pourquoi le moyen âge désespéra"; *Histoire de France*, bk. VI, chap. 3: "La jacquerie, la peste"; *Histoire de la Révolution française*, introduction.

wolves when the hunger gleamed in their eyes, and mad dogs engendered by their mad dogs biting them. Monsters.[6]

Many causes, or currents, converged in the events of 1789. The poverty of the countryside had its part in them, at least as a pretext—or a form of remorse?—in the minds of the bourgeois notables who took the initiative. But there will never be an adequate assessment—especially since a current in historiography has been busy blurring it—of the extent to which the peasant insurgency (half *Jacquerie* and half panic), which is known as *la Grande Peur* and covered France from end to end (except for Brittany, the Landes, and Lorraine) in the summer of 1789, contributed to clarifying the hesitations in Paris and compelling a clean sweep. The night of August 4, for all its mythology, exudes the sweat of fear in the face of the manors ablaze and the assembled masses of the poor. The "feudal" order collapsed under their pressure. And the evidence becomes yet more cogent in that, despite the Assembly's legal pettifogging in laying down strict clauses for the purchase of seigneurial rights, the peasantry confirmed their *de facto* abolition by a collective refusal to pay them. This is what is meant by revolution.[7]

The result in the countryside was a huge transfer of ownership, even though it did not affect the mass of those whose sole property was the hire of their hands. But regardless of whether they did or did not have a plot of land, all of them placed great hopes in the legal liberation which they believed they had gained: equality of rights, status as citizens. Now, "free and equal in law," they were men, at last identical with all others. As such, they could make con-

---

[6] On the Royal Society of Medicine (1776–93) and the relation between medical discourse and the world of the countryside at the end of the 18th century, see Jean-Pierre Peter, "Les mots et les objets de la maladie," *Revue historique*, July-Sept. 1971; *idem*, "Le corps du délit," *Nouvelle Revue de psychanalyse*, no. 3, Spring 1971.

[7] Georges Lefèbvre, *La Grande Peur de 1789*, Paris, 1932, reprinted 1970.

tracts. Peasant life thereafter was invested in the contract and in the greed for land, governed, satiated, and renewed by the contract. Pierre Rivière's father was one such, basing on a piece of ground perhaps acquired by his own parents through the Revolution[8] an ambition for an ever-larger property which he wished to bequeath to his children. Buyer and lessor of lands, faithful steward of the desirable properties of his wife and their laborer who worked free of charge, he identified himself with the being of the Contract, alienated himself in it, and lost himself in it.

THE STRAIGHT AND THE CROOKED

For it was certainly here that the snares still existed. The order of the new liberal society mounted its control apparatus at this very place—the contract, the desire for property, the work incentive engendered by them—to control and perpetuate hierarchies and inequalities, but now under the false pretense of a relation "voluntarily" accepted. Here it was that power worked in secret.[9]

[8] This is merely an assumption. A hasty search turned up an only approximately contemporary cadastral survey, but lacking a nominal roll. The Rivière family "lands" cannot be identified on it. There is no land-tax register before the second half of the century. (The Calvados archives will have to be searched again.) A more thorough search, which we wanted to make but did not have time for, would have to be made in the files for the sales of the *biens nationaux*. The Abbey of Aunay and its domain were dismembered as Church properties, and the Rivière family probably began to acquire lands at that time.

[9] It will be recalled that under the Old Regime power controlled not only the status of persons, and hence their freedom by exercising some degree of pressure upon their bodies, but especially that its immediate instrument was taxation (royal, seigneurial, and so on), which creamed off the peasants' labor product and capital. It was no accident that the peasants looted the manors and held a reckoning with the tax farmers, tithers, and so on whenever they could. Henceforward the peasants' labor product was controlled from within by the indirect means of the contract. Hence the hatreds among contracting parties and, as Michel Foucault has suggested to us, the new type of peasant criminality (crimes within families or penalizing ownership, tenancy, sharecropping, and other relationships).

Victoire Rivière, the mother, is an exemplary case. No doubt because as a woman and even more so as a wife married to thwart by rule a rule which itself was irregular, she felt that any contract remained a trick, an institution-alized assault—as if in a frozen, arrested, perpetual combat. She set herself up as the everlasting canceller of contracts, perpetually put them in doubt, and shifted their signs by setting them moving again—which is tantamount to repudi-ation and challenge.

As a child of this confrontation, Pierre Rivière inherited a fascination with contracts that became enshrined in his memoir. But he also gained an inkling that this war con-cerned something over and above the pettifogging terms in which the conflict was couched, and hence descried over and above the choices he himself had to make in it some evidence that, more generally, something somewhere had been falsified. The world around him, around all of them, waved and teased like the red rags used to deflect and wear down the strength of animals. He became aware that a snare lurked somewhere. What called itself order was a lie, or rather the existing order was the reverse of an order. Pierre Rivière assumed the stance of a questioner of the straight and the crooked, the just and the unjust. Here he too was exemplary.

If he was to put such a question, however, he had to have the right to speak. But that was precisely what he did not have; the tally of his resentments is endless.

For once the revolutionary tempest had passed over and society had been forcibly remolded by the Empire, what picture did the country people present in the resur-rected society? What were the tidings announced to these beings by the wholly formal equality of rights and the free-dom to acquire property? The truth is that nothing had changed. Animals they remained; the discourse of ascend-ancy had not shifted. They were as alienated as they could be—beasts or things, something close to nothing, who could not seriously be thought to have anything to say.

The compassionate doctors continued to give detailed accounts of their monstrosities, invariably ascribing them to evil nature.

But was this really possible? If we were still monsters and henceforth your equals, what were you? The new deal no longer allowed for such a play of contempt without generating a backlash. And it came.

BLOOD AND CRY

Indeed, unexpected incidents began to occur at about the time of Pierre Rivière's birth. The countryside, the silent universe of ill-hap, no longer merely dumbly suffered its lot, but externalized it, and this resulted in significant symptoms—the most frightful crimes. Symptoms is the word for them, since we know of these cases through medicine, which promptly extracts from them the juice it needs for its annals. For instance, peasant servant girls butchered the frail babes they loved and that were entrusted to their care, for no reason, but with the utmost cruelty. A needy day-laborer's wife, unable to bear her fifteen-month-old child's hungry squalling, slashed its throat with a cleaver, drained its blood and cut off and ate one of its thighs. Yet amid all the dearth she kept a goat, a garden plot, and a few cabbages. Antoine Léger, a vine grower, left his village community, lived in the woods like a savage, attacked a little girl and, failing to rape her, sliced her open, sucked her heart, and drank the blood.[10]

All of them were appalled by their deeds. "I wished," said the girl, "to spare the child from having to live as I

[10] Most of these cases were discussed in the seminar on criminology under Michel Foucault in 1971. They were first published either in the files of the *Annales d'hygiène publique* or in Georget, *Examen des procès Léger, etc.*, 1835 and C. H. H. Marc, *De la folie*, 1840. We have recently reprinted two cases of cannibalism: "Ogres d'archives," *Nouvelle Revue de psychanalyse*, no. 6, Fall 1972.

do, solitary, joyless; death is better." "It is the misery of it," the ogress said. "God abandoned me. I was thirsty," says the ogre. In some sort their stammered confessions declared: It was me that I was killing. And Pierre Rivière, the culmination of this memorable line of descent, called to the neighbors, not "I have killed," but "I am dying . . . for my father."[11]

It seems to us now that the silent people of the countryside had just become aware of the testimony and the opportunity of some of them who sacrificed their lives as if they knew of a knowledge that staggers reason and that the native had to start by killing and consequently dying in order to speak up and be heard. Their acts were discourses; but what were they saying and why did they speak this terrifying language of crime?

We have only to appreciate the disarray in the customarily secure and composed discourses of the lawyers and doctors caused by these fine and tragic monstrosities of horror to see that something important was happening.

EXAMPLE AND EVENT

Indeed, something basic had already occurred, and it is one of the crucial points in all these cases. Traditionally, the years of the Revolution and their prolongations until 1815 are studied for their social and political significance. And quite rightly. On the other hand, too little attention is paid to their impact on, and the consequent shifts in, what historians awkwardly call mentalities.

To begin with, the assumption of violence and death. It must be said that some tolerably fine butcheries went on for over twenty years. The taste for blood may have profited from them and made some progress during these years. These new citizens, peasants freed from the feudal yoke, were politely invited freely to sow all the fields of

[11] Pierre Rivière's memoir, p. 112 and p. 105.

Europe with their entrails and their bones. Others were to reap the harvest. To die for liberty and then to die for the benefit of the monsters; to kill for it and for them. To kill and to die. What they gained were baubles; at the end of the road there awaited the mass of the peasant herd (again the peasants), the prospects of disablement or death. They paid very dearly for their new and fallacious rights. Pierre Rivière's birth is direct evidence that they tried to elude such obligations; he was conceived so that his father could evade the draft.

At this period some ogres presented an imposing appearance to the world's gaze, Jacobin, Imperial, or Royal ogres, most of them highly decorated, ribbonned, and bemedalled. The most illustrious of them finally rotted on a small island. But so many others, before and after him, were able to set a splendid table, digesting Poland, champing their jaws on the nations and on freedom. A crew of well-fed monsters. At one degree below them, what, after all, was a prefect or a judge, revolutionary or otherwise? They too quaffed their goblet of blood here and there. Willingly or perforce, the fathers bit into this universe of violence; it is not surprising that their children's teeth should have been set on edge. Pierre Rivière and his brothers in murder, village ogres or ogresses, frail women cutting off children's heads, did not invent violence by themselves, nor did the parricide athirst for glory invent the holocausts that had to be performed that good might come.

The fact remains that, from the Bastille to Thermidor, a few very crowded years left their impress on the memory, because the *event* as such arose from them, the long-awaited and finally assured revelation that no one was safe from the event, not even the tyrant.[12] Nothing was in-

12 At the time of the diabolic possession at Loudon most of the pamphlets and broadsides which interpreted and distorted it day after day placed themselves in a privileged relationship to the truth by their title-heads: "Truthful account of . . . ," "True narrative of the righteous proceedings . . . ," "Defense of the truth concerning the possession . . . ,"

tangible any more. Everything could henceforth happen, since *it* had happened. In this festival of death people learned, and never ceased remembering thereafter, that death, if risked, caused a shift.

Saint-Just awaited this dawn (all unknowing that it would come one day), Saint-Just who, as Michelet relates, driven to despair by a frozen world and raging at it ("the world has been empty since the Romans"), shut himself up in his room to read of the life and death of the heroes of antiquity; and when he, who was soon to be the first funeral orator to demand a king's head, emerged from it, "he was seen beheading (like a Tarquin) poppies with a stick."[13] Pierre Rivière and his impatient gestures with the

---

or "Examination of . . ." With the Revolution the event as such was the area in which the headings proclaimed not the whole truth, but the evidence of the fact or movement. Hence the repetitious titles of the leaflets and broadsides: "Memoirs on what happened on . . ." (or "what happened at . . ."), "Documents designed for the history of the events which . . . ," "Particulars (or "Particulars and explanation") of the occurrence . . ." This is the title Pierre Rivière chose for his memoir. On the frequency of a similar form of words in the titles of the tales of crime at this period, see Michel Foucault's essay (Note 2).

[13] Michelet, *Histoire de la Révolution française*, bk. IX, chap. 5. We have been constantly struck by the way in which Pierre Rivière's story duplicated illustrious models of whom he knew nothing. Thus he is subsumed in many ways, but without knowing it, under the universe of exemplarity. "A pupil of Plutarch's," Stendhal said of Julien Sorel. This obscure peasant resembles Julien Sorel, as he does Saint-Just and Don Quixote, in the role that the reading of basic works played in determining his crusade. Like each of them, bringing other exemplary lives to life again in his own person, he testified to the absolute obligation of an ancient code (Roman rigidity in the case of Saint-Just, chivalry in that of Don Quixote, the Napoleonic adventure in that of Julien Sorel, and so on), whose proclamation alone and re-enactment should suffice to return to its nullity the degraded world in which he lived as an exile and whose values were, to one whose eyes were fixed on other texts, lies and deceit. Hence, like the Knight of the Rueful Countenance, he seems mad; like Julien, a criminal rebel; like Saint-Just, sullen and abstracted. Like all of them—and like Hamlet—he holds in hand or in memory a little book which speaks the truth in terms unintelligible to any Polonius, a book which at least proclaims the model to which each of them refers in order to produce his own truth.

cabbages turned on a date and already spoke, in the guise of the whim of a child's game, of the existence of leaders and the execution of tyrants.

When the curtain fell again after 1815, and once again after 1830, and the established order said, as it always says, "You better come quiet," some (a woman who insulted God and who, like him, sacrificed a son, a Pierre Rivière who thought that everything was lies, a Lacenaire, and a Fieschi in the same year as he), killed and consented to die in order that amid the deathly immobility something should happen, start to live, to move, to question, to disturb. The event was freedom; it cut like a blade, perturbed, thwarted, or took every sort of institution in the rear. An exemplary event, murder, here aimed, in a frozen world, at the timelessness of oppression and the order of power.

KING AND MONSTER

From the Bastille to the death of Louis XVI another shift occurred from which, time after time, certain effects of truth were to well up and explode.

In the divine order from which the Old Regime issued the king was the keystone of an edifice in which everyone was assigned his place, but in which only the man wellborn was fully a man. Each person possessed a demonstrable being, speech, or evident existence only by virtue of the avowal he made of this position, of his membership of his estate. Anyone who claimed to be anything else (or used any other form of speech) was false to the divine order and cut himself off radically from mankind. Thus, the sorcerer, the atheist, and the rebel eluded all classification.

After July 1789 God and the truth changed sides and passed over to the people by secularizing themselves. The king suddenly found himself isolated from his own truth and severed from God. And so no longer credible. The result was that his head fell less than four years later. "A

king is unnatural; there is no natural link between the
people and a king," was the Mountain's contention. We do
not pass judgment; we exterminate a monster.[14]

Thereafter, everyone was among his fellows, all the
more since the idea had been emerging, for some time, of
a contract among equals, and this was at last possible; never
again would there be subjects; all were to be alike. There
would now be nothing to limit anyone's belonging to the
full human condition. But the fact that the sovereign had
once been designated the monster, in a prodigious reversal
of all signs, was enough to raise a problem about the
frontier between the human and the inhuman.

Henceforth it had no basis in law. Nevertheless its
trace was not erased and served to support the ascendancy's
illusory picture of itself by virtue of the power it exercised.
But here the effects of a lie and the potentialities of nega-
tion began to flare up.

In a world now subject to the abstract violences of
money, the peasant and his like, the native after the conquest, were henceforth defined only as the negative of the
ascendancy. The member of the ascendancy alone was a
"notable," that is to say, identifiable on a scale of values
established by himself and one which would be seen as the
scale of "humanity." But there was no antonym for
"notable," so that the "other" (native, savage, or yokel)
could not even give himself a name. Under the Old Regime
he was almost nothing (the absolute degree of subjection,
but recognized in that status). Here, as soon as he ceased
to define himself by the vise of the contract (by his relation
to the economic nexus), he was nothing at all in humanity.
Then the only possibility left him was a reversal of values.

[14] Saint-Just expressed himself to this effect. See Michelet, *loc cit.*;
Albert Mathiez, *La Révolution française*, vol. II, bk. 2, chap. 4. "We
know all too well," the Abbé Grégoire said in September 1792, "that
all dynasties have always been nothing but predatory races living on
human flesh." And, he added, "in the moral order the king is what the
monster is in the physical." See Michelet, *op. cit.*, VIII, 3.

Only to those who are excluded from the social nexus comes the idea of raising a question about the limits of human nature.

CRIME AND ASSERTION

It was at this point that a few delegates from the countryside intervened and stood surety for the right they assumed to utter their speech by casting the weight of their life and their reason into the scales. In point of fact, this speech was so negligible that it had become customary never to record it. There is evidence of this over the ages in the archives, where one has to read between the lines to grasp beneath the discourse of the master (overlord, bailiff, notary, doctor, judge, tax-collector, policeman, and the like) what was being said and was what being carefully obliterated. Even when it shouts aloud, this voice is heard only as the mutterings of a dying man. If he had anything to say, the native was the only person who was not taken at his word. If he was to be heard, he had to be killed.

It was precisely on this point that the dark precursors beat. What would happen if they ceased to recognize the fundamentals of a society which had believed that it was founded by excluding them? Since by rejecting them a frontier had been drawn, if there was something inhuman here or there—and this is tacitly postulated—could the orderly world of the notables remain what it said it was? If they wanted monsters, here they were. But it was no longer possible not to see oneself in them. For, once the feudal world had been swept away, notability was no longer safe-guarded by the wish or command of a god; and every person in law (the law of the ascendancy) was equal to every other person; the have-nots to the haves. All that the former had to do merely to test the imaginary frontier which the latter had tried to make credible was to elude it, and they would no longer be able to maintain their role.

These radical murders attacked the very principle of

civility. In the code, civility was defined within a twofold frontier; one was stated—parricide (any person who committed it was unnatural); the other was implicit—cannibalism (there are no words to describe it, even in statute law). Against these frontiers the native struck blow on blow, and from this place he stated his terms: Tell us what nature you are willing to concede to those with whom you are willing to contract, but let it be as among equals. That is to say, fix truly, and not as a snare, a frontier for the human nature in which we can recognize ourselves. Then I will cease terrifying you with these monstrous masks.

A statement of this sort can be voiced only in the moment of hesitation which opens between an absolute act (in which a victim falls) and the death (on the scaffold or in the nothingness of madness) of those who have dared to make it. At least two deaths, of which none could fail to talk, unlike as they were to the everyday deaths of the countryside, the monotonous deaths that were celebrated merely in silence. Pierre Rivière, moreover, added a written statement over which every notable was to stumble.

Each of these tragedies set in motion the garrulous machinery of the law and medicine, partners and rivals in this operation of trying to contain the question that comes to them and smother it in a fog of words. In point of fact, it was rather that all these operations of discourse whereby they distorted the literal meaning of the facts served to enable the lawyers and the doctors to look at themselves in a glass without shuddering. But, secure holders of power as they were, could they really make us believe that they did not tremble when they discovered every time that the aggressive monstrosity of the "other" fell back on them, that in them someone was speaking the same language, that desire can leap barriers, and that normal is simply a word one applies to oneself? If not, why was there this itch that irked their knowledge, why this medical logorrhea visible in the ever-increasingly incomplete, always ill-fitting catalog of madness, whether monomaniac or not?

When Fodéré was asked for his expert opinion at the assize court in the Sélestat case and had to say what the ogress-mother was, he was troubled. The woman showed none of the patterns of signs by which madness was recognized; dispersed and uncoordinated traits, and that was all. Then, and because otherwise he could not have borne it, "he felt obliged to consider that the accused was deprived of her reason and so to enable the judges and prosecution to rule out" (for the sake of the honor of humanity) "liability for so heinous a crime."[15] He added—a Parthian shot —that the neighborhood of the tragedy was populated by imbeciles and cretins. Though shaken for a moment, the ascendancy swiftly regained power by a racist discourse.

It was indeed because this vise was so powerful that fresh murderers were constantly needed to put the same question yet again. But these forward reconnoitrers of a distant cause ventured so rashly into the heart of darkness and found themselves so much alone that, in killing to testify, they came to grief. Exemplars of the dominated, it was precisely because of their predicament as natives that they did not think of killing those who secured against them the power of the law—the law of lies. The native terrorist kills innocent children, and above all those he loves; he kills his brothers in slavery, the everlasting victims, the disarmed. In them, in killing his nearest, in killing something of his own, it is himself that he strikes, and blow upon blow: at one and the same time to kill several people, to kill several times.[16]

---

[15] "Examen d'un cas extraordinaire d'infanticide, par le docteur Reisseisen de Strasbourg," *Annales d'hygiène publique*, vol. VIII, 1832; Fodéré, *Essai médico-légal sur les diverses espèces de folie*, Strasbourg, 1832.

[16] "And I committed that fearful crime . . . after that I struck them again and again." (Pierre Rivière, Memoir, p. 112.) "The savagery of the [native] shows itself especially in the number of wounds he inflicts, some of these being unnecessary once death has already occurred. Autopsies establish one fact beyond shadow of a doubt: The murderer gives the impression, by inflicting many wounds of equal deadliness, that he wished to kill an incalculable number of times." (Frantz Fanon,

To his father, who played in good faith, but blindly, at a fallacious emancipation by collecting plots of land, Pierre Rivière wished to oppose, at the cost of his life, the radical violence of the liberated word. He would have chosen rightly if, in so doing, he had not happened to cut down his mother and his sister, two other rebels, engaged in the same confused struggle for emancipation, women desperate to undermine from one side (their own) an unjust order at which Pierre was aiming from the other. It was their misfortune that they acted too early in this age. It was a misfortune, too, for the other; but his rigor lay in the very fact that in this confusion about themselves in which the ascendancy keeps the weak, thereby frustrating their revolt, he should have recognized coherent symbols, isolated a tyrant, identified the original dupe (the worn-out old horse, the people, his father) and himself have put a question which will never cease to haunt us.

MOTHER AND TYRANT

Neither the judges nor the doctors seem to have seen Pierre Rivière as this peasant, the perpetual loser, who believed he would herald a new era by slaughtering a tyrant. The publication of his memoir in the *Annales d'hygiène* is evidence enough of the misunderstanding in which they confined him beforehand; the fact that in this case the person who made contracts ridiculous was the mother, not the king, enabled medicine to reduce the murder to its symptomatic dimension and the murderer to the abstraction of a clinical case.[17]

Les Damnés de la terre, Paris, 1961, p. 226.) [English trans., section on "Criminal impulses found in North Africans," in *The Wretched of the Earth*, London: Penguin Books, 1967, p. 240.]

[17] The doctors interested in Pierre Rivière's case considered the first part of his memoir, entitled "Summary of the tribulations and afflictions which my father suffered at the hands of my mother from 1813 to 1835," lacking in clinical interest, and so did not publish it.

In the introduction to his memoir Rivière demands attention: "but all I ask is that what I mean shall be understood" (p. 55), he concludes. The least we can do, therefore, is to look at how he justifies his murder and the way in which he couples Napoleon's crimes with his mother's in a disconcerting discord. "I conjured up Bonaparte in 1815. I also said to myself: that man sent thousands to their death to satisfy mere caprices, it is not right therefore that I should let a woman live who is disturbing my father's peace and happiness" (p. 108). Further, it is time to set an example and overthrow the morale of "this fine age which calls itself the age of enlightenment, this nation which seems to be so avid for liberty and glory obeys women" (p. 108).

Thus, a tyrant had risen again in this age. This time it was woman. The law she instituted was the arbitrary. Never again! In my family this tyrant is my mother; she renders every contract void of meaning; she makes my father forfeit his rights and loads him with dues.[18] At the same time, she was a stumbling-block to the son: I desire her constantly, perhaps because of the vacant place in her bed where, from the very first, she has not wanted my father, and he was not strong enough to take it. I hate her.[19] By killing her I am setting an example so that the law may be restored, the contract honored, and tyranny over-

[18] Pierre Rivière invariably presents his father as the mild one, the weak, the oppressed. When the mother wins her case with the judge before whom she has dragged her husband, the son at once comments: "so my unfortunate father was left to his fate and the mighty prevailed" (i.e. the tyrant mother), p. 92, footnote.

[19] Compare the testimony of the surviving relations as reported by the district prosecutor: "his mother especially was odious to him. At times he felt a wave of something like repulsion and frenzy when she approached him" (p. 10). Rivière expresses his own feelings quite plainly: At a time when he "was *consumed by ideas of greatness and immortality, carnal passion troubled* [*him,*] above all [he had] a *horror of incest*" (p. 102) which caused him to shun the women of his family and, if he could not do so, he tried to repair the harm he believed he had done by rituals which surprised those around him.

thrown.[20] I am thus executing the justice of God.[21] Human contracts are monstrous, I appeal to another justice, of which I, monster in semblance, am the providential executor.

ANIMAL AND MADMAN

It is not surprising, therefore, that no means was left untried to reduce the significance of his act; since it was aimed at the social order, the order of the contract, it could only be something done by a beast or a madman, the opposite of a man. The district prosecutor, representing those laws of men which seemed "ignoble and shameful" to Rivière, did precisely this: "solitary, wild, and cruel," he said, Rivière "is . . . a savage not subject to the ordinary laws of sympathy and sociability" (pp. 10–11). He hastened to identify the murderer's appearance with that of an ape or a primitive: "He is short, his forehead is narrow and low, his eyebrows arch and meet, he constantly keeps his head down, and his furtive glances seem to shun meeting the gaze of others, as if for fear of betraying his secret thoughts; his gait is jerky and he moves in bounds, he leaps rather than walks" (p. 11). Pierre Rivière, the ultra-rustic and therefore the ultra-bestial. Perhaps he seemed so only because he himself appreciated how dangerous his secret thoughts were and because he was sometimes uncertain when he wondered in what order (superhuman or animal) this thought classified him.[22]

[20] "I regarded my father as being in the power of mad dogs or barbarians against whom I must take up arms" (p. 105). "In former times one saw Jaels against Siseras, Judiths against Holoferneses, Charlotte Cordays against Marats; now it must be men who employ this mania" (p. 108) (i.e. kill and recover the power).

[21] "It even seemed to me that God had destined me for this and that I would be executing his justice. I knew the rules of man and the rules of ordered society, but I deemed myself wiser than they, I regarded them as ignoble and shameful" (p. 105).

[22] He told his father that he was going to do like the horned beasts,

Thus, he accounted for his solitude by "some acts of stupidity which I had done since the beginnings and which, as I thought, had discredited me for ever" (p. 101). He certainly had some idea that these "acts of stupidity" were simply incestuous thoughts, obsessive enough to make him keep silent about them, to shun an exchange of glances with anyone, and to accept the verdict of animality or savagery: "thus he asked his father whether a man could not live in the woods on plants and roots" (p. 11). Far from the object of desire, far from the tyranny of women, far from humiliated fathers. To reach that, he would need three murders and the inability to kill himself as he had purposed; for in this universe governed by the law of women it was permissible to be a man only for the space of a moment; kill and then die, exhaust the possible in a flash. Failing to achieve this, he decided to become temporarily animal: "at last I resolved *to abide by my condition* since the evil was irremediable, I resolved to live on plants and roots until whatever events might come"[23] (p. 114). Killing and then surviving and enduring is the opposite of being a human. All that is left is to try to return to nature.

But he did not live in it like Robinson Crusoe, who, wholly mindful of his father's words, labored, cleared the land, constantly transformed nature, accumulated goods in case he succeeded in rejoining society, and, naturally, did succeed in doing so. The only word Pierre Rivière's father gave him to determine his destiny ("you will become a priest"), precisely unlike Crusoe's, became inoperative, just like his wish to induce his wife to honor the marriage contract. That is why his son's survival was impossible.

---

that he was going to "scamper about" (p. 45); "Sometimes he uttered terrifying cries" (statement by the widow Quesnel, p. 48). Cf. Michelet, *La Sorcière*, chap. 2: "We, sad beasts, having lost man's speech, the only one that God is willing to hear [Latin], what can we do now but low and bleat?"

[23] Italics added.

When he fell back on nature, he could not cope with it, he could neither remain in it nor exploit it. Since he debarred himself from enjoying it, all the knowledge he had as a humble peasant became useless. He wandered for a long time, like a man without culture, an animal without instinct, that is to say, like something which, specifically, did not exist; a mythical being, a monstrous being impossible to define because it does not belong to any identifiable order.

This is no doubt why, however much he showed himself in the villages or tried to draw attention to himself in order to put an end to this insensate situation, he was never recognized or denounced by the peasants. For the man who was being hunted was "the man from Aunay," guilty of three murders. But the man who was seen was literally no one, neither man nor beast, a ghost, but a ghost of what?

He then decided to rejoin society, but under the mask or with the trappings of a madman.[24] When he was at last arrested, he said he came "from everywhere" (p. 120) and was going where God commanded him. We see what rigor his simulated madness preserved, how much of the truth the mask let through when he still tried, despite all, to utter the impossible, in which he henceforth stood as firm as if he were in the front line of battle.

But everyone was caught up in this playing with labels, all those who judged possible the impossible which his murder denounced: the fallacious rule of contracts. Especially those around him, so prompt to declare him mad. His silence, his savage demeanor had always frightened them; these yokels whom doctors and judges called beasts always saw him as the ultra-beast, "Rivière's brute"; whether or not it was the consequence of an original fault in this child of man, he had been outlawed from society,

[24] He gave more and more signs: sleeping in ditches, lying down on the public highway, giving strange answers when questioned. But his madness was taken seriously only when he was seen carrying the anachronistic weapon he had made. See Michel Foucault's essay (Note 2 below).

had been imprisoned in an impossible animality. But as if that were not enough, as if two outlawries were always better than one with a being of this sort, he was called madman or idiot. Because he was silent when he was in society and spoke when he was alone. But above all because he laughed interminably, with a terrible laughter, if asked the reason for his bizarre behavior. After his arrest his fellow-peasants spoke of his laughter as of the intolerable accompaniment of morbid symptoms. Only the parish priest thought to minimize them: "Certainly no one would have thought anything more of it had it not been for the murders he has committed," he said (p. 26). What peasant did not remember taking pleasure in such acts of cruelty to children and animals and such mimic battles with cabbages and imaginary enemies? But once Pierre Rivière killed, all his games became signs of madness. He himself, who believed he was pursued by the consequences of ridicule from the start, noted—often enough—the laughter of others only whenever it appeared. For them the intolerable thing consisted in this, that he should reinforce with his own laughter the pale within which he was kept by the laughter of others, just as the sorceress, with a great peal of laughter, surrounded herself with a circle of fire.[25]

THE DEAD AND WORDS

When imprisoned and questioned about the motives for his act, Rivière no longer flung his intolerable laughter in the faces of his questioners; he answered tersely and calmly. When left to himself once more, "he immediately took up his pen again and continued writing his memoirs as if he had not been interrupted" (p. 123). The line from the murder to the text was continuous. It was broken, however, for the space of a flash, only after he had fled into the woods and thrown away his weapon, when he suddenly realized that the impossible had happened, that it had come

[25] Michelet, *La Sorcière.*

upon him at the close of a long history of which he alone could tell the course and the trenchant logic. Then he cried out: "chasms gape beneath my feet, earth swallow me" (p. 113). The final stifling, all at once.

Life went on, however, over his dead body, as it were, and his "ideas of glory" repossessed him. He fled toward his judges in order to defy them and immortalize himself by dying and thus give weight to the words of his text.[26]

He had at first thought of writing a memoir in which he would set out the deed and the motives for it, commit the triple murder, mail his text, and then kill himself. Some weeks later he changed his project: write, kill dressed in his Sunday clothes, thus challenging the judges' black robes (each Law has its own accoutrements and tawdry finery), and then die, convicted of expressing opinions contrary to the established order. But every time he set to writing, he was disturbed or went to sleep; and every time he donned his Sunday clothes, his victims scattered. To finish with it all he resolved to compose his text in his mind and to kill without dressing up; there would always be time to write and defy later, in the interval between the tyrant's execution and his own.

Be that as it may, killing and dying are the two sides of one and the same medal: the death of the murderer, the lonely and livid death which Pierre Rivière was to give himself in the solitude of the cell, having exhausted every remedy, every chance of being heard by those whom he was asking to kill him fairly and not to let him rot; his death without redemption came as a necessary consequence of those he had consigned in his text and ballasted him with a final truth. "I can only follow them," he had said of his victims, "so I therefore await the penalty I deserve, and the day which shall put an end to all my resentments" (p. 121).

---

[26] Before the murder he purposed to write a memoir, at the end of which he would set out "my reasons for committing it at the end and the way I intended to flout the law, that I was defying it, that I was immortalizing myself" (p. 107).

This was the death of which a clumsy psychiatry had tried to cheat him. By having him reprieved they were refusing to hear him, they were declaring that, all things considered, the native's speech had no weight, was not even an effect of monstrosity; such criminals were only disturbed children who played with corpses as they played with words. The resentment they displayed had no reason for its existence; it was merely a product of their imagination.

The suicide came precisely to frustrate these paternalist reasonings. This death which Pierre Rivière voluntarily gave himself when there was no longer anything to inflict it on him compels the later reader to give its full weight to a text which quite obviously is that neither of a madman nor of a savage. Though "very crudely styled" (p. 55) by someone who had not mastered the rules of spelling and punctuation, it found a tone, a rhythm, a breathing—all of them calm—for describing suffocation. In so doing, it demonstrates its major virtue of taking in the rear every dominating ideology, even if humanist. By its content and its prosody, by its "obliquity," it smashes the images in which everyone was forever trying to catch Pierre Rivière and in which he himself at times consented to catch himself. This text, proclaimed by a being who played in the margins—it is quite uncertain whether he insisted on this or whether he was made to do so—turned out to be the most successful of the "completely new instruments" (p. 103) he liked to conceive,[27] a potent instrument to dislodge himself at last from the margins and to put to everyone, his judges included, the central question which they always evaded: What is the place of a law which is beyond the law?

[27] When he felt he had been turned to ridicule by girls, he planned to avenge himself by *making writings* against those who mocked him and to distinguish himself as well by inventing *completely new instruments*: a "calibene" to kill birds, an automatic butter churn (i.e. one that would not need a woman to work it), a carriage to go all by itself, and so on (p. 103).

No one makes his way to where it is with impunity. A man falls apart if he looks God in the face.

And what of us confronted with these broken lives which cannot be appeased?

There would be no end to adding words to words in order to avoid being engulfed and scorching in the torrid abyss of these documents.

Jean-Pierre Peter,
Jeanne Favret

2

Tales of Murder

AFTER NEARLY 150 YEARS Pierre Rivière's memoir strikes us as a text of singular strangeness. Its beauty alone is sufficient justification for it today. We can hardly help feeling that it has needed a century and a half of accumulated and reconstituted knowledge to enable us at last not perhaps so much to understand it as to read it—and, even so, to read it none too well and to grasp so little of it. How much less, then, could the doctors, lawyers, and jury make of it when they had merely a preliminary investigation and a court hearing to enable them to determine the grounds for deciding between madness and death in the 1830s?

Yet it caused no particular stir. It did, it is true, arouse some surprise, but only at the very last moment; someone who had been held to be a "kind of idiot" in his village turned out to be able to write and reason; someone whom the newspapers had depicted as a "raving madman" and a "maniac" had written forty pages in explanation. And, in the months following, the text gave rise to a battle of medical experts, caused the jury to change its mind, lent support to Chauveau's appeal to the Court of Cassation, furnished the justification for the reprieve, thanks to support from Esquirol, Marc, and Orfila, and documented an article in the *Annales d'hygiène* in the long debate on monomania: a definite indication of interest and of a great deal of indecision.

But, on the whole, it fell into place among the rest of the documents in the file of the case without attracting too much attention. Everyone seems to have thought that it did not so much throw light on, or account for, the crime as form part of it. The judge in charge of the investigation, noting that the memoir had been so to speak fabricated along with the crime, asked Rivière to set it down in black and white and thus in fact complete what he had set out to do. The text immediately became, as the order for committal to the assize court put it, "an exhibit in evidence." In its contemporaries' opinion the narrative of the crime was definitely not something aside from, or over and above, the crime which would enable them to grasp the reasons for it, but simply one element in Rivière's rationality or irrationality. Some said that the same signs of madness could be found alike in the *fact* of premeditated murder and in the particulars of what was narrated; others said that the same signs of lucidity could be found both in the *preparation* and *circumstances* of the murder and in the *fact* that Rivière had written it down. In short, the fact of killing and the fact of writing, the deeds done and the things narrated, coincided since they were elements of a like nature.

His contemporaries seem, therefore, to have accepted Rivière's own game: The murder and the narrative of the murder were consubstantial. They might all have wondered whether one of the two was a sign of madness or a proof of lucidity as against the other; no one seemed really surprised that a humble Norman peasant "barely able to read

and write" should have been able to couple his crime with
a narrative of this sort, that this triple murder should have
been interwoven with the discourse of the murder, or that
when Rivière undertook to kill half his family he should
have conceived of writing a text which was neither confession nor defense, but rather a factor in the crime. In short,
that Rivière could have been, in two different ways but
in virtually a single deed, an "author."

TEXT AND MURDER

For in Rivière's behavior memoir and murder were not
ranged simply in chronological sequence—crime and then
narrative. The text does not relate directly to the deed; a
whole web of relations is woven between the one and the
other; they support one another and carry one another in
ever-changing relations.

If Rivière's text is to be believed, his first project was
that the memoir was to surround the murder. Pierre Rivière
intended to start by writing the memoir; the announcement
of the crime would have come first; then the explanation
of his father's and mother's life; and, at the end, the reasons
for the deed. Once he had finished the draft, he would
have committed the murder; then, after he had mailed the
manuscript, Rivière would have killed himself.

Second project: The murder would no longer be interwoven with the text; it would be shifted from the center,
placed outside, at the culminating point, and at the same
time moved to the far end of the text, and would, so to
speak, be finally produced by it. Rivière planned to narrate
his parents' life in a memoir which everyone might read;
then to write a secret text narrating the murder to come,
what he called "the reasons of the end and the beginning";
and only then would he commit the crime.

Final decision, taken because a *fatal* drowsiness prevented him from writing and caused him virtually to forget
his memoir: He would kill, then get himself taken, then

make his declarations, and then die. This is the decision he finally put into execution. Except, however, that, instead of writing, he wandered for a whole month before he was taken and, after making *false* statements, wrote down his true narrative at the examining judge's request. But though he wrote so long after killing, he emphasized that his memoir had all been drafted in his head beforehand; he had "considered most of the words he would put in it"; this is why, though the murder had been accomplished, the harsh and unnecessarily wounding words about his victims were still in it. A memoir stored beforehand in the memory.

In all these transformations the text and the murder kept changing places, or, to put it more precisely, moved one another around. The narrative of the murder, originally intended to come at the beginning of the memoir, fuses with it and becomes diffused in it; it is concealed by the text, which would not now narrate a premeditated murder, but would be a secret codicil to it; and in the end, the proclamation of the murder is placed not only at the end of the memoir, but after the murder itself. The murder, too, has been reversed and has gradually become disengaged from the memoir; from the original intention that it should happen after the memoir was written and simply for the purpose of triggering its dispatch it has broken free and has at length arisen to stand alone and to happen first, propelled by a decision which had determined the narrating of it, word for word, but without being written down.

Basically, the successive placing of the text and the deed are simply stages in the operation and production of a mechanism: the murder/narrative. The murder would rather appear to be a projectile concealed at first in the engine of a discourse which recoils and becomes unnecessary in the propulsion discharging it. We might well call this mechanism the mechanism of the "calibene" or "alba-lester," from the names of the instruments invented by Rivière, fabricated words, instruments to discharge arrows, weapons to bring down clouds and birds, wrought names that brought death and nailed animals to trees, all at the same time.

The equivalence weapon/discourse is brought out clearly enough in the murderer's wanderings after his crime. For after the murder was accomplished, Rivière did not make the declaration to which he had committed himself. He fled, though he did not really hide, keeping always to the outskirts of the woods and towns; for a month he became invisible, not through any cunning on his part, but seemingly because of a peculiar property of his being a parricide or because of the systematic blindness of all those who passed him by. It was then that he decided to make a bow or arbalest, for "it might rather serve . . . the role I would be playing"; and this it was, an escutcheon and a confession, a lethal weapon and a fool's bladder, which he carried at arm's length; and it was by this that, by a strange complicity, he was finally recognized: "Oh look, there is a fellow carrying a bow." The bow was, so to speak, a mute declaration which became a substitute for the dark discourse engendered with the crime and intended to make him, by the narrating of it, glorious.

And the reason why it did play that role may be that Pierre Rivière's games, his imagination, his theater, what he called his "ideas" and "thoughts" were one day (was it the day on which a girl succeeded in kissing him on the mouth?) transformed into discourse/weapon, poem/invectives, verboballistic inventions, instruments for "enceepharing"; into those engines of death whose names were fabricated and whose corpses were buried, those words/projectiles which were from now on never to cease springing from his lips and spurting from his hands.

THE HISTORICAL AND THE EVERYDAY

Fly sheet and infernal machine, Rivière's narrative is subsumed—at least so far as its form is concerned—under a vast number of narratives which at that period formed a kind of popular memoir of crimes. "Particulars and explanation of the occurrence on June 3 at la Faucterie" seems to fit into the multitude of similar narratives reproduced in the contemporary broadsides and fly sheets: "Tragic occurrence at the Palais-Royal in Paris," "Particulars of a double suicide pact," "Particulars of a horrid crime of jealousy committed on the person of a Polish woman," "Authentic and circumstantial account of a frightful crime in a pretty little hermitage near the capital," "Curious and circumstantial details of the recent discovery of two escaped convicts at Saint-Germain-en-Laye."[1]

We should note carefully the words that were so often repeated in the titles of the broadsheets—"particulars," "circumstance," "explanation," "occurrence"—for they denote very plainly the function of this sort of discourse as compared with the importance given to the same facts in newspapers or books; their purpose was to alter the scale, to enlarge the proportions, to bring out the microscopic seed of the story, and make narrative accessible to the everyday. The first requisite in bringing about this change was to introduce into the narrative the elements, personages, deeds, dialogues, and subjects which normally had no place in them because they were undignified or lacking in social importance, and the second was to see that all these minor events, however commonplace and monotonous they may be, appeared "singular," "curious," "extraordinary," unique, or very nearly so, in the memory of man.

In this way such narratives could make the transition from the familiar to the remarkable, the everyday to the historical. And in this transition three essential processes came into play. First, what people had seen with their own eyes, what one muttered to another, and all the tales that spread by word of mouth within the confines of a village or district became universally transcribable by becoming out of the ordinary, and so ultimately became worthy of set-

[1] See J.-P. Seguin, *Canards du siècle passé*, Paris, 1969.

ting down on paper in print: the transition to writing. Secondly, the narrative simultaneously changed its status; it was no longer a vague tale carried from one posting stage to the next; it became news, with all its canonical details fixed once and for all: floating rumor was transformed into statement. And thirdly, the village or the streets, of their own accord and with no outside intervention, came to produce history; and, in turn, history stamped the dates, places, and personages with the mark of its instantaneous passage. No king or potentate had been needed to make them memorable. All these narratives spoke of a history in which there were no rulers, peopled with frantic and autonomous events, a history below the level of power, one which clashed with the law.

Hence the relations of proximity, opposition, and reversibility set up by the fly sheets among the "curious" news items, the "extraordinary" facts, and the great events and personages of history. For the broadsheets narrated both contemporary crimes and episodes of the recent past; the battles of the Empire, the great days of the Revolution and the war in the Vendée, 1814, and the conquest of Algeria rubbed shoulders with murders; Napoleon and La Rochejaquelin took their place beside brigands and bandits, patriotic officers beside cannibal shipwrecked sailors.

On the surface the two sets were contraries, like crime and glory, illegality and patriotism, the scaffold and the annals of immortality. From the far side of the law the memorial of battles corresponded to the shameful renown of murderers. But in fact they were such near neighbors that they were always on the point of intersection. When all is said and done, battles simply stamp the mark of history on nameless slaughters, while narrative makes the stuff of history from mere street brawls. The frontier between the two is perpetually crossed. It is crossed in the case of an event of prime interest—murder. Murder is where history and crime intersect. Murder it is that makes for the warrior's immortality (they kill, they order killings, they themselves accept the risk of death); murder it is that ensures criminals their dark renown (by shedding blood, they have accepted the risk of the scaffold). Murder establishes the ambiguity of the lawful and the unlawful.

This doubtless accounts for the fact that to the popular memory—as it was woven from the circulation of these sheets with their news or their commemorations—murder is the supreme event. It posits the relation between power and the people, stripped down to essentials: the command to kill, the prohibition against killing; to be killed, to be executed; voluntary sacrifice, punishment inflicted; memory, oblivion. Murder prowls the confines of the law, on one side or the other, above or below it; it frequents power, sometimes against and sometimes with it. The narrative of murder settles into this dangerous area; it provides the communication between interdict and subjection, anonymity and heroism; through it infamy attains immortality.

These narratives of crime will certainly have to be carefully examined some day and their place in popular knowledge demonstrated. The protagonists in those we find in the 19th century are no longer positive heroes of illegality like Mandrin and Cartouche. It is not that they no longer originate in a true expression of the popular mind. All the sheets disseminated in the 19th century are very conformist and moralistic. They tend to be didactic. They draw a careful distinction between the glorious feats of the soldier and the disgusting deeds of the murderer. In a way, they illustrate the Code and convey the political morality underlying it. And yet by their very existence these narratives magnify the two faces of murder; their universal success obviously shows the desire to know and narrate how men have been able to rise against power, traverse the law, and expose themselves to death through death.

The ambiguous existence of these sheets undoubtedly

masks the processes of a subterranean battle which continued in the aftermath of the Revolutionary struggles and the Empire's wars around two rights, perhaps less heterogeneous than they seem at first sight—the right to kill and be killed and the right to speak and narrate.

It was in the background of this underground battle that Pierre Rivière enrolled his narrative/murder, and it was through it that he provided the communication between it and the history of sacrificial and glorious murders, or, rather, with his own hand accomplished a historical murder.

THE SONGS OF MURDER

The broadsheets of the early 19th century were usually divided into two parts, the first being the "objective" narration of the events by an anonymous speaker, the second the criminal's "sorrowful lamentation." In these strange poems the guilty man was depicted as coming forward to rehearse his deed to his hearers; he gave a brief outline of his life, drew the lessons of his adventure, expressed his remorse, and at the very moment of dying invoked pity and terror. In 1811 a nineteen-year-old female parricide had had her hand struck off and her head cut off on the main square at Melun. The story was related and distorted in the broadsheets for years after; one of them in 1836 ascribed a lament to the dead girl, beginning:

> *You shudder, I see, feeling hearts,*
> *And the sight of me inspires terror.*
> *Yes, my felonies, my crimes are horrible*
> *And I have deserved the rigor of heaven.*
> *Take heart, my torment is ready.*

There are some noteworthy characteristics in these lamentations. Firstly, the use of the first person and the verse; in some cases the air or tune is given. It is the song of crime; it is intended to travel from singer to singer; everyone is presumed able to sing it as his own crime, by a lyrical fiction. (The Melun murderess's lament, for example, is sung to the air of "*Le Chien Fidèle*.") The criminal freely confesses his fault; he not only does not excuse it, but proclaims it; he calls down upon himself his condign punishment; he assumes for himself a law whose consequences he accepts. ("They condemn me to suffer death/My hand struck off and my severed head/Will deter all the great villains.") Secondly, the criminal confesses openly, clothed with a horror that inspires horror in himself, but a horror which he claims for himself unshared; he makes no concession to his own monstrosity. ("Let us recognize this execrable girl/Yes, it is I, it is Magdeleine Albert/This monster, frightful, cruel, abominable.") Thirdly, the criminal is depicted as speaking up when the punishment is imminent; in the very moment before death, at the very instant of departure for the hulks, he raises his voice to summon the justice which is about to engulf him; the song is placed between two deaths—murder and execution. ("I hear the last toll of the hour/My head, alas, belongs to the executioner/ And then my soul will appear before God.")

It marks the place—fictitious, of course—of a subject who both speaks and is murderous. This place is not that of the confession (in the judicial sense) nor of the defense or justification; nor is it the starting point for begging for reprieve or reconciliation. The speaker displays his murder for all to see, isolates himself in it, summons the law, and calls for both memory and execration. It is, as it were, the lyrical position of the murderous subject, a position defined from outside it by those responsible for composing the fly sheets.

Pierre Rivière came, in fact, to fill his place in this fictional lyricism. He filled it by a real murder which he had purposed beforehand to narrate and by composing an exact account of it at the judge's request. He came to lodge his deed and his speech in a defined place in a certain type of discourse and a certain field of knowledge. None of the historical memories to which he appealed in his text was an ornament or a justification after the event. From Biblical history as learned at school to recent events taught or commemorated in the fly sheets or broadsides there was a whole province of knowledge with which his murder/narrative was vested and to which the murder/narrative was committed. The historical field was not so much the brand or explanatory substance as the condition which made this premeditated murder/memoir possible.

Pierre Rivière was the subject of the memoir in a dual sense: It was he who remembered, remorselessly remembered it all, and it was he whose memoir summoned the crime, the horrible and glorious crime, to take its place beside so many other crimes. He contrived the engineering of the narrative/murder as both projectile and target, and he was propelled by the working of the mechanism into the real murder. And, after all, he was the author of it all in a dual sense: author of the crime and author of the text. The very title of the memoir expresses this plainly enough: "Particulars and explanation of the occurrence on June 3 at la Faucterie by Pierre Rivière, author of this deed."

Rivière, there is little doubt, accomplished his crime at the level of a certain discursive practice and of the knowledge bound up with it. In the inextricable unity of his parricide and his text he *really* played the game of the law, the murder and the memoir which at this period governed a whole body of "narratives of crime." Was it an irrational game? The majority of the jury seem to have decided that the fact that he played this familiar game both in the text and in the deed, that he was the dual author and appeared as the dual subject, was monstrous rather than insane.

A DIFFERENT GAME

But precisely there, in the institution of criminal justice, Rivière's murder/discourse confronted a quite different game. There it was not only that subjects who spoke did

not have the same status, but that the discourses were not
the same type of event and did not produce the same effects.
Rivière was the accused; the point at issue, therefore, was
whether he really was the author of the crime. He was up
before an assize court jury which had had the right to grant
extenuating circumstances since 1832; what it had to do,
therefore, was to form an opinion of him in accordance with
what he had done, what he had said, how he had lived, the
education he had been given, and so forth. And lastly, he
was subjected to a medical examination; here the question
was whether his action and discourse fitted the criteria of a
nosographic table. In short, his deed/text was subjected to a
threefold question of truth: truth of fact, truth of opinion,
and truth of science. To a discursive act, a discourse in act,
profoundly committed to the rules of popular knowledge
there was applied a question derived elsewhere and administered by others.

Pierre Rivière's parricide was paid for, however, in the
glory he sought. In the small change of it at least. Like so
many other crimes of the period, it was sung in the fly
sheets.[2] Sung and distorted, as was the custom, and with

[2] Thanks to Mme. Coisel, we were able to find a copy of it among
the uncatalogued pamphlets in the Bibliothèque nationale:

JUDGMENT OF THE CAEN ASSIZE COURT

on December 5, 1836

sentencing to death
the person known as PIERRE RIVIÈRE, aged twenty

convicted as charged of murdering his pregnant
mother, his sister aged eighteen, his brother aged eleven,
and his other brother aged seven.

He was executed on February 15, 1837

PARTICULARS

Vainly the reader's curious eye would seek in the annals of crime
a deed so horrid as that committed recently by Pierre Rivière, born at
la Fouquetrie, commune of Aunay, department of Calvados, district of
Vire. This fiend in human shape was twenty years of age and was to be
drawn by lot in the next draft. On Wednesday, June 3, ready to leave

elements belonging to other crimes and the conventional passages obligatory in this genre of writing mixed in as well. Rivière was even given a death which he had desired, which was prescribed by the law, but which, perhaps precisely because he had written the memoir and it spared him the ignominy of a felon's death, though it was written the better to prepare for himself a glorious death, was not to be his.

---

that morning to go to work the fields, he told his father that he could not go till noon and let him leave alone. The father had long been at odds with his wife, who lived alone on a property on her land a quarter of a league distant from her husband's dwelling. A week before the crime they went together to apply for a separation of persons and properties. The wife answered the judge who sought to reconcile the household by his advice that she had long harbored no more love for her husband and that the child she was carrying was not his. Nevertheless, she returned to the conjugal hearth and brought back her children with her, an eighteen-year-old daughter, a boy of eleven, and another of seven. On Wednesday October 3, after stating, as the reader has seen, that he would not go to work the fields, left alone with his mother and his sister, Pierre Rivière, impelled by a hellish spirit, seized a bill such as is used to prune trees, and the fiend hurled himself on his mother who was lighting the fire, struck her cruelly on the head and stretched her dead at his feet; immediately thereafter he flung himself on his sister and treated her in like fashion as he had his mother. Their bodies were still quivering when his young brother on his way back from school was stopped by a neighboring farmer who asked him why he was running so fast. I am going, the child said, to dine. The farmer who knew him tried to persuade him to stay for dinner; but his fatal destiny had to be fulfilled. He therefore refused the invitation and hurried home. His brother fell on him with lightning speed and struck his head a blow which practically severed it. On the morning of the murder his mother [sic] had asked him what he proposed to do. You will know this evening, the villain replied.

After committing the crime, Rivière took to flight in the belief that he could evade the law.

On October 4, 1836, the funeral procession was seen advancing silently through a crowd of villagers. On each visage was imprinted every sign of horror.

The venerable priest, in tears, said the prayers for the dead, and the earth covered the four victims for ever.

(There follows a Sorrowful Lamentation in four verses, to the air of "Le Chien fidèle.")

But a newspaper informs us that in his prison he considered himself already dead.

Michel Foucault

3

Extenuating Circumstances

"In June 1835 a young man of decent family cold-bloodedly and with premeditation killed his six-months-pregnant mother, his sister, and his brother. The jury, bringing in a verdict of guilty, deprecated his execution, for though they had found that he had discernment sufficient to render him responsible for his actions, they believed that his reason, of which he had never been fully in possession, might have been strongly affected by the circumstances in which he had been involved. Accordingly, they petitioned the king to commute the sentence."[1]

The sensitive question of the use of extenuating circumstances is summed up in these few paradoxical sentences as it related to the sentence passed on Pierre Rivière by the Calvados assize court on November 11, 1835. As the culmination of a long process of development, the law of 1832 had finally been passed three years before Rivière's conviction to extend the possibility of pleading extenuating circumstances to all crimes.

In 1835 there were, therefore, two means whereby sen-

[1] *Annales d'hygiène publique et de médecine légale*, 1836.

tences might be modified: Either the king might be petitioned for a reprieve, in other words, to modify a court's final sentence, or the jury might admit extenuating circumstances, which implied that it recognized that a crime existed, but also accepted the fact that circumstances external to the crime itself limited the offense committed by the accused and were accordingly grounds for mitigating the punishment. The Revolution had substituted a principle of codifying penalties by means of legislation for the judge's discretionary decision on the penalty under the Old Regime. The Penal Code of 1811 had enlarged the differentiation of penalties by introducing the notion of minimum and maximum sentences and had gone so far as to introduce the actual term "extenuating circumstances" in article 463, but had restricted its application to certain felonies only. Finally, however, after the law of 1824 had extended the application of extenuating circumstances to certain narrowly defined offenses and had left their appraisal to the court, the law of 1832 had made extenuating circumstances the rule and their disallowance the exception and had left it to the jury to decide whether they should be admitted.

A THREEFOLD CONFLICT

This development, culminating as it did in a liberalization of extenuating circumstances, should have worked to Pierre Rivière's advantage. A threefold conflict had in fact arisen with Pierre Rivière in the midst: a conflict between power and general consensus, a conflict on the seat of the punitive power, and a conflict between scientific knowledge and judicial power.

The conflict between punitive power and public consensus derived from the unduly repressive character of the law. This led to sympathy for the offender and a number of unjustified acquittals either for lack of extenuating circumstances or for fear lest the court disallow them under the law of 1824. The problem was, then, to ensure condign punishment. Two means could be envisaged: either to reduce penalties or to lower their minimum. Extenuating circumstances represent the second alternative. They do in fact satisfy a twofold concern to preserve the arsenal of primitive weapons, unused but ready for use when needed, and to adapt the law to the state of public opinion. Opinion could no longer be regarded as a negligible quantity after two revolutions. Extenuating circumstances made it possible *to correct the general appraisal by the law by the circumstantial appraisal by conscience.* They individualized punishments in the first instance and attenuated the feeling against the law; but the main point was that the law could be modernized and adapted if they were used systematically. Their principal function was, therefore, to reduce any excessive conflicts between public opinion and the law, all the more so because they were granted by the juries and not by judges who were out of touch with the nation at large. Consequently, they palliated any further questioning of power as such.

A second conflict turns on the seat of the punitive power. This problem might be examined at the level of the relations between the executive and the legislative powers, but these relations are relevant to general policy only and have no direct bearing on extenuating circumstances themselves, being mainly concerned with the relations between political power in general and judicial power in particular in respect of the possession of the punitive power. The Revolution had attached punishment solely to legislation, the aim being to eliminate the Old Regime's arbitrary discretion in the exercise of the punitive power. In 1832 extenuating circumstances may appear to be a reversion to the judges' arbitrary discretion, since they permitted the modification of penalties specified by legislation, but in fact the law of 1832 led to the crystallization of a power relation which was to remain unchanged thereafter. Law-making and the definition of punishable offenses now became the sole preserve of the legislature. The courts adapted the general provisions to the current state of public opinion and so recovered some latitude within the legal framework. They also adapted them to the facts, inasmuch as they considered not only the offense itself, but in addition to it the entire behavior of the offender and its relation to the total situation.

Thus, psychiatric knowledge, then in full spate of development, was introduced in this indirect fashion into the enforcement of the law. An early sign of this conflict was article 64, exempting the insane from responsibility. The criminal lunatic, as harmful, if not more harmful to the social order than any other criminal, had to be condemned, but his status as madman took precedence over his status as criminal. Any and all experts on the facts concerned were as qualified as the judges to determine responsibility by the primacy conferred on the facts of a case and the context of the offender's behavior over the offense itself. This paved the way for greater intervention by psychiatry, and hence to the development of the theory of limited responsibility and the introduction of all the various degrees of insanity into the concept of responsibility before the law. Indeed, the existence of extenuating circumstances opened the way to introducing not merely psychiatry, but all the social and human sciences (psychology, sociology, genetics, and so on), into the judicial procedure. Their existence may be decided by the jury, as the representative of public opinion, just as much as by the judges. The result, therefore, is to diminish the specific character of law enforcement and to reduce the power of the judges, since their specific jurisdiction is invaded by experts of various kinds.

FROM INDECISION TO ARBITRARY DISCRETION

The introduction of extenuating circumstances was, then, a sign of three conflicts, and Pierre Rivière was situated at the confluence of these conflicts both because of the date at which he committed his crime and because of his personal position.

Pierre Rivière came up before the assize court soon after the jury had acquired the faculty of granting extenuating circumstances, and his was a case in which there could be doubts about the accused's guilt and one in which, as the presiding judge of the assize court informed the Director of Criminal Affairs, "the effect of his execution will only be undesirable."

Furthermore, Pierre Rivière, a parricide and accordingly to be equated with a regicide from the penal point of view, raised a political problem in which the revival of the judicial power would have symbolically occurred if the case had been decided by the granting of extenuating circumstances.

For since Pierre Rivière was held "never to have been in full possession of his reason," this plea could have been used to grant him the benefit of extenuating circumstances, since insanity was no longer the only case in which full responsibility applied.

Rivière should, then, have been given the benefit of extenuating circumstances, but the jury refused to grant them and petitioned the king for a commutation of the sentence a few days later. The decision looks inconsistent. It was in fact based on the grounds of Rivière's character and the nature of the crime itself, but equally on the specific nature of parricide in the circumstances of 1835.

In Pierre Rivière's case the interrelationships of the three conflicts are complex in the extreme; there are contradictions at every level of knowledge. At the level of popular knowledge the witnesses contradicted each other, unable as they were to agree about Riviere's madness, and the public "which followed the hearings in court with the liveliest interest is divided in its opinion." At the level of psychiatric knowledge, the doctors were divided, though they were regarded as "all equally trustworthy." At the legal level, the jury, "some of whose members were persons of outstanding education and intelligence," was unable to come to a definite conclusion, since six of its members wished to grant extenuating circumstances, and six refused them. "Grave doubts would have arisen in the minds of the members of the Court if they had been called upon to hand down a decision."[2]

These divisions and these contradictions, visible at all levels, caused the apparent inconsistency of the decision. The jury, lacking proper information, could not come to a conclusion, found itself unable to use its new powers and the discretion with which it had recently been vested, and referred back to the supreme authority vested with discretion, the king. The limits of its power were defined as against those of psychiatric knowledge; it refused to recognize as partially responsible a madman who did not fit into the traditional canons of madness as laid down by the law and public opinion, but it could not wholly deny an ambiguous reality referred to it by certain psychiatrists. All it could do, therefore, was to relieve itself of the new responsibilities it was incapable of assuming.

The decision of the court at Caen was influenced, too, by political motives. Parricide was equated with regicide, so much so that violent debates had taken place in the Chamber when the vote had been taken on the law concerning extenuating circumstances. The conservatives had considered it inconceivable that regicide, and hence parricide, should be granted the benefit of extenuating circumstances.

Furthermore, on July 28, 1835, Fieschi had fired an infernal machine at Louis-Philippe and had not yet been judged; the Court of Peers did not pass sentence until February 15, 1836. To grant extenuating circumstances to a parricide in these circumstances would therefore have been tantamount to an affront to the king. The close connection between parricide and political crime was too much in everyone's mind.

This constraint must have been felt all the more strongly

2 See Report by the Presiding Judge of the Assize Court to the Director of Criminal Affairs (pp. 142–7 above).

because the Director of Criminal Affairs and Pardons had blamed the Prefect of the department of la Manche for selecting unduly indulgent persons for the jury at the December 1834 assize sessions: "a majority of countrymen devoid of education and incapable of appreciating the importance of the functions they were performing and the danger of undue indulgence."[3] Close attention must therefore very certainly have been paid to the composition of juries in Calvados too, since its Assize Court also sat at Caen, and especially to the conservative and punitive disposition of its individual members.

The jury could not possibly, therefore, take a decision in such a politically ticklish area. A further fact too had to be taken into consideration, that Philippe Egalité, Louis-Philippe's father, had himself voted for the king's death and might therefore be regarded as a regicide. An independent decision by the court without reference to the king's authority would therefore have set the judicial power on a firmer basis, but perhaps at the expense of a conflict with the king, and hence of a risk it could not possibly take upon itself.

The judges' decision, the refusal of attenuating circumstances and the petition to the king for the sentence to be commuted, was thus perfectly justified. The judicial power suddenly found itself equipped to decide even very awkward cases such as Rivière's. But despite the strictly juridical powers it had acquired, it could not but abdicate its prerogatives when confronted with a factual situation as well as an impossible political situation and it could only request the king to take its place. The court's decision, paradoxical as it is on the face of it, is therefore perfectly logical in its political context.

Patricia Moulin

[3] Report by the Presiding Judge of the Assize Court to the Director of Criminal Affairs, 1st quarter, 1835.

4

Regicide and Parricide

WHY WAS PIERRE RIVIÈRE REFUSED, by a slight majority, the benefit of extenuating circumstances which had removed a fair number of parricides from guillotine and acquittal alike after the amendment of the Penal Code in 1832, and why was he granted the commutation of his sentence by virtue of the royal prerogative of mercy?

To the first question we would be tempted to answer by reference to the conflict between the two institutions which were claiming power over Rivière, the law and medicine, and the relative weakness of the latter due in part to its internal divisions, since, despite the authority of the diagnosis by some doctors such as Vastel and Esquirol, others refused to recognize the existence of his madness and so stated in court (Bouchard, Le Bidois, Trouvé).

It is an indisputable fact that the personality of Rivière disconcerted medical knowledge by his act and his memoir, both of them inextricably linked, and that this knowledge in some sort abdicated from its faculty of arbitration, as is explained elsewhere, simply by exposing its divisions.

THE CRIME OF CRIMES

But in 1835 the law had additional reasons for displaying all its rigor; at the very moment when the Calvados Assize Court was trying the parricide, the Court of Peers, with Portalis presiding, was beginning the trial of Fieschi and his fellow-conspirators, who, as accomplices in the attempt to assassinate the sovereign and his family[1] on July 28, 1835, were liable to the penalty for regicide. Under the terms of the Penal Code itself Rivière's trial set up a "resonance" with the Fieschi trial.

The specific term "regicide" does not appear in the Penal Code of 1835, several times amended since it was originally drafted by Treilhard in 1810; it is subsumed under the head of offense against the security of the state, the basic article (art. 86) stipulating that: "The penalty for a criminal attempt against the life or person of the sovereign is the punishment for parricide," the offense being defined in article 88: "The compassing and the attempt to compass are the sole constituent factors of the offense termed assassination."

Besides the coincidence of date—on November 12, 1835 Pierre Rivière was sentenced to the punishment for parricide, on January 15, 1836 the Court of Cassation disallowed his appeal at the very moment when the complicated examination was being conducted at the Fieschi trial, and Pierre Rivière's reprieve was announced on February 15, the day after the judgment sentencing Fieschi to the penalty for parricide and the eve of his execution amid a countless throng—the coupling of these two cases, of parricide and of regicide, stamps a deeper impress on the criminal history of the 19th century.

The Penal Code made parricide the most heinous of all crimes, more heinous and more total even than premeditated murder, infanticide, or poisoning, all of which, however, were punishable by death (art. 302). The Penal Code complemented the Civil Code, which established the paternal authority and consecrated the family, devoting to it the major part of its regulatory provisions, and stamped with the seal of its severest punishment the most inviolable of all sacred things. "This heinous felony, the very name of which

[1] The king was not hit, but eighteen persons were killed, including Marshal Mortier.

cannot be uttered without a shudder, is the crime of crimes. The monster who perpetrates it is capable of every atrocious felony that can be invented by a perverse imagination," a deputy, Gaillard de Kébertin, stated (debate on the Reform of the Penal Code, December 7, 1831).

Until the reform of 1832, "the prisoner convicted and sentenced to death for parricide shall be taken to the place of execution in his shirt, barefoot, his head covered with a black veil, he shall be exhibited on the scaffold while a sheriff's officer reads the writ of sentence aloud to the people. He shall then have his hand struck off and shall immediately be executed and put to death" (art. 13). After 1832 the law renounced the hand but kept the black veil and the head; it retained body and soul alike within the precincts of the prison in perpetuity.

Punishing regicide with the penalty for parricide before 1832 was a method of inflicting upon conspirators a mutilating and ignominious penalty, as attested by the reasons given by the members of the Emperor's Council of State: " . . . the crime so termed is the most heinous of all crimes, it will be punished by the capital penalty specially reserved for parricide, that is to say, the only one which subjects the convicted man to mutilation before he is put to death."[2]

FAMILY AND HIERARCHY

But in the context of a code which set the death penalty "for many and many a crime and even for the mere attempt"[3] and attached to a number of punishments a whole train of ignominious, cruel, and unusual corporal punishments, such as branding, the pillory, and exposure, the coupling of regicide and parricide had yet a further significance: It testified to the fact that the sovereign—first the emperor and later the monarch—wished to be, and presented him-

[2] Berliet, Corsini, Pelet, *Conseil d'Etat, Séance du 5 février 1810 du Code Pénal, précédé de l'exposé des motifs par Mrs les orateurs.*

[3] Solimène, *De la réforme du Code pénal français.*

self as, a father. The equating of regicide with parricide is not intelligible unless it is linked with the promotion of the family as the model of society.

It is true, however, that, relatively to the Old Regime, the Civil Code liberalized the family and considerably diminished the paternal authority, which under Roman law was overwhelming, especially by its abolition of the father's lifelong domination over the son[4] for explicitly economic reasons.

Hence parricide became the most monstrous of crimes, and regicide was equated with it inasmuch as the family functioned as the ideal model of an *inegalitarian natural institution*. If the theme of the family was promoted not only through the operation of the two codes, the Civil and the Penal, but also in the works of the authors who framed the doctrines of the French Restoration (such as Bonald and Joseph de Maistre) and was so to the men of order of the party of resistance under the July Monarchy "in right-wing thinking with a long-standing and brilliant fortune . . . if the state and every community are conceived on the model of the family in which minors are placed under the tutelage of the adults, it is because society must be constructed of a *hierarchy* of groups and orders" (R. Rémond).

The family model set the seal of law on the political organization of the Empire and the two "parliamentary" monarchies in substituting a more inegalitarian society based on a hierarchy of authority and obedience for the ultra-egalitarian society established by the Revolution.

Thus, the accusations of monstrosity and of a totally unnatural disposition launched against parricide and regicide alike testify to an identical effort to denounce the two

4 "In the last state of this legislation the son of the family remains legally under the paternal authority for his father's entire lifetime. He remains so even if he is sixty years old, unless his father is pleased to emancipate him" (Address by Comte Réal in *Procès-Verbaux du Conseil d'Etat contenant la discussion du Projet de Code Civil Public, par le comte Locré*).

possible and irremediable forms of treason to the state of society in the 19th century. The Penal Code of 1810 set apart for regicide a space symmetrically equal to that which the members of the Convention, except those who followed Robespierre and Saint-Just, had assigned to the Tyrant.

Regicide was to be tried by a special court set up for the particular case, sharing as it did with parricide—though the latter was tried in the ordinary way by the assize courts—the opprobrium of breaching the "social compact."[5]

The exceptional gravity of these two types of crime, regicide and parricide, was so strongly appreciated that when the decision to amend the Penal Code was being debated in 1831, at least two voices were raised in an attempt to exclude them from the benefit of extenuating circumstances, that of Gaillard de Kébertin, whose amendment was rejected, and that of Roger deprecating giving too much power to the jury: "Give them a Ravaillac to try and they will declare that there are circumstances which extenuate even that fearful crime" (*Archives parlementaires*, November 22, 1831).

Legal though it was after 1832, the application of extenuating circumstances to the crime of parricide neverthe-

---

[5] It is noteworthy that the gravity of the crime of regicide was attested by all the successive political regimes in the 19th century, whether monarchical or republican. There is nothing surprising in the fact that the rapporteur for the Second Empire law on regicide should have stated: "For this crime [regicide], the greatest of all crimes, the most formidable and terrible of expiations, the penalty for parricide, is not excessive." But it is also worth emphasizing that under the Decree of February 7, 1869 "the provision in article 87 of the Penal Code protects the Republican government in the same manner as it previously protected the Monarchical government" and that the Third Republic should have incorporated articles 86 and 90 of the Penal Code in its statutory legislation; the legislator's constant concern has been to ensure the security and stability of the state, despite periodic convulsions, in the person of the head of state, regardless of its provisional embodiment, whether monarchical, imperial, or presidential.

less gave rise to objections and even indignation, as revealed in this outburst by the Counsel-General for the Crown in connection with a case of parricide: "He killed his father, but there are extenuating circumstances. Extenuating circumstances for parricide! Let us beware lest a declaration of this sort be not sacrilege against nature and against society!" (Leuret's case, *Gazette des Tribunaux*, August 30, 1840).

This caution, indeed this hostility, constantly echoed in the *Gazette des Tribunaux*, in no way prevented the application of the benefit of extenuating circumstances to a large number of parricides after 1832, the effect of which would perhaps have made itself felt in Pierre Rivière's case had it not been for the coincidence in date of his crimes with Fieschi's.

The reform of the Penal Code in 1832, confirming and broadening a number of amendments introduced in 1824, rescinded the corporal punishments associated with several penalties and accordingly abolished mutilation, branding, the pillory, and exposure, enabled the application of extenuating circumstances to parricide and regicide, and adjusted the range of punishments more closely to the gravity of crimes, which consequently restricted the jury's role in mitigating them.

A LEGAL DEVELOPMENT

We shall concentrate on two of the many basic reasons for this reform of the Penal Code which reveal the effect of Fieschi's trial on Rivière's inasmuch as, far from increasing the inevitability of a death sentence on a parricide, they made it less probable:

(1) The concern to render the enforcement of the law more effective.

"The idea has been to make penalties severe, but more equal and more certain and to balance too great a chance of impunity with a modicum of indulgence," stated Du-mon, the rapporteur for the amended Code (November 11, 1831).

The result was indeed a noteworthy reduction in the number of acquittals brought in by juries who did not want the death sentence, but had no alternative other than acquittal.

Thus, there were from 1826 to 1830 32% jury acquittals
	in 1831	37%	"	"
	from 1832 to 1835	33%	"	"
	in 1840	28%	"	"
	" 1880	17%	"	"

In other words, the severity of punishment was alleviated, but its scope was broadened. The number of death sentences and sentences to life imprisonment fell, whereas sentences to a term not exceeding five years increased appreciably. On the other hand, acquittals became less frequent in the period from 1825 to 1839.

As in the case of other felonies, the reform of the Penal Code considerably modified the penalties inflicted for parricide, even aside from altering the legal definition of the crime, a procedure used by the jury before the reform in order to mitigate the severity of sentence;[6] extenuating circumstances were a means of saving criminals from the guillotine, and capital punishment was no longer uniformly the sentence in all cases of parricide.

If Pierre Rivière's case had followed the statistical trend whereby extenuating circumstances were granted to a majority of parricides, he would in the ordinary course have had a good chance of receiving the benefit of them in view of the factor of uncertainty introduced by the defense's plea of the possibility of unsound mind.

---

[6] As witness the following table for parricides granted the benefit of extenuating circumstances:

1833	7/8	of sentences	1836	5/7	of sentences	
1834	13/14	" "	1837	3/4	" "	
1835	7/12	" "	1838	9/11	" "	

A further reason, a second reason for the reform of the Code, would also have operated against sentencing him to death, had his trial not been contemporaneous with Fieschi's.

(2) The arguments against unduly broad extension of the death penalty.

In practice an opposition to the unfettered use of the death sentence had developed in the juries' stand against the practice of applying the death penalty under the Empire's Penal Code too indiscriminately to crimes committed in circumstances which differed appreciably from each other. This position was supported by the considerations—political in this case—advanced by Guizot and others in taking a public stand against the death penalty in political cases after Louvel's assassination of the Duc de Berry, on the grounds that while it had been really efficacious under the Old Regime, when the issue at stake had been the repression of peasant revolt by massacre or putting a stop to aristocratic conspiracy, it was no longer an appropriate means of combating political disturbances under the new French regime. It meant, Guizot explained in substance, treating any opposition on the same footing as a conspiracy when opposition was now widespread in quite a different way; it further meant amalgamating in political crime what was dangerous to the state with what was immoral.

But inasmuch as the Fieschi case was an attempted assassination directed against the person of the king, and the prosecution insinuated that it was closely linked with the republican secret society known as the Society for the Rights of Man and the Citizen, political opposition reassumed the form of conspiracy and terrorism and so was brought within the scope of the death penalty. This was, of course, the twofold stimulus both to the September repressive laws muzzling the press and prohibiting any public demonstration of republican convictions or action and to a long-lasting train of attempts at assassination directed against Louis-Philippe and his family.[7]

RESONANT ECHOES

The sense of outrage aroused by the attempted assassination was therefore to affect the trial of Pierre Rivière, whose crime assumed a more monstrous resonance in that it was committed at the same time as Fieschi's.

The two trials, though they had no apparent common denominator, since one was of concern to the whole of France, whereas the other concerned merely a humble family in Calvados, interrelated not merely the dates of two atrocious crimes and their punishment but also the similar incidence of extenuating circumstances, madness, and reprieve.

Pierre Rivière's counsel put forward the defense of madness and pleaded extenuating circumstances for him; Maître Patorni, Fieschi's counsel, was to do the same, attempting to demonstrate his client's mental derangement, declaring that he was suffering from melancholia and demanding extenuating circumstances on these grounds, to the general indignation.

Fieschi's trial was held, of course, *after* Pierre Rivière's, but the former accounts to some extent for the outcome of the latter. For the caution and refusal of the court which tried Pierre Rivière implied that the plea of madness could not lightly be accepted to evade condign punishment. The judges and prosecution could not but fear the contagious effects inherent in all judgments by a court, and the parricide became more serious and more irremediable at the very moment when the regicide was to be sentenced. Any mitigation of the gravity of the crime of one of them might well have attenuated the horror of the other's felony.

[7] Alibaud, 1836; Meunier, 1836; Darnies, 1840; Lecomte, 1846; Henri, 1846; and Quénisset, who shot at the Duc d'Aumale in 1841.

The reciprocal atrocity of the two crimes became absolute, Rivière's infected by Fieschi's, and the two criminals' punishment became more terrible, Fieschi's borrowing its terror from Rivière's. So Rivière's configuration could not take form clearly under the signs of madness, for that would have meant that he would escape condign punishment. Hence the prosecution's description of Rivière as the savage, the monster, but by no means the madman: "Solitary, wild, and cruel, that is Rivière as seen from the moral point of view; he is, so to speak, a being apart, a savage not subject to the ordinary laws of sympathy and sociability, for society was as odious to him as his family, thus he asked his father whether a man could not live in the woods on plants and roots" (pp. 10–11), an arraignment which muffled the doctors' assertions of insanity and demanded a lack of sympathy on the jury's part correlative with his savagery. In Fieschi's case the prosecutor, Martin, depicted him as a monster of pride devoid of human feelings.

The answer to the second question raised by Rivière's case, its upshot in the grant of the reprieve, becomes clear only if we observe that the echoes from one trial to the other, the trial for parricide and the trial for regicide, become consolidated and the situations reversed. Pierre Rivière was reprieved, Fieschi and his associates were punished; worse than that, their counsel did not even petition for a reprieve, and word was conveyed to the convicted men's families that the king could not display magnanimity because none of his near relations had been hit, whereas innocent bystanders had been killed.

It is worth recalling once more that Pierre Rivière was reprieved after Fieschi had been sentenced to the punishment for parricide and the guillotine had topped Fieschi and his fellow-criminals the following day. It was as if Pierre Rivière could be cleansed of the immensity of his crime and restored to solitude, madness, and prison only if he were first doomed to punishment by the law, and it seems as if the royal prerogative of mercy could be exercised only after so heavy a debt had been paid.

It was only after the death sentence on the regicide had finally silenced the echoes that the parricide Rivière, a figure symbolical of Fieschi, could be restored to himself and could benefit from the king's mercy.

Blandine Barret-Kriegel

5

The Parallel Lives of Pierre Rivière

FOUR SETS OF DISCOURSES: Pierre Rivière's memoir and the substance of his interrogations by the examining judge, the depositions collected from witnesses by the judicial authorities, the medical opinions by Dr. Vastel and his Paris colleagues, and the legal documents drawn before the end of the proceedings.[1] The purpose of this Note is to detect the

[1] The main legal documents we have used are the report of June 5, 1835, by the District Prosecutor Royal attached to the civil court at Vire (hereinafter designated by the initials PRV), the application for a warrant for committal to the pre-trial court drawn by the district prosecutor at Vire on July 20, 1835 (AWC), the decision of the pre-trial court, and the bill of indictment drawn up by the regional prosecutor at the Caen Assize Court on July 28, 1835 (BI). One medical document, Dr. Bouchard's report, has not been used, since it does not deal with Rivière's life before the crime, nor (except in the table) has one legal document, the report by the Presiding Judge of the Caen Assize Court (RPJCA), since it is not, strictly speaking, a document in the proceedings and because it includes heterogeneous materials derived from both the legal documents and the medical reports.

shifts in meaning and the contradictions among and within these four, to discover how they work and what determines them, and to do so by identifying the effects of some of these discourses on others due to the operation of a system of selection and interpretation.

The comparison will deal with the account of Pierre Rivière's life up to the moment at which he decided to commit his crime. There are several reasons for this: The narrative (or at least some of its elements) appears in all four of the discourses; it is necessarily constructed both in the legal documents and in the medical reports from materials presented in Rivière's memoir and interrogations and in the witnesses' depositions, with all of which we are familiar; this is of considerable strategic importance, because it provides some means of deciding whether Rivière was mad or not. The main purpose of this Note will be to show how two conflicting arguments (that advanced by the doctors and that put forward by the judges and prosecution) could be constructed from two different accounts of Rivière's life, both of them based on the same sources of information. First we shall compare the two conflicting arguments as a whole with the relevant texts (Rivière's memoir and the depositions of witnesses) and then we shall try to demonstrate the coding system determining the choice of the elements retained or omitted from the basic texts and their interpretation, and we shall do so by using a body of specific facts, namely instances of Rivière's "bizarre behavior."

FUNCTIONS OF THE NARRATIVE

It is easy to delimit the two conflicting arguments: In the doctors' case, "Rivière has suffered from mental deficiency since his early childhood" (the summing up in Vastel's report, p. 135); in the lawyer's case, "Rivière was visited and observed in prison by a qualified doctor; in this professional practitioner's opinion nothing about him reveals any sign of mental derangement, and even if his flight after his crime and this attempt of his to pass for a madman in order to evade the ends of justice did not evidence on his part his perfect understanding of what he was doing and of the consequences which must ensue, his rationality would yet be quite evident from a very detailed memoir written by him since his arrest" (BI, p. 50). It was, above all, the circumstances attendant on the crime which furnished, in the prosecution's view, cogent evidence of Rivière's sanity; so that the primary significance of this retrospective view entailed by the narrative of Rivière's life was to fill in the traditional portrait of the guilty man, to show that "like all heinous criminals, he stifled the voice of conscience and did not struggle hard enough to control the propensities of his evil character" (AWC, p. 40).

But it would also necessarily have another and more polemical significance, to establish that not only was Rivière not mad, but that he never had been. There is, indeed, a problem here—the many instances of "bizarre behavior, extravagance, and oddity" ascribed to Rivière by the witnesses. This is the point on which the doctors dwelt to sustain their argument, so that the account of Rivière's life assumed considerable importance in their reports. Following a reminder that "Rivière comes from a family in which mental deficiency is hereditary" (Vastel, p. 126), it places before us a long sequence of instances of extravagant and bizarre behavior summed up as "numerous signs of insanity." The ensuing crime then plainly appears as yet one more sign of mental deficiency, or rather the result of this mental deficiency: "I became deeply and fully convinced that Rivière was not sane and that the act which the prosecution considered to be an atrocious crime was simply the deplorable result of true mental alienation" (Vastel, p. 125).

Thus the account of Rivière's life performed a very

different function in the two sets of texts. To the doctors it supplied cogent evidence that the crime was the result of mental deficiency dating right back to Rivière's early childhood; it absolved the guilty and at the same time relieved the defense from having to plead homicidal monomania (how valid this plea was in 1835 has been shown in another of these Notes); it enabled Rivière to "evade the ends of justice," to quote the bill of indictment (BI, p. 50). Taken up as it was by the judges and prosecution, this account had a dual function: the traditional function of accounting for the criminal's acts by his "evil nature" and the polemical function of establishing against the doctors that Rivière had never been mad and thereby of ruining the line of defense adopted by his counsel. Since both these sets of accounts were constructed from the depositions of the witnesses, we must now turn to them.

Of the thirteen witnesses questioned (including Rivière's family), only one (Hamel) asserted that Rivière was mad; another (Grelley) said that Rivière was generally held to be mad or imbecile, and three others (Suriray, Fortin, and Colleville) reported that Rivière passed in his village for an idiot or imbecile. Incidentally, it should be noted that the witnesses were certainly not using these terms in their accepted psychiatric sense. Except for Hamel, they did not explicitly take it upon themselves to confirm what they reported as the common opinion. Suriray, the parish priest, even expressed a contrary view: "The accused had always seemed to me a very gentle character, he was held to be an idiot in his village and even throughout the parish, but having talked to him sometimes, I did not think he was" (p. 25). The other eight witnesses did not even allude to any reputation for imbecility on Rivière's part. Yet Vastel wrote: "Until the age of four, the witnesses state, he was like other children of his age, but from that time on he was always held to be an idiot or imbecile" (p. 127). It is true that all the depositions (except Harson's) attribute

one or more instances of "extravagant or bizarre" behavior
to Rivière, but they do not explicitly describe him as mad
or imbecile; and two witnesses (Suriray and Fortin) mention Rivière's intellectual talents. The impression of ambiguity given by these depositions is accounted for by a
reading of Pierre Rivière's memoir; in it there is a very
distinct break dividing his life into two separate parts.

PORTRAIT, MATRIX, CODE

The first period began at Rivière's birth and ended
when he was ten or eleven. It covered the larger part of his
schooling and a period of great religious devoutness which,
according to him, began when he was seven or eight and
lasted for two or three years. It seems undeniable that
Rivière was a good pupil; he said so himself in his memoir,
Suriray and Fortin confirmed this, and no witness denied
it. Seemingly Rivière's relations with those around him
were then normal. There was some talk of his becoming
a priest, he preached sermons; none of the witnesses reported
any instances of bizarre behavior during this period, and
Rivière does not yet seem to have gained his reputation as
an idiot or imbecile. The break came when Rivière had
given up the idea of becoming a priest (that is, when he
was ten or eleven): "Later my ideas changed and I thought
I should be as other men. Nevertheless I displayed singularities. My schoolmates noticed this and laughed at me,
I ascribed their contempt to some acts of stupidity which
I had done since the beginnings and which, as I thought,
had discredited me for ever. I amused myself all by myself,
I walked in our garden and since I had read some things
about armies, I imagined our cabbages drawn up in battle
array" (Memoir, p. 101). From that time on Rivière
conceived his ideas of glory and sought solitude. Witnesses
reported the earliest instances of his bizarre behavior, which
were to continue until the murder. Rivière's reputation as

an imbecile seems to date back to this time; Fortin's deposition at any rate seems to indicate this: "I knew Rivière when he was a child, he seemed very eager to learn to read and write. When he was ten to twelve years old he did not seem the same any more, he appeared to become an idiot" (pp. 26–7). We might also refer to the certificate drawn up on November 4, 1835 and signed by fifty-two inhabitants of the commune of Aunay who had known Rivière (p. 138).

The reason why the two sets of texts do not mention this break is a matter of necessity rather than an oversight; their purpose is to outline a portrait rather than reconstitute a narrative. The two portraits, that of Rivière as "criminal-having-given-way-to-the-propensities-of-his-evil-nature" and that of Rivière as "deluded maniac," were not put together at the same period. The portrait devised by the judges and prosecution was constructed by reference to the crime; in it are depicted at work Rivière's intelligence, his gloomy and unsociable character, his "evil nature." The whole purpose of the account of his life was to find instances to fill out this portrait and to justify its perpetuation. For the doctors' purposes it was necessary for the portrait of Rivière as "deluded maniac" to be established well before the crime and to be practically continuous; it was constructed by reference to the account of Rivière's life from his childhood up to the crime. In the Paris doctors' report, as in Vastel's, this account was reduced to an enumeration of the many instances of "bizarre" behavior reported by the witnesses. Compare the title of the third part of Vastel's report: "Condition of his mental faculties since his childhood. Numerous signs of insanity." Rivière was the same at the ages of four and eighteen and at the time he committed his crime; this does not mean that nothing had happened, but that everything that had happened was juxtaposed against the same background, Rivière's insanity. The "signs of insanity" in Rivière did not follow each other in any particular order; each of them was given only the time needed for its own occurrence: the time the frog took to die, the time for which Prosper Rivière's legs were tied over the fire. Here, too, the purpose was certainly to fill in a portrait which began to take shape and had to be perpetuated.

The judges and prosecution built up Rivière's portrait around the crime and extrapolated it to cover the first and second periods of his life. The doctors constructed their portrait from the materials furnished by the witnesses on the second part of Rivière's life and extrapolated it to cover his early childhood and the events surrounding the crime. Thus, the Paris doctors wrote: "Pierre Rivière consistently showed signs of mental deficiency since the age of four" (p. 165). The judges and prosecution, on the other hand, dwelt on the earlier period, in accordance with the depositions and the memoir: ". . . he attracted notice among his fellows by his aptitude for learning, equalled only by his avidity for instruction" (BI, p. 49), but they did not mention the break in Rivière's life that occurred when he was ten or eleven. It is clear that if these two periods and the break between them did not exist, it would not have been possible to construct two such conflicting accounts of Rivière's life; Rivière would always have been mad, as the doctors presented him, or always sane, as the lawyers claimed. But it was also necessary that this break should not appear in either of these two types of account, in order that Rivière's portrait and the argument bound up with it should be consistent as they appeared in each of the two cases. The construction of Rivière's portrait in both accounts does not amount to the reconstruction of a case history, but determines a matrix which operates by a selection among the whole body of facts reported by Rivière and the witnesses and sets up a coding system for their interpretation.

BREAKDOWN OF REFERENCES TO RIVIÈRE'S "BIZARRE BEHAVIOR"

Facts noted	Depositions	Medical reports	Legal documents	Pierre Rivière
Story of cabbages	Colleville	Vastel and Paris doctors		Memoir
Obstinacy	Riv. fam., Binet, Hars., Mor., Fort., Coll., Ham.	Vastel	BI	2nd interrog. (contested)
Taste for solitude	Riv. fam., Hars., Mor., Fort., Ques.	Vastel and Paris doctors	BI	Memoir
Talking alone and strange gestures	Riv. fam., Retout, Fortin	Vastel and Paris doctors		Memoir
Unmotivated and prolonged laughter	Nativel, Quesnel	Vastel and Paris doctors		Hearings (RPJCA)
Cruelty to animals	Riv. fam., Marie, Nat., Ham., Grel.	Vastel and Paris doctors	AWC BI	Memoir, 1st and 2nd interrog.
Cruelty to children	Suriray (contested), Marie, Nativel	Vastel	AWC	2nd interrog (contested)
"Calibene" and albalesters	Quesnel		AWC	Memoir, 1st and 2nd interrog.
Fear of incest		Vastel (indirectly)		Memoir
Aversion to women	Riv. fam., Coll., Ques.	Vastel and Paris doctors		Memoir
"Fecundating fluid"		Vastel and Paris doctors		
Devils and fairies	Riv. fam., Coll., Ques.	Vastel and Paris doctors		Memoir

1. The double lines contain the "instances of bizarre behavior" which are examined together.
2. The facts which are connected with each other in each set of discourses are divided by dotted lines in the last part of the table.
3. Abbreviations: Rivière family, Harson, Moret, Fortin, Colleville, Quesnel, Hamel, Grelley, Nativel.

BIZARRE BEHAVIOR AND CRUELTY

The doctors and the lawyers did not accord equal importance to Rivière's "bizarre behavior." To the former it was both the result and the most manifest sign of his madness; since it helped confirm the portrait of Rivière as madman, it was therefore of the utmost significance. The legal documents did not dwell on this point, since it did not suit their interpretation of Rivière's life. By way of bringing this out more clearly, we have thought it worthwhile to draw up a table showing the distribution of instances of Rivière's bizarre behavior among the various discourses (see table on p. 236).

It should be noted at the outset that the greater part of the instances of bizarre behavior entered in the table appeared both in the witnesses' depositions and in Rivière's memoir. It should be noted, too, that all of them (except the "calibene") were referred to in the medical reports. The lawyers, on the other hand, made a stricter selection; they mentioned only a few instances and tried to minimize the relevance of those they did mention: "some extravagant *but misunderstood* actions . . . would probably have secured his acquittal on the grounds of insanity"[2] (decision of the pre-trial court, p. 43) or again: "The bizarre behavior of a character universally considered to be sullen and unsociable and certain circumstances, which were little noticed *when they seemed insignificant and were promptly distorted by imperfect recollection and by prejudice against him*, soon rendered this opinion general"[3] (BI, p. 48). The latter passage can be supported by Suriray's statement in connection with some instances of Rivière's bizarre behavior: "Certainly no one would have thought anything more of it had it not been for the murders he has committed" (p. 26).

[2] Italics added.
[3] *Idem.*

The "judicial" portrait of Rivière has two aspects. We have already spoken of the first; by stressing Rivière's intelligence the lawyers ascribed to him full responsibility for his crime. The second aspect is that which accounts for the crime: "Such is the accused, taciturn and reflective, with an ardent, cruel, and violent imagination," said the regional prosecutor at Caen (BI, p. 49); "solitary, wild, and cruel," said the district prosecutor at Vire (PRV, p. 10). It is defined in terms of the explanation adopted by the prosecution: "Daily witnessing his father's distresses and knowing their cause, the thought of putting an end to them occurred to him. Once it had taken hold of *an imagination somber and accustomed to hold firmly to the object which took possession of it*, this thought never left him; it became the subject of his constant preoccupation, his *solitary meditations*. Ceaselessly beset as he was by this lethal purpose, all the powers of his ill-organized brain, heightened by reading books which he misunderstood, were directed toward a purpose and its fulfillment, and his *sanguinary instinct* was to indicate to him the frightful means to accomplish it"[4] (BI, pp. 49–50).

We can easily observe here the items in the table stressed by the judges and prosecution: "obstinacy" and "taste for solitude" and "acts of cruelty." The reading matrix dictated by the judicial portrait of Rivière makes for a strict selection; no other "instance of bizarre behavior" appears in the column headed "legal documents." A corresponding system of coding and interpreting the facts which fit into the matrix operates in the direction required. "Obstinacy" and "taste for solitude" are primarily consistent traits of character; they need no commentary. The only example of an application of these character traits to a specific instance comes in the account of the preparation of the crime. To everything mentioned by the witnesses (specific examples of obstinacy and of acts,

4 *Idem.*

238

words, and gestures connected with Rivière's solitary expeditions) the lawyers made no reference at all. Questions which had in fact been asked during the judicial examination—questions on specific instances of obstinacy in the second interrogation—disappeared in the ensuing legal documents. The fact is that all this is extremely ambiguous: "Returning from these nocturnal excursions he said that he had seen the devil and had made a pact with him" (PRV, p. 10, statements by Rivière's family). Here, as in the other statements by witnesses, the specific instances relate to those twilight zones of Rivière's personality which the doctors exploited but which the lawyers passed over in silence. They report specific facts only where their interpretation does not seem to raise any problem; thus the torturings of animals were necessarily a consequence of Rivière's "sanguinary instinct."

Yet even on this ground the lawyers ventured cautiously; the facts of cruelty toward children quoted in the application to the pre-trial court do not appear in the bill of indictment. This is probably because there is no conclusive evidence that they were "acts of cruelty." Rivière, at any rate, maintained that he never meant to harm children (second interrogation, p. 35). The "calibene," called "an instrument of torture to kill birds" in the application to the pre-trial court (p. 40), also disappeared from the bill of indictment; the reason is that in Rivière's memoir the "calibene" is mentioned alongside "an instrument to churn butter all by itself and a carriage to go all by itself with springs, which I wanted to produce only in my imagination" (p. 103). What emerges from this conjunction is not the cruelty of Rivière's ideas, but their "bizarre character"; besides, the widow Quesnel reported that a strange ceremony was connected with this instrument: "He went one day, followed by the village children, and buried it in a meadow. Two or three months later he went, again followed by children, and dug it up again" (p. 31).

The lawyers did not tackle the obstacle, they simply ignored it. The coding system operative in the legal documents is based primarily on a reading matrix; certain types of "bizarre behavior" are first selected (precisely those which can be presented otherwise than as "bizarre," namely the "acts of cruelty"); then within each type some particular instances of "bizarre behavior" (the acts of cruelty to animals, but not to children); and then, for each instance of "bizarre behavior" selected discourse relating to it (the "'calibene' as instrument of torture" and nothing else). Obviously, in detecting these procedures we are making no claim whatever to reproduce the processes of thought, calculated or innocent, conscious or unconscious, of the authors of these legal documents; we are simply trying to bring to light the texture of a discourse, the texture being composed not only of what was said, but of all that was needed for it to be said. This will also apply later when we are trying to determine the system of coding and the matrix on which the doctors' discourse is based.

BIZARRE BEHAVIOR AND UNITY OF DELUSION

The portrait of Rivière as "deluded maniac" is not based, as the lawyers' portrait is, on the consistency of a number of character traits (intelligence, obstinacy, cruelty), but on the continuity of a delusion through its various manifestations. Rivière was simply the place at which a delusion, which had its own determinants and its own logic, settled in and took command; the madman was someone who was no longer in possession of himself. Rivière's portrait became indistinguishable from the description of his delusion. (It was only after the crime, when Rivière had partly recovered his faculties, that the doctors came to speak of memory, imagination, and so on.) We have already seen how the continuity of this delusion was assured over the various periods in Rivière's life; we still have to show how its description worked. Though present at all places and at all times, this delusion was nevertheless revealed only through its manifestations; so that the doctors did not proceed, as the lawyers did, by a selection of a set of "acceptable" instances of bizarre behavior; sections were cut within the discourses themselves relating to each instance and were interpreted; each instance of bizarre behavior had to be built up into a sign of insanity. The matrix excluded everything that could not be related to delusion; the coding system ensured the transition from the level of mere "bizarre behavior" to that of "sign of mental insanity."

The features of the version of the story of the cabbages presented in the medical reports are: The fact is only one sign of insanity among others; it is narrated in such a way as to produce the impression that Rivière believed that he was really fighting against men. Apparently he gave way to this strange propensity when he was in a state of complete delusion. This version is inaccurate; it is not stated that Rivière was ten or eleven years old at the time and that it clearly emerges from his memoir that it was simply a game. If we consider this first example of the fabrication of a sign of insanity from a mere child's game, we may well wonder —so clumsy is the proceeding—whether this was really worthwhile. The fact is that something more important than one more or one less instance of bizarre behavior is at stake here; we have already shown that this story of the cabbages was not merely one instance of bizarre behavior among others, because it marked a break in Rivière's life; we are inclined to think that at this same moment a second break began, which comes in between the instances of bizarre behavior and divides them into two groups. Rivière realized the consequences of the cabbage incident; people jeered at him and gave him a reputation as an idiot or imbecile. From then on he would indulge in certain acts of bizarre behavior in secret (at least from adults) and in solitude (such as making the "calibene" and the "albalesters"), whereas others, as we shall see, were deliberately displayed quite openly either for fun or to conceal the true motives for an act (such as the stories about devils and fairies). This already brings up the question of simulation.

It may be put in this way: How could Rivière, who was mad, make a game of madness designed for others, who were not mad, and how could they be taken in by it? The answer is simple enough, the same for both doctors and lawyers: he could not. And yet he did so after his arrest by trying to pass himself off as a "religious monomaniac," to use the words of the district prosecutor at Vire. So that it must either be said, as the lawyers said, that Rivière was not mad, or else, as the doctors said, that he was no longer mad, having partly recovered the use of his faculties after his crime. But, in the doctors' view, Rivière was always mad, from his birth to his crime; he could not, therefore, have simulated madness during that period. The story of the cabbages, in so far as it was a game, was already a simulacrum; for what distinguishes play from delusion here is an awareness of playing, whereas in fact a person is the unconscious plaything of delusion. If Rivière was playing and if therefore he was wrongly taken for mad, and if he perceived this, it means that he was not mad and it means that thereafter he would be simulating. The story of the cabbages must necessarily be presented as "one sign of insanity among others" in order that the second break, which we have just identified, should not appear, any more than the first one did.

SIGNS

"Obstinacy" and "taste for solitude" were deemed by almost all the witnesses outstanding traits of Rivière's character; they are indeed the mark of a certain oddity, but it is another matter to call them "signs of insanity," as the doctors did. In fact, they did so only after a number of manipulations in Vastel's report, the conclusions of which

were adopted by the Paris doctors. In the first place, "obstinacy" and "taste for solitude" are not presented as "signs
of insanity" in themselves; they promote the appearance of
these signs and are likewise its consequence; it was because
he was jeered at that Rivière took refuge in solitude; it was
because he had lost his reason that he was obstinate in the
face of all the evident impediments and the most authoritative advice (such as his father's) in trying to accomplish
extravagant or dangerous feats. They promoted its appearance; it was in solitude that "[Rivière] bent his mind in a
direction the more vicious in that, since he never confided
in anyone, no one could correct his errors" (Vastel, pp.
127–8); it was because Rivière was extremely obstinate that
he carried through to the end aberrant acts in which his
insanity revealed itself. The main function of "taste for
solitude" and "obstinacy" is to "designate" Rivière's insanity through the manifestations of them, promoted by
them, and simultaneously resulting from them; they in turn
thus insensibly become signs of insanity.

The system of coding in operation here is readily deter-
minable; the aim is systematically to relate "obstinacy" and
"taste for solitude" to more manifest signs of insanity and
only to them. (We have already seen how the lawyers, conversely, avoided referring to specific examples.) It is precisely this that determines a reading matrix and a system of
exclusions. Vastel forgot that in his second interrogation
Rivière vigorously contested with "reasonable" arguments
all the specific cases of extravagant obstinacy ascribed to
him by the witnesses. He noted that Rivière sought solitude
and said that in solitude he worked out his delusion, but
about this delusion he said only what the witnesses reported
—the facts about torturing animals, the battles with the
cabbages, the stories of devils and fairies, and so on. If we
read Rivière's memoir, we note that, in his solitude, he devised many other ideas, of which the doctors breathed not
a word; it is true that at the start this search for solitude was
equally a flight, but, after a kiss which a girl forced him to

give her, it first of all led to "anti-social" projects, such as the songs Rivière wanted to compose to revenge himself on his mockers. Such, too, were the "instruments" he invented to "distinguish himself," to gain glory, and which he wished "to be created in his imagination" and "never to have been seen." Some of these "instruments" were machines of war (the "calibene" and the albalesters), others were intended to work "all by themselves" (the carriage with springs, the butter churn). Without going into an interpretation of Rivière's memoir, we can easily observe that the doctors dodged this dimension. The lawyers had shown themselves more alert by associating the word "solitary" with "wild" and "cruel." We have already observed in connection with the story of the cabbages that the "instances of bizarre behavior" performed *quite openly* (precisely those of which the witnesses spoke) are to be distinguished from those carried out in secret and solitude; we also pointed out that the doctors could not make this distinction; this is confirmed here.

"He was often overheard talking to himself and conversing with invisible interlocutors, or laughing loudly, or uttering plaintive cries. At times he was seen rolling on the ground, at others making the most bizarre gestures" (Vastel, p. 128). ". . . he was often seen talking to himself and conversing with invisible interlocutors, roaring with laughter for no reasonable motive" (Paris doctors, p. 164).

In this gesticulating puppet that talked and laughed but to whom no one listened we recognize Rivière's body; the strings were pulled by delusion. Yet more sinisterly, there emerged the ancient image of the possessed; the madman lurks on the verge, unceasingly gliding from one image to the other; he is possessed by his delusion. The coding system operates on the connotations of the discourse; nothing is said, but all is clear. Rivière, indeed, had not been wrong; he had explained his strange acts precisely in this way. The widow Quesnel reported some scenes she had witnessed:

". . . he talked to himself with his head lifted, as if speaking to the trees; sometimes he uttered terrifying cries. When asked what he was doing, he sometimes answered that he was conversing with the fairies, sometimes that he was conversing with the devil" (p. 30; Marguerite Colleville's statement contains similar details). These two images turned out to be opportune in filling the space left empty by the failure to reproduce Rivière's words; they opened out on to the idea of the madman's irresponsibility as a plaything of a higher power, and this excused the crime; they affected the twilight zones of discernment and disqualified the discourses that presented Rivière as a "normal" person. The coding system based on the image of the gesticulating puppet and the rule of exclusion which arises from it are simple: everything calculated to specify or modify this primal image must be excluded. This applies to the words spoken by Rivière; a reading of the memoir can give us some idea of this: ". . . on my solitary walks I made up stories in which I imagined myself playing a role, I was forever filling my head with personages I imagined" (pp. 102–3). In his statement the witness Retout reports that he saw Rivière acting in this way. Obviously this does not square with the connotations we have identified; Rivière was aware that he invented stories, he did not seem to be a prey to any driving force; and this activity, though certainly somewhat uncommon, has nothing particularly extraordinary about it. About the gestures and peals of laughter we shall say little here; they seem to be connected with the stories about devils and fairies, and their meaning will become clearer when we come to examine that point. We shall see that they relate in essence to the simulation-dissimulation of which we have already spoken.

In dealing with acts of cruelty the doctors took as many precautions as did the lawyers, but for the opposite reason; in their view, these acts related to delusion rather than cruelty. It must be acknowledged that this was no easy task; all the witnesses who spoke of these acts ascribed them to Rivière's cruel propensities, and so did the lawyers; Rivière himself explained in his second interrogation that he acted in this way because he took pleasure in it; and everyone would agree that taking pleasure in inflicting suffering on other beings is cruelty. Thereupon Vastel added this extraordinary remark: "Religious ideas passed through his head, he sacrificed and tortured small animals to reproduce the scenes of Christ's passion" (p. 128). The act merges with the religious delusion which produces it and gives it meaning; the madman takes the place left free by the sadist. This does not operate without a movement in reverse, and a large one at that; no mention of any such explanation is to be found either in the witnesses' statements or in Rivière's memoir or in his interrogations. But Vastel, like the judges and prosecution—and like us—had no other source of information on this period of Rivière's life. The coding system no longer applied only by means of a reading matrix; it introduced arbitrarily (in relation to the facts) fresh pertinent elements (for its interpretation of the facts). Another example of this procedure is to be found where Vastel says that Rivière amused himself by terrifying children to exercise "some notion of power and superiority" (p. 128). The fact remains that it cannot be applied without a matrix which excludes from the medical discourse the elements which do not fit, namely the witnesses' views of Rivière's behavior, all of which related to cruelty, and what Rivière says of the pleasure he took in torturing animals and the amusement he gained by frightening children (second interrogation).

SIMULATION

The last part of the table is the one which presents the greatest complexity: Rivière, the witnesses, and the doctors did not speak of the same facts and did not connect them in the same way; as to the lawyers, they did not speak of them at all—which is not at all surprising.

Pierre Rivière reports in his memoir that he was always

troubled by carnal passion and especially for a period of about a year (by cross-checking we find that it was when he was between sixteen and eighteen) and had a great horror of incest: "Above all I had a horror of incest which caused me to shun approaching the women of my family. When I thought I had come too close to them, I made signs with my hand as if to repair the harm I believed I had done" (p. 102). People expressed surprise at what he was doing, and he later explained what he did to conceal its true meaning: "When they asked me why I made these signs, I tried to evade the questions by saying that I was trying to drive away the devil. They said too that I had a horror of other women" (p. 102). There can be no question that these diversionary tactics were successful; no witness even alluded to any fear of incest that Rivière may have felt, they simply observed his aversion to women; nor did they perceive the true meaning of the stories of devils and fairies, but usually reported them as independent facts. It is true that in some cases these stories do not seem to be connected with the presence of any female; and, indeed, they continued (the widow Quesnel reports one which occurred a fortnight before the crime), whereas the fear of incest ceased to trouble Rivière. Without going far into any interpretation of Rivière's acts, we may venture the following explanations: He wished to divert suspicion by ensuring that these stories and the presence of women of his family never appear connected, to make use of a convenient and well-tried means of making sure that he did not have to furnish any explanations (compare the statement by the widow Quesnel quoted above: "he talked to himself with his head lifted," and so on) and to amuse himself, since, according to the report by the Presiding Judge of the Caen Assize Court, Rivière stated during the hearing that he told stories about devils and fairies "to mock at those who believe in such absurdities" (p. 144). This may perhaps account for the unintelligible gestures and the "peals of laughter without reasonable motive" previously mentioned.

Is there any reason, therefore, why after reading Rivière's memoir we should laugh at the doctors for seeming to fall into the same snare as the witnesses? The stories of devils and fairies are set out in their reports quite independently of the question of incest: "The devil and the fairies held an important place in his diseased brain, and by dint of thinking of them he came to believe that he saw and heard them. He held conversations and made pacts with them" (Vastel, p. 128). According to Vastel, Rivière really believed he saw the devil and made a pact with him, just as he really believed that he was fighting with men when he cut off the heads of cabbages. But the fear of incest was not the origin of these varied manifestations (Freud had not yet been born), but the consequence of a general fear of "females" allegedly felt by Rivière because he imagined that "a fecundating fluid incessantly flowed from his person and could thus, in his own despite, render him guilty of crimes of incest and of others yet more revolting" (Vastel, p. 129). The doctors had at all costs to avoid admitting that Rivière might have been able to play a comedy and simulate a delusion of which he was not the blind instrument but the author; otherwise, the whole personage of the "deluded maniac" falls to pieces; as we have already seen (as regards the story of the cabbages), madness and simulation are incompatible.

Simulation comes out so clearly from a reading of the memoir that it cannot be entirely dismissed; so the whole story has to be reconstructed. The "fecundating fluid" is the keystone of the edifice; as the cause—and manifestly the delusional cause—of Rivière's strange acts, it is enough to exhaust its meaning and direct it along the right lines, toward insanity; but *only the doctors* spoke of this fecundating fluid. Here we see all the procedures of the above-mentioned coding system at work: the use of a reading matrix (which excludes Rivière's discourse); play on the connotations of the discourse ("those who make pacts with the devil"); dissociation of discourses relating to one and the same body of facts (the devil, fear of incest, aversion to women); reversal of the internal order of the instances of bizarre behavior (by virtue of the fecundating fluid the fear of females is placed before the fear of incest, which is simply a special case of it); the arbitrary introduction of fresh elements of significance which became the keystone of a fabricated edifice (the "fecundating fluid," like the phrase "to reproduce the scenes of Christ's passion," of which we have already spoken). We also see that the doctors, despite all this work, could not avoid plunging headlong into a trap which Rivière had nevertheless indicated.

TRAPS

Two essential points emerge from this comparison.

The first relates to a reading of the legal and medical texts; a parallel examination of them shows that selections and interpretations match from one set of texts to the other. The doctors remained silent on points on which the lawyers dwelt strongly; one and the same fact was related either to cruelty or to insanity, and so on. We believe that these selections and interpretations are not only the expression of a certain level of medical knowledge or the effect of the operation of the judicial machinery, but mark the border where two types of discourse confront one another and, through them, two powers; the question was which of them, the medical institution or the judicial institution, was to take Rivière into its charge.

The second point concerns the relation between these two sets of texts and Rivière's memoir; the reconstruction of Rivière's life, as analyzed, requires and entails discarding his memoir. It requires this not only because the memoir often contradicts the doctors' and lawyers' allegations on specific points, but also because it does not square as a whole with their interpretation. The memoir does not paint a portrait, but narrates a history; Rivière is not always the same; this history is obviously not that either of a madman or of a sadist; it eludes the ordinary classifications. It entails this because the doctors and lawyers managed to fulfill the requirement that Rivière's acts should make sense by substituting for the memoir two "acceptable," though conflicting, versions of his life. Smothered under the whole weight of the official texts and the official interpretations, Rivière's text was to vanish into the archives for nearly 150 years. But precisely because it was kept out of circulation for so long, this memoir which we are reading today has lost nothing of its strange power of trapping any interpretation which has any pretension to be a total one. If it unveils the hidden meaning of a gesture or a word, we cannot register this without burning our fingers; we think we have demonstrated this in the course of our study; and if this were not enough, the very choice we have made in refusing to interpret it would be yet a further proof of this contention.

Philippe Riot

6

The Doctors and Judges

"PIERRE RIVIÈRE ought to have been placed in confinement; the young man was too ill to be left at large."

Such is the conclusion to the postcript which Lenter appended to the seventy-five pages in the *Annales d'hygiène publique et de médecine légale* devoted to Pierre Rivière.

With this sentence, then, the prisoner's medical dossier was closed. We may venture to view it also as a statement of what was intended in opening it, to which we owe the transmission of this collection of texts by the *Annales*. It was not simply a taste for the picturesque that induced the editor of a medical journal to devote a third of his issue to a murderer. Indeed, the same note as Leuret's was sounded in the conclusion by Vastel, the author of the second medical report:

"Society is therefore entitled to demand, not the punishment of this wretched man, since there can be no culpability in the absence of moral freedom, but his restraint and confinement by administrative process as the only means of reassuring itself about what this madman may do in the future."

These are the only two references in the *Annales'* reproduction of the doctors' opinions to what was to become of Pierre Rivière if he was recognized to be insane. Not a word about the possibility of a cure, or even treatment. This seemingly surprising silence on the part of therapists in conjunction with the evident care to emphasize that to declare a man mad did not mean neglecting all social procedures for controlling a dangerous person enables us to identify the real purposes of these attempts to pathologize a sector of criminality in which Rivière's case is a very significant episode.

SOCIAL CONTROL

We may say, by and large, at the outset that the principal issue at stake in the contemporary competition between the penal and medical authorities was the partial replacement of one method of control by another. Not that the two balanced. Between them there was the difference of a judicial murder, *the special punishment for parricides*. But the fact that we find the consequences of a shift from verdict to diagnosis are the essence of the matter is by no means a reason for regarding it as the recognition by a new form of knowledge of a diseased subjectivity which may thus elude the sanctions of power.

The fact that the law and medicine each tried to appropriate Rivière's act to itself raises in the first place a problem of nomenclature with regard to two kernels of knowledge, guilt and madness. Behind this theoretical issue is concealed, too, a competition between actors defending their position in the division of social labor: To what type of specialist is he to be entrusted and what will be his "career"; is it to depend on verdict or diagnosis? But, in the third place, we may observe in the unanimity of the emergent psychiatry the attempt to gain a space for its intervention between the after and the before, between consequential punishment and preventive action, for the future of mental medicine to deploy in. In a sense, the judicial machinery was set in motion as soon as the stakes were on the table, whereas mental medicine was trying to erect a new apparatus, to which Leuret's observation gives the clue—that is, an intervention which would not always be bound to come too late, for it would be based on a knowledge capable of *anticipating the possibility* of criminal behavior before the act was put into execution.

In relation to these three dimensions Rivière's case was the tragic pretext for a relatively exceptional attempt at demonstration. The profound ambiguity of his crime, the enigmas it posed to a knowledge that was in the course of elaboration and the gaps it disclosed in the legislative and institutional apparatus prior to the law of 1838 present us with a representative range of the possible medical attitudes toward this sort of problem. The knowledge assembled in the several medical reports concerned primarily a human destiny. But the issue was also a turning point in the development of a new apparatus for social control, the ramifications of which have gone on constantly spreading to this day. Schematically speaking, we can identify:

I, Pierre Rivière . . .

1. The Bouchard report, or the zero degree of psychiatric knowledge, abandoning Rivière to the traditional punitive authority, criminal justice;

2. Vastel's report, or the application of a specific semiology of madness, whose relatively archaic features failed to embrace a sector of criminality in mental medicine in any convincing manner;

3. The report by the leading Paris specialists, or the conjunction of the maximum psychiatric knowledge and power to annex Rivière to the new medical apparatus within a strategy which was also to instigate the legislative recasting of the law of 1838.

(1) BOUCHARD

Bouchard represents here the level of knowledge of a "non-specialist" doctor (let us avoid the term "general practitioner," since what we are talking about is the state of the discipline before the birth of specialties, of which mental medicine is truly the first—if we except surgery, whose status is peculiar to itself). Probably selected by the examining judge from among his colleagues for his local reputation, Bouchard concluded that Rivière was responsible only because, so far as the knowledge he expressed went (the knowledge of the non-specialist medical training of the period), *there was no specific semiology of madness.*

Bouchard first fell back on the ancient theory of humors which has pervaded medicine since antiquity. He also looked for a direct organic etiology, internal or external, which "might have acted on his brain in a way likely to have impaired its functions," such as hemorrhages, organic diseases, falls, blows on the head, and the like. Lastly, he did not find from direct observation of Rivière's behavior any evidence of a manifest pathology as sometimes observed (in, for example—to take the contemporary categories— fits of mania, dementia, or idiocy). Rivière's behavior—and this is why his "case" was so difficult that it required three medical reports and the final diagnosis remained ambiguous —raised a problem of *interpretation*. Bouchard himself did not have a coherent conceptual matrix to interpret it, that is to say, to relate the various traits he observed to a pathological whole in which they would assume the significance of symptoms.

Bouchard was, however, of all the experts the one who had spent most, and by far the most, time observing Rivière. He noted the main characteristics from which those who considered Rivière mad were to draw precisely the opposite conclusions. But lacking a *medical* matrix capable of interpreting them, he confined himself to a sort of popular phenomenology which tried to comprehend the crime in the light of the almost accidental conjunction of independent causal series: the father's misfortunes, a temperament prone to melancholy, its black humors enhanced by solitude, a state of momentary over-excitement, and so on. In the light of common sense, too, an unforeseeable "misfortune" arose from the fortuitous encounter of causes with events, each of them representing a practically "normal" sequence.

Bouchard's "defect" relative to the other experts was not, therefore, that he did not see or even that he did not understand. It was merely that he lacked categories to situate what he saw in a specialized knowledge. Hence his concluding sentence:

"The triple murder of which he was guilty can be ascribed, I believe, only to a state of momentary over-excitement brought on by his father's tribulations."

A Restrictive Use

The third section of Hoffbauer's *Treatise of Forensic Medicine*, which had recently been translated in France (1827), is entitled "*Of the temporary states of mind which may fall within the scope of mental medicine.*" It comprises four chapters: 1. *Of drunkenness*; 2. *Of the state intermediate between sleep and waking*; 3. *Of momentary aberration*;

and 4. *Of inhabitual impulsion to a specific action.* The last two sections especially are particularly confused, for Hoffbauer could not relate such acts to his classical conception of madness, which presupposed an aggravated disturbance of the mental faculties.

Hoffbauer was, in short, virtually in the same theoretical situation as Bouchard. But his strategy was different. Impelled by the purpose of his work, which was to found a forensic medicine and to show the wide scope of its applications, he established a category of "states which cannot be termed madness, but in which it is impossible to overcome the compulsion to some action or other." According to him, therefore, there are cases in which a subject must be declared irresponsible though· he cannot nevertheless be said to be mad. A very equivocal means of evasion, this. Hoffbauer did of course equate such states with those in which an individual compelled by forces stronger than himself is no longer a free agent. (This, under article 64 of the Penal Code, is the other cause in French law besides a habitual state of frenzy or insanity for exemption from responsibility.) But here the compulsion, regardless of whether it was "momentary aberration" or "inhabitual impulsion," was not an external compulsion which, *de facto*, abolished free agency. Nor was it, as Hoffbauer himself admitted, the internal compulsion which exempted from responsibility under the Code, namely madness. So that Hoffbauer remained imprisoned in a contradiction from which he escaped only by main force.

Significantly enough, it was precisely to this chapter of the translation of Hoffbauer that Esquirol attached his famous "Note on monomania." It was the escape from the contradiction. In order to relate these ambiguous cases to mental pathology it was necessary—and it was all that was necessary—to broaden the concept of madness and to break down the intellectualistic sclerosis inherited from the 18th century, which held madness to be a delusion of the reason. What was needed was to dare to conceive of a pathology of the feelings and the will without aggravated disturbances of the intellect—a solution for which Pinel had paved the way with his observations on "madness without delusion," but which had been, so to speak, held in reserve.[1] It was an aporia necessarily arising in practice from the series of concrete problems set by the medico-legal consultation that reactivated it and made the transition feasible.

Here we may grasp precisely how an act becomes "pathological" through an advance in psychiatric knowledge. Henceforth mental medicine possessed a new category, monomania, enabling it to interpret a new area of behavior which had lain outside its scope and had had necessarily to be left to the operation of justice.

Because of his situation as regards the contemporary knowledge, however, Bouchard fell short of this decisive leap. Yet, it will be objected, Bouchard was aware of the concept of monomania, since he referred to it in his statement to the assize court, if only to rule it out: "Pierre Rivière is not a monomaniac because he does not harbor delusions on one and only one subject." In point of fact, when Bouchard made this statement he was referring to the classification by Esquirol and modern mental medicine: monomania, idiocy, mania, dementia, insanity. But in this tardy application of it (he probably consulted a modern textbook on psychiatry between drawing up his report and the trial) he had assimilated only the letter of the new nosography, for he confined himself to a definition of monomania as "partial delusion," as it appeared in the article on monomania written by Esquirol in 1819 for the

[1] "One may have all due admiration for Locke's writings and yet concede that the notions he gives of mania are very incomplete in that he regards it as inseparable from delusion. I myself thought as he did when I resumed my investigations into this disease at Bicêtre, and I was somewhat surprised to find several madmen who were not suffering at the time from any impairment of the understanding, but were dominated by a species of instinctual frenzy, as if the affective faculties alone had been impaired." (*Traité médico-philosophique sur l'aliénation mentale*, 2nd ed., Paris, 1809, pp. 155–6).

Dictionnaire des sciences médicales. This is precisely the definition which cannot fit Rivière's case. This type of monomania is really only a micromania, it is still characterized by delusion, the sole difference from mania being due to the fact that mania is here restricted to a narrow category of subjects. Taken in this sense, the notion provides no escape from an intellectualist context defining madness exclusively as a disturbance of the understanding.

In any case, it was not the use of the concept of monomania that mattered as such here (we shall see that the other medical reports made use of it cautiously, to say the least). What was sought through this notion was an indirect means to pathologize, with the assent and active support of all the psychiatrists of the period, a new area of behavior. Bouchard was interesting *a contrario* because he remained outside this movement and thus traced its outer frontier. Out of ignorance, it will be said. No doubt Bouchard was not well informed on the latest state of knowledge. But, above all, he had *a different strategy.* Clearly, he did not feel committed to the task of pathologizing Rivière. He did not interpret the fact that he had to declare him guilty as a setback to medicine. Of the scanty knowledge he had he made a *restrictive* use by remaining solidly entrenched in the traditional corpus of medicine. Thus, he had heard of phrenology, but distrusted it; the issues at stake in a verdict of parricide seemed to him too serious to depend on what might only be a Paris fad. He had also been willing to make an effort to bring himself up to date in the classifications of the new mental medicine, but here too he made the most restrictive possible use of these categories by applying them in their formal rigidity.

Bouchard was not a "specialist." Just as he put his trust in traditional medicine, so he also put his trust in the traditional punitive authority: Let the law decide, medicine has no say in this case. The two went hand in hand. The theoretical division between madness and normality with no frontier zone and based on a physical etiology of madness was matched by an institutional division without risk of encroachment by the medical system on the judicial system. The traditionalism of knowledge and institutional conservatism were the two complementary aspects of this status quo between the law and medicine which the new mental medicine was beginning to disturb.

(2) VASTEL

Vastel, assistant head physician at the Bon Sauveur asylum at Caen, to which were sent all the insane from the department of Calvados, was called for the defense, whereas Bouchard, the "general practitioner," was called for the prosecution, an indication that the idea that "specialists" were preferable for saving a murderer's head in doubtful cases was already widespread. Vastel's medical report was, in fact, an expression of the consensus among psychiatrists that there was to be wrested from the judicial power a new sector in which they might intervene. But while the specialists as a whole were at one in this joint enterprise, not all of them had worked out the theoretical grounds for undertaking it to the same degree. Vastel's report gives the appearance of an intervention by a specialist who was not yet fully aware of all the weapons which mental medicine had become capable of deploying by 1835. We may perhaps try to interpret this deficiency by looking at Vastel's situation—or rather the situation of the type of training represented by him—in relation to the psychiatric knowledge of his period and the psychiatric institution then in course of erection.

Unlike Bouchard, Vastel was in possession of a wholly specific semiology of madness. This theoretical code for interpretation, equipping him to decide whether Rivière was or was not mad, was based on, and built up from, the tradition of Pinel as developed by Esquirol and his disciples. Vastel related to and manipulated this whole corpus of knowledge. But the significant point is his restrictive use of it. It was as if he assembled the concepts which were beginning to be the gospel of mental medicine only to push them in the most archaic direction possible.

There are at least thirty references to delusion, disturbance of judgment, or feebleness of intellect in the few pages comprising Vastel's report. Vastel's reading of Rivière's behavior swings between two poles: intellectual incoherence and mental deficiency. In both cases the aim was to show a lacuna—dysfunction or primary feebleness —in the faculty of thinking. This bias began in the physical description of the defendant, served as a clue to the interpretation of his childhood by emphasizing the slightest indications along these lines, and culminated at the instant of the crime. In Vastel's opinion, Rivière "proceeds from delusion to delusion" on to the murder, the apocalyptic apogee of deluded thinking. The act of murder thus tended to dissolve in the phantasmagoria of delusion. At the very most, it imprinted on reality the bloody trace of a madness which had existed in its perpetrator's mind ever since the age of four.

Esquirol's great discovery, which he named monomania, had been to demonstrate—or believe he was demonstrating —that a certain type of crime was cogent evidence of madness *in itself alone*, by its mere presence. In Vastel's report there is only a single reference to monomania, and that an indirect one: "Never have I seen a more manifest case of insanity among the hundreds of monomaniacs I have treated." This is either too much or too little. If Vastel had treated *hundreds* of monomaniacs, the only explanation is that he did not construe the concept in the most recent specific sense given it by Esquirol. Indeed, the whole structure of his demonstration was based on a reading precisely the reverse of the new mode of thought signified by the concept of monomania. If homicidal monomania were beyond all doubt the singular conjunction in which the existence of the criminal act in itself is a sign of madness, then Vastel was trying to "exteriorize" the relation of crime to madness; and this was precisely the reverse method. He made great efforts to find prior to it, elsewhere, and by way of a multiplicity of delusions an insanity of which murder is merely the paroxysmal crystallization. And, as though he were afraid that this was not convincing, he developed the complementary aspect of this demonstration, directed entirely toward seeking for a disturbance of the understanding. Alongside aberration of mind he made desperate efforts to show congenital feebleness of mind, Rivière's quasi-idiocy, contrary to the evidence provided by his narrative of the crime.

A Marginal Situation

Thus, even while he used the categories of the new mental medicine, Vastel's epistemology was still solidly rooted in a concept of madness that ran through the 18th century and the early years of the 19th. (Georget was still giving it expression in 1820 by making delusion the indispensable symptom of mental disease.) Vastel's relatively marginal position in the psychiatric institution might account for this backwardness. From the standpoint of his training, in the first place—like most contemporary provincials, he completed his medical training in Paris. But as soon as he had taken his degree he returned to Caen. He had not, therefore, attended the school at la Salpétrière, where a revision of the concept of madness which was to leave its impress on the whole of the 19th century was being worked out around Esquirol, concerned with attention to behavior and the disturbance of faculties other than the understanding.

Vastel must also have owed his position as assistant head physician at the Bon Sauveur asylum at Caen, before becoming head physician on his predecessor's death, to accidental circumstances due to his network of local connections.[2] It was not his only occupation. Successively physician to the *lycée* and the hospitals, then director of the Caen School of Medicine, vice-president of the Departmental Board of Health and Hygiene, president of the jury for the inspection of pharmacies and of the Calvados Medical Association, member of the General Council of the Medical Association of France, his profile is that of a provincial medical notable rather than of the young "medical specialists" out of the school of Esquirol, who were starting to disseminate the new psychiatric ideology rather in the way that the Third Republic's primary school teachers were to take instruction to the people.

Vastel, therefore, was a sort of semi-specialist like the alienists who, including even Pinel, devoted only part of their activity to mental medicine. Situated on the periphery of the new science's propagation area, he shared its strategy. But he did not represent the center of psychiatric power and knowledge.

(3) THE PARIS DOCTORS' REPORT

This center was in Paris. It intervened directly in the third medical report, after Rivière's sentencing to death,

[2] His biographer states that he returned to Caen "invited first to several educational establishments, thanks to certain family connections. Appointed assistant head physician at the Bon Sauveur asylum, which was to provide him with an inexhaustible source of useful and curious observations, M. Vastel soon acquired a respectable situation without having to experience the uncertainties and difficulties of a laborious start" (biography of J. C. E. Vastel by Denis-Dumont, *Mémoires de l'Académie de Caen*, 1876). The Bon Sauveur at Caen, a private institution directed by Abbé Jaumet, a member of a monastic order, was one of the dozen or so institutions organized specially for the treatment of the insane before the law of 1838. The inmates were classified by their symptoms, as Pinel advocated. Esquirol praised the institution in his report "on hospitals for the insane" in *Des malades mentales*, vol. II, 1838. It was not irreproachable, however, in relation to contemporary knowledge, since Esquirol expressed his regret, in connection with certain organizational details, that "studies with a greater emphasis on medicine were not the principal factor in determining the administration of this institution" (*ibid.*, p. 477).

for the purpose of at least securing the royal reprieve. But the way in which the intervention was orchestrated seems at first sight somewhat puzzling, for this last report did not introduce any new element. The signatories had not seen the condemned man; they had worked at second hand on the documents in the dossier. They confined themselves to identifying the main elements in it likely to render the thesis of Rivière's madness credible and presenting them in a clear and coherent order. The text, brief and cautious, eschewed polemics and did not labor the most controversial points too heavily.

To take only one example, the curious way in which the concept of monomania was presented in silhouette, so to speak. It was introduced indirectly by means of a comparison between Rivière's behavior after his crime and the behavior of monomaniacs who seemed to recover their reason after a paroxysmal fit. But it is nowhere stated explicitly that Pierre Rivière was a monomaniac. Vastel too, as we have seen, made discreet use of the notion of monomania. But in the case of the second report we might wonder whether this caution may not have been due to ignorance of the resources that the notion could muster when applied to Rivière's case or to tactical prudence. For monomania, whose golden age was around 1825, seems to have become somewhat threadbare by frequent use by this time and liable to antagonize a court (see Note 7). It is quite certainly this prudential consideration that accounts for the third report. Three of the names in French mental medicine who had undoubtedly done most to make this notion reputable are among the signatories to the report (but not Georget, since he had died in the meantime). Esquirol was the creator of the concept. Leuret led the counter-polemic in the *Annales* against Elias Regnault and the trend in legal circles toward construing monomania as a mere invention by the doctors to encroach upon the province of the law. Marc was preparing to give the theory its most systematic form by drawing the distinction

between "instinctive monomania" and "reasoning monomania" in his *De la folie considerée du point de vue médico-
légal,* 1840.

The signatories thus had all the requisite theoretical
resources on which to ground their diagnosis. There is one
sentence in their text which indeed does point to this possibility of going beyond the intellectualist conception of
madness in which Vastel remained enclosed, though marked
by a rather eclectic formulation: "considering that the
narrative of his life written by Pierre Rivière demonstrates
a profound aberration of his mental faculties and moral
feelings." But the signatories slid over this essential doc-
trinal point very quickly. Similarly, when confronted with
Bouchard's "rebuttal" of Rivière's monomania presuppos-
ing a reduction of the concept to partial delusion, they confined themselves to a diplomatic allusion to the relativity
of nosographic categories by stating that one cannot "claim
to impose immutable boundaries on nature." In the contemporary texts, however, the authors in fact emphasized
the prescriptive role of nosography. But this was not the
time to enter into a theoretical discussion on monomania.
The point was to carry conviction without grating on sus-
ceptibilities. Lack of discernment is a better argument to
put to a court than a pathology of the will. The third report, therefore, by and large endorsed Vastel's. It did not
stress a specific theory of madness; it even avoided advancing a precise diagnosis.

The most important element in the text is the signatures.
The report is couched in the form of a petition introduced
by the formula, "we the undersigned," each name being
followed by the signatory's main professional qualification.
This means that the active nucleus of the medical world
interested in the social applications of medicine was throwing its entire weight in the scales to affirm Rivière's madness. It may be useful to spell out what this group signified
in terms of power:

· Esquirol, the continuator in the direct line of succession of Pinel's work and the unchallenged leader of the new school of mental medicine, Head Physician at the Royal Charenton Asylum, Inspector-General of the Faculties of Medicine, member of the General Council and the Board of Public Health and Hygiene, later to become its President, member of the Academy of Political and Moral Sciences;

· Marc, First Physician to the King, member of the Higher Board of Health, the Board of Hygiene, and the Royal Academy of Medicine;

· Pariset, Head Physician at la Salpétrière, succeeding to Pinel's post, member of the Board of Health, of the General Prisons Board, the Higher Board of Health, the Academy of Moral Sciences, and the Royal Academy of Medicine, of which he was to become permanent secretary in 1842;

· Orfila, the leading authority on forensic medicine with his four-volume *Traité de médecine légale*, member of the Royal Board of Education and the General Welfare Institutions Board, *conseiller général* of the department of the Seine, Dean of the Faculty of Medicine;

· Rostan, Resident Professor of Clinical Medicine, member of the Royal Academy of Medicine;

· And two of Esquirol's closest disciples, his nephew Mitivié, physician at la Salpétrière and his associate at the private clinic at Ivry-sur-Seine, and Leuret, whom Esquirol had had appointed secretary of the *Annales d'hygiène publique et de médecine légale* from the date of its first publication in 1829.

A couple of notes on the composition of this constellation of medical authorities: The school of la Salpétrière was over-represented, but its concurrence in the views of the most eminent representatives of hygienic medicine was absolute. The Board of Health was in fact the key institution in which all these eminent personalities coincided. The *Annales d'hygiène publique et de médecine légale*, established at the prompting of Esquirol and Marc in 1829, expressed the ideology of this group, which also included Villermé and Parent-Duchâtel. The prospectus announcing the journal's publication carried an extremely significant statement of the contributors' intentions, and seven out of twelve on the editorial board were also members of the Board of Health:

"The purpose of medicine is not only to study and cure diseases, it also bears upon social organization; it sometimes assists the legislator in framing laws, it frequently enlightens judges in their application, and it invariably joins with the administration in the supervision of public health. Applied in this manner to the needs of society, this branch of our specialized knowledge includes *public hygiene* and *forensic medicine*."[3]

This statement sums up the political consensus of the signatories to the third report on Rivière. The theoretical consensus itself is essentially that derived from the principles of the Salpétrière school, especially its overriding emphasis on the "moral causes" as against "the physical causes" of madness; but *this is not the essential point*. For example, one of the signatories was Rostan, a former pupil of Pinel's, it is true, but primarily the leading upholder of the organicist theory. The contemporary theoretical divisions between the materialist "somatists" and the "ideologists," the partisans of a physical etiology and a psychical etiology of mental illness respectively, were transcended by a more fundamental tactical and political accord. They shared the same strategy aimed at putting the spread of the new medical specialty on a rational basis and defending its social applications.

A Medical Strategy

The substance and function of the third report must be viewed in the context of this logic of medical power.

[3] *Annales d'hygiène publique*, 1829, vol. I.

Mental medicine had to demonstrate that it was able to take its rightful place beside the law by advancing into the breach in hard cases. Rivière's was just such a case. If he was mad, his conviction by a jury was a setback to the entire medical profession. Seven of the most eminent medical authorities were not mustering in 1835 for just any murderer whom they had never even seen. They were staging a demonstration of power. They were called in by the defense, but they were also alerted by the press to the magnitude of the issue at stake. (See extract from *Le Pilote du Calvados*, pp. 154–6 above.)

Leuret threw open the columns of the *Annales* and gave space to its most distinguished contributors. There is perhaps reason to believe that the operation was mounted in tactical detail, since Marc, as First Physician to the King, was particularly well placed to intercede with Louis-Philippe.

The "petition" achieved its purpose, since the jury's verdict was erased by a commutation of the penalty, secured through a petition for reprieve based on medical considerations. It was only a semi-victory, however. Pierre Rivière was, as we know, to hang himself in his cell five years later. The doctors' intervention wrested him from the hands of the executioner, but not from the prison administration. Apart from any humanitarian motivation—medical humanitarianism did not go so far as contravening the exigencies of law and order, as we have seen—such a conclusion to the whole case reveals a state of legislation which ran counter to the expansionist policy of mental medicine. A reader of the *Gazette des Tribunaux* drew attention to the difficulty (p. 158): If the court had found Rivière not guilty, what guarantees would there have been that he would be prevented from doing harm in the future? In point of fact, there was no legal provision which specifically applied to dangerous maniacs who had been found irresponsible. The practice of the courts in such circumstances is illustrated by the following excerpt from a judgment, in which an assize court decided not to proceed with a case of homicidal monomania (on the basis of an expert opinion by Esquirol and Ferrus):

"The Court, having consulted together, considering that the exhibits in evidence and the examination in court furnish good and sufficient proof that Jacques Baptiste D. was in a state of dementia on the night of May 3 to 4, 1828, during which was committed the act to him imputed and that therefore under the terms of article 64 of the Penal Code no felony nor misdemeanor existed, decides that no case need be stated for the prosecution nor further proceedings taken against D.; nonetheless orders that he be placed at the disposal of the Chief Counsel to the Crown, who shall take in his regard such measures as may be necessary for the safety of the public and for the private interests of D."[5]

Thus, psychiatric power could be only a power to intercept. It suspended the exercise of judicial punishment in its extreme form, but had not yet secured for itself a specific legal and institutional frame in which to set its victories. Nevertheless—as Vastel and Leuret pointed out—the decision on irresponsibility based on the opinion of medical experts required a system involving personal restraint and even intervention (Leuret) prior to the act which set the legal machinery in motion. Because they concurred in the prevailing standards with regard to punishment and because at the same time they needed a new apparatus to deploy the resources of mental medicine, the psychiatrists' relationship with the judicial power was ambiguous. All the texts on forensic medicine of the period stressed the fact that the purpose of the psychiatric consultation was neither to deprive crime of its guilt nor to restore dangerous maniacs to freedom or leave them at large. Leuret went so far as to suggest here that it was

[5] *Annales d'hygiène publique*, 1829, vol. II, p. 403.

capable of introducing a more effective, a preventive, means of control. But mental medicine would be able to gain a position as a controlling authority supplementing the judicial process only if it could equip itself with the twofold primary institutional and legislative structure it lacked.

Medical Isolation

A solution began to take shape in 1835. The same persons who mustered on behalf of Rivière were already committed to a far more ambitious enterprise. The law of 1838 was being prepared with the active assistance of the leading figures in psychiatry. They were to succeed in gaining acceptance for a new synthesis—which has lasted to this very day—signifying, besides much else, a decisive change in the relations between the medical and the penal. The twofold requirement which, as we have seen, came to the surface in Rivière's case was to be met by carefully institutionalizing the conditions for committal—"by judicial warrant" or "voluntary"—to "special institutions" (i.e. asylums). Committal by judicial warrant made provision for speedy confinement, as effective and peremptory as penal restraint, but with the additional advantage that it could be applied before a punishable offense had been committed and also before incapacitation, which was legally required in cases of madness before the law of 1838, had been certified. The confirmation of the medical certificate by the prefectoral authority and the additional safeguard of the faculty of judicial inspection became an effective means for detecting states of *potential* danger.

This did not, of course, solve the entire problem, for there was no provision specifying the *duration* of confinement; and voices were soon to be raised deprecating this gap in the law as regards dangerous madmen who needed to be confined for life. But a specific provision to this effect may not have been necessary. Since a medical certificate of recovery was still required before a discharge could be granted, nineteenth-century society could trust the "specialists" sufficiently to rest assured that they would not be lax in their exercise of a power which lay beyond the courts' jurisdiction. There was a further safeguard in the requirement that endorsement must be obtained from the prefectoral authority for any discharge from a committal by judicial warrant. The room for maneuver gained by mental medicine in this period therefore remained firmly circumscribed within a specific social commitment. The power with which it was vested was a delegated power to administer a particularly difficult sector of the area of what is now called "deviance" in complete conformity with the prevailing norms. The fact remains that some of these "deviants" were still threatened with two separate sanctions: the machinery of criminal justice, with the shadow of the guillotine hanging over it, and medical isolation, with the shadow of the asylum.

Robert Castel

7

The Intermittences of Rationality

THE PROBLEM

ALL OF A SUDDEN, the criminal was made to speak, to write. On the one side there were the doctors and lawyers, on the other the criminal, who in this particular case was also a "madman." But why, it may be asked, this new emphasis on speech in interrogations, why the writing of the memoir? What were they trying to get him to say, what did they want to know?

This is the question to which we are addressing ourselves in a Note which is intended simply to raise the question. As to the solution, if solution there can be, the place to look for it is in an intrinsic, a virtually inherent, difficulty in the mental medicine of the early decades of the 19th century turning on the concept of "monomania" and a difficulty in the practice of judicial investigation, with its procedure of investigation, observation, and interrogation, suggested, and even elevated to a theory, in the manuals of forensic medicine in cases of suspected madness.

Putting the criminal to the question was thus introduced, by means of a surreptitious complicity, into a new complex of forms involving reason, delusion, and simulation against the background of the inexpiable crime, for the purpose of identifying madness or unmasking imposture. "Write out the memoir you were going to write, then," said the prosecutor, "and we shall know, after you have done it, whether the fitting fate for you is the asylum, the prison or the scaffold. Was there motive and interest in the criminal act or was there not? Was there discernment and responsibility in it or was there not?"

But be that as it may, even if this writing was strongly requested or even ordered, and this discourse closely watched and even listened to, it still did not answer the question with any precision when those who made the statements seemed strangely and dangerously impassive, unconcerned and indifferent to the legal consequences of the crime. So, since there undoubtedly was something that was expressed in this writing, it may be that the question was wrongly put, or even that it had no meaning except that of giving away its non-meaning and its inherent uncertainty. Possibly this may be what Rivière was trying to say in his own way (the only possible way, in any case), and so we shall try to understand it as Rivière wished it to be understood ("but all I ask is that what I mean shall be understood and I have written it all down as well as I can").

THE UNCERTAINTY

The *Journal de médecine et de chirurgie pratique* introduced its account of Rivière's case as follows:

"The very important yet very obscure question of homicidal mania has been raised several times in this journal. We are adding to the facts already noted a new one which has been published recently and which in more than one respect deserves our colleagues' full attention. Since the opinions of the doctors called by the legal authorities were divided about the existence of monomania in the case of the subject observed here, we are setting it out in broad outline."

According to the journal, indeed, "three of the six doctors who were heard by the court gave as their opinion that he was insane, while the other three stated that he was not."

Of the opinions included in the file of the case, Bouchard, as we know, asserted that "Pierre Rivière is not a monomaniac since he does not harbor delusions on one and only one subject," while Vastel (though for reasons of prudence he did not bring in the concept of monomania, since the notion was unacceptable to the judges and prosecution and had already become a subject of controversy among the doctors themselves) did not rule out in several passages the possibility that Rivière might recover his reason after the "moral shock of the crime"; and the signatories to the medical report drawn up in the form of a petition for reprieve (Esquirol, Orfila, and others) alluded discreetly but explicitly to homicidal maniacs who "sometimes become calm and even rational again after accomplishing the act toward which they were impelled."

The jury itself seemed to be divided on the question of Rivière's madness (and therefore on that of his moral freedom, his responsibility, and his discernment with regard to his act), for "though they found that he had enough discernment to be liable to be held responsible for his actions, they believe that the circumstances in which he was involved may have strongly affected his reason, of which he had never been in full possession in any case."

Here is the question: Rivière's crime, in which the frontier between rationality and madness is hard to establish and which seems therefore to take its place in the sequence of crimes which had held the judicial stage in the 1820's—crimes disproportionate, excessive, and incomprehensible, for they seemed to violate the natural and social order (parents killed, children killed, the criminal feeding on his victims' flesh[1], while the criminals seemed to have acted without apparent motive and to have been in possession of their full intellectual faculties[2]—Rivière's crime, then, seems to have brought once again to the fore the

---

[1] See the account in Georget, *Examen des procès criminels de Léger, Lecouffe . . .* , 1825.

[2] In the indictment of Henriette Cornier, who killed a neighbor's child and threw its head into the street, it is stated that the guilty woman "seems never to have lost her presence of mind, discernment, and even the coolness of which she seems capable, either in premeditating and preparing her act or in consummating it." "Moreover," Marc writes, "despite the very careful investigation of the case before the trial, no motive, in the legal sense, which could have impelled the accused to act could be discovered or even suspected" (H. Marc, *Consultation médico-légale pour H. Cornier*, 1826). As to Léger, after confessing his atrocious crime (he had eaten his victim's heart), "he does not try to conceal anything," the indictment states, "he wholly recovers his coolness and himself unfolds the series of crimes of which he has been guilty; he reveals their minutest details; he produces the evidence for them and informs the law both of the scene of the crime and of the way in which he perpetrated it; the judge has no need to question him; the criminal himself speaks" (Georget, *op. cit.*, p. 4).

dangerous question of the coexistence of madness and rationality, of partial delusion and the lucid interval.

Is it possible for a criminal to keep his reason entire or lose it for an instant and then recover it? Was he aware of what he was doing? Did he harbor delusions about a single subject only, keeping the remainder of his faculties intact? Was only one of his faculties affected, to the exclusion of all the others? These were the questions with which the emergent mental medicine had been dealing since the beginning of the century, and they gave rise to a number of divisions among the doctors themselves and between doctors and lawyers, the theoretical (as well as political) stake at issue being whether and in what way rationality could be criminal and how it all, crime and knowledge, could be "borne" by what was called the "social order."[3]

So, in order to grasp whether the *uncertainty* displayed in various ways by the doctors' contradictory reports, the jury's verdict, and even the witnesses' opinions (to almost all of them Rivière "passed for" mad, if he was not really so) was accidental or inherent in a certain type of knowledge of mental disease, we shall have for a moment to retrace its theoretical structure, starting from Pinel's teaching, of which the medicine of the period was continuously conscious as an inauguration and as a major precedent.

[3] With regard to monomania, Marc was to say, for example: "The general principle that can be derived from it is that whenever homicidal monomania appears, it has constantly been preceded by phenomena such as would indicate at least a commencing disordering of the intellectual faculties, and this circumstance is reassuring to the social order, because it may serve to distinguish crime from delusion and pretense from reality" (*op. cit.*, p. 58); and Orfila added later: "We do not conceal how difficult it may be at times to determine the existence of monomania and how dangerous to the social order it will be if the principle we are upholding is improperly applied." (*Traité de médecine légale*, 3rd ed., 1836).

LOCALIZING MADNESS

In his *Nosographie philosophique* Pinel[4] recognized that neuroses are lesions of the feelings and impulse which cause an impairment or perversion of the moral qualities without inflammation or structural lesion and with properties "more directly affecting the nervous system, the known origin of which is the encephalic organ." Pinel had also observed eight cases of madness in which patients appeared to have kept their intellectual functions intact, and from this observation sprang the important distinction between a "mania without delusion (in which no appreciable impairment of the functions of understanding, perception, judgment, imagination, or memory is observed, but a perversion of the affective functions, a blind impulse to acts of violence or even sanguinary frenzy, without any dominating idea or any delusion of the imagination assignable as the determining cause of this fatal propensity) and a mania with delusion (with lesion of one or more functions of the understanding or the will, with gay or sad, extravagant or frenzied emotions)."

Pinel therefore seems to rule out the possibility of showing that an organic lesion is the origin of the malady, and consequently of assigning a single seat to it in conformity

---

[4] We do not of course intend to recount the history of the emergent mental medicine here, but simply to recall the fundamentals of the problem with which we are concerned, how the concepts of reasoning madness (*folie raisonnante*), partial delusion, and monomania led to wide study of the speech and writing of the criminal insane. A useful survey of monomania and the questions relating to moral responsibility can be found in P. Dubuisson, "De l'évolution des opinions en matière de responsabilité," in *Archives d'anthropologie criminelle et des sciences pénales*, 1887.

[*Isaac Ray's A Treatise on the Medical Jurisprudence of Insanity (Edinburgh, 1839) was the authoritative American textbook of the period. Much of Ray's material is based on the findings of Esquirol, and his book is useful for finding equivalents of the French terms for the medico-legal categories of the time. (Translator's note.)*]

with Condillac's system, to which Pinel refers explicitly;[5] in this sort of division of labor governing the mental faculties, the malady affects one function to the exclusion of the others, the affective functions if there is no delusion, the understanding or the will if there is.

Thus madness could only be the perversion of a secondary faculty or a partial dysfunction produced by accidental and external causes. Pinel certainly *saw* that there is a "madness power"[6] intrinsic in reason, but only to impute it either to the affective functions or to the lesion of one function of the understanding. The dual postulate of the nonexistence of the single seat and the relative autonomy of the various functions of the mind simultaneously preserved the principle of a universal reason, inherently sound in its fundamentals and effects, and ruled out the possibility of considering madness as *intrinsically* produced and engendered by this same reason and the "social order" which bears it. Henceforth madness, in its manic form, would be only aberration, deviance, perversion, or malfunctioning in relation to a universal norm;[7] it would be total loss of

---

[5] "Similarly, is it not of importance to the history of human understanding to be able to consider in isolation its various functions, such as attention, comparison, judgment, reflection, imagination, memory, and reasoning, with the impairments to which these functions are liable?" And, with regard to the seat: "Can this whole body of facts [about mania with or without delusion] be reconciled with the opinion that there is one single and indivisible seat of the understanding?"

[6] In the same way as Ricardian economics isolates the concept of labor power, but is not able to determine its *value*.

[7] We do not know how much Pinel could have known of the Kantian doctrine. (Kant is quoted by the doctors in connection with his claim that philosophers alone are competent—to the exclusion of forensic medicine—to decide the question "whether the accused was in possession of his faculties of discernment and judgment at the time of his act.") But here it is less a matter of influence than of belonging to a single conceptual system; for to Kant madness does not breach the principle of a universal functioning of reason, in relation to which madness is only a counter-reason with its own laws and specific rules: "For unreason," he says in his *Anthropology* (1797), "(which is something positive, not simply a lack of reason) is, like reason itself, a pure form

reason in its manic form and non-access to reason in its idiotic form.

Pinel's disciples were not to change his theoretical fabric fundamentally; they would endeavor to give a name to the dangerous cohabitation of madness and reason which Pinel had already called "reasoning madness" and would localize the impaired faculties more accurately; they would seek to identify the "accidents" which cause it.

OF MONOMANIA

Thus, upon that special area delimited by Pinel where madness has ambiguous contacts with reason Esquirol erected around 1810 and onward the edifice of monomania or partial insanity, a term, he was to say, which fits all partial delusions: "The madman, retaining the use of almost his entire reason, harbors delusions on any one subject or on a very few subjects; feeling, reasoning, thinking, and acting just as he felt, thought, and acted before he fell ill."[8] When homicidal, monomania was, he said, "a partial delusion, characterized by a relatively violent impulse to murder," itself provoked either by an intimate but deluded conviction, by overexcitement of the imagination, by a false reasoning, or by deluded passions, or else, if no impairment of the intelligence or affections is observed, by a blind instinct, by an irresistible propensity or by something in-

to which objects can correspond and both of them rise to the universal."

J. Fairet was to assert in this connection in 1866 ("De la folie raisonnante ou folie morale" in *Annales médico-psychologiques*): "Let us see whether his [the so-called monomaniac's] behavior is consistent with common sense or ordinary good sense and whether he has not run head on and too violently against all the ordinary notions, all the received ideas, all the general conventions, in short, the shared fund of ideas which constitutes the *general reason* of mankind; for it is in this appraisal of the common reason, with its many possible individual variations and shifts, that resides the fundamental point of comparison by which madness can be distinguished, in the last analysis, from reason."

[8] *Note sur la monomanie homicide*, 1827. In 1860 Griesinger, a German doctor, said that "Pinel's creation of mania has been a misfortune to science."

definable (what criminals themselves call "voices, the evil spirit, something that drove me"). Be that as it may, monomania remained in essence a mental state "which presents to the observer the strangest and most varied phenomena," which "embraces all the mysterious anomalies of the sensibility" (1820), and its study "is inseparable from the knowledge of the passions; its seat is man's heart; it is there that one must explore in order to grasp all the fine shades." Curiously, and in an inevitably mechanistic manner, Esquirol made monomania a species of *"mal du siècle"* due to the development of the intellectual faculties and more generally to the "state of society." (The police, for example, could, he thought, contribute to the disturbance of "weak imaginations," because the former demonomania no longer had such hold on them.)

Georget introduced the concept of instinctive monomania in 1825, due essentially to a perversion or obnubilation of the will for causes as diverse as the vicissitudes of life, enfeeblement by illness, or the perversion of the passions; this assumption could be derived from the crimes by the "ogres" (Papavoine, Feldtman, Léger), seemingly motiveless crimes if the criminals were rational, of whom he gives an account in his *Examen*, claiming that madness was involved here to some degree.

Henceforward instinctive, intellectual, and reasoning monomaniacs intersected and overlapped in a blend which the doctors themselves often found inextricable; what is of more account than terminology and definitions is the fact that an alarming twilight zone seemed partly to obscure medical knowledge; it was a zone frequently traversed by a crime with eclipses of reason and recoveries of rationality. This is why Esquirol issued a warning in 1827 against the tendency to erect monomania (which, according to him, was merely an observed fact) into a theory or system,[9] and

[9] Monomania was indeed taxed—rather strangely, perhaps—with fatalism and materialism because it seemed to cast doubt on free will, a fact which had caused Esquirol to utter his well-known disclaimer:

doctors like Marc, when called in by lawyers to give expert testimony, insisted that not too much use should be made of the concept of monomania, since it was only an exception and should only be accepted "with extreme caution, in the interest of the social order." Advising similar precautions and a similar circumspection, Orfila observed in his *Traité*: "We do not conceal how difficult it may be at times to determine the existence of monomania and how dangerous to the social order it will be if the principle we are upholding is applied improperly; the right to judge each particular case and to give the courts the only data on which equitable decisions can reasonably be based should be reserved solely for the informed opinion and probity of doctors."

The doctrine of monomania attracted the hostility of jurists and the courts alike and, among the doctors, of the upholders of the emergent anatomo-pathological conceptions of madness. Though there was no doubt in cases of dementia (since article 64 of the Penal Code at that time excluded culpability and hence the existence of felony or misdemeanor in such cases), the former considered that the principle of irresistible propensity in monomania should on the contrary be reduced to the more general principle of the culpable perversion of the passions, the will in this case retaining its full sway,[10] whereas the latter were concerned

---

"Heaven forfend that we should be fomenters of materialism and fatalism and wilfully try to establish or defend theories subversive of morality, society, or religion!"

[10] Dupin and Tardif had asserted in an opinion of March 30, 1826: "When they could not say that he (the monomaniac criminal) is guilty, they would say that he is mad; and Charenton would come to replace the Bastille." Collard de Martigny maintained in his *Questions de jurisprudence médico-légale* (1828) that "homicidal monomania can be regarded as a species of insanity only insofar as the passions themselves are to be assimilated to madness. In both cases there is delusion. The intelligence remains intact; all monomanias are passions and all passions monomanias." Thus, he added, at about the same date: "If monomania is an illness, it must, when it leads to capital crimes, be cured on the Place de Grève, that is to say by the guillotine."

I, Pierre Rivière . . .

with putting on a physiological basis, visible when cadavers were opened, the far too "spiritualist" and "metaphysical" concepts of Pinel's pupils.[11]

[11] In his treatise of 1810–12 (*Anatomy and Physiology of the Brain*) Gall had already recognized the existence of intermittent, partial, and reasoning diseases of the mind and asserted that "the cause of these diseases must be sought neither in the seat of the emotions nor in a supposed perversion of the imagination, but in the physical structures"; he noted that when the skulls of insane persons were opened it was to be observed that the membranes had thickened and hardened; the propensity to murder derived from a "carnivorous instinct," with its seat probably localized in the temporal and lower parietal area above the ears, whose action was tempered and regulated by moral factors such as education, habit, and religion. More specifically, J. Bayle noted in his *Nouvelle doctrine de la maladie mentale* (1825) that organic distempers in the region of the stomach and intestines had already been observed (Pinel), in lesion of the vital forces of the brain (Esquirol), in the impairment of a vital principle residing in the blood (Fodéré), in the accumulation of bile (Prost), and in a cerebral ailment (Georget), though he apparently "did not attach much importance to it"; he was thus trying to think of madness as a unified trajectory characterized by chronic inflammation of the meninges "in which monomania is probably only the first episode (with local or general paralysis) followed by mania proper and dementia." This was the line adopted by Broussais (*De l'irritation de la folie*, 1828), Calmeil (*De la paralysie chez les aliénés*, 1826), and Brierre de Boismont (*Observations médico-légales sur la monomanie homicide*, 1827). This research was finally to lead both to Fairet's conclusions ("De la folie raisonnante ou folie morale" in *Annales médico-psychologiques*, 1866) that monomania does not have the characteristics of a species or special variety of mental illness and from the clinical point of view is not to be classified as one of the complex syndromes compounded of manic excitement, general paralysis, hysterical madness, and moral hypochondria, and also to Morel's theories about degeneration and heredity, thus paving the way to the concept of madness as a measurable deviation from a norm, within which Lombrosian anthropometry was to lodge itself.

But in the 1830s, at the time of Rivière's crime, F. Leuret, a cosignatory to Esquirol's report, was still stating the following propositions:

"I. General paralysis is not a terminal form of madness; and any deformations found on opening the cadavers of paralytics, though only in them, should not be regarded as the effects of delusion (*Fragments psychologiques sur la folie*, 1834).

II. Madness consists in the aberration of the faculties of understanding; it is not, as ordinary maladies are, characterized by physical symptoms; and the causes producing it, while sometimes appreciable by the

There is no getting away from the fact, however, that this concept of monomania, disputed and controversial though it was, continued to embrace a number of facts (partial delusion, absence of delusion, lucid intervals) which remained basically "mysterious" and "incomprehensible" in the system used by Pinel and his disciples, in which it fostered an "uncertainty" which can only be described as "inherent." Reasoning madness and monomania were the flaw, the twilight zone, the point of opacity in the system, at which there had, simultaneously and necessarily, to be enrolled a semiology of external lineaments visible in the area of signs, an etiology of mechanistic determinism in the area of symptoms and remote causes, and a recognition or failure to recognize blind accident in the area of the impelling factor.[12]

---

senses, are usually part of an order of phenomena completely alien to the relevant general laws (*Du traitement moral de la folie*, 1840).

III. Though it is true that madness arises from an impairment of the encephalon, we have no knowledge whatever of what this impairment may consist in (*ibid.*).

IV. Such applications of phrenology to the study of mental disease as have been attemped are as irrelevant as they are unfounded (*ibid.*)."

[12] As regards the signs: In behavior they are the oddity and singularity displayed by the madman ever since his childhood, singling him out essentially as a "savage," a marginal figure relative to the norms of sociability; in the appearance they are the ashen and livid color of the face, the sunken and bloodshot eyes, and the vacant expression to which Zacchias had already drawn attention in his *Traité* and which are reproduced, with very slight variations, in the manuals of physiognomy (cf. Moreau's *L'Art de connaître les hommes par la physionomie*, Paris, 1807), in the treatises on forensic medicine (Metzger, Fodéré, Orfila), and in the depositions of witnesses. For here the cogent evidence is supplied by the opinion of those who have known the madman or criminal, based on the stereotyped semiology which seems to move, with only slight differences, between learned textbooks and the popular imagination.

In the area of symptoms, they are ailments as heterogeneous as insomnia, choking fits, hot flushes, headaches, stomach aches, and palpitations, though more often regarded as effects rather than causes of the malady. In the area of causes the physical series (hereditary factors, climate, age) is placed alongside the moral series (passions, fanaticism,

With monomania visible as regards signs in external lineaments, as regards symptoms and causes in mechanistic determinism, and in blind accident as regards the impelling factor, it meant that monomania operated as a sort of "bad form" between the "good forms" of manic insanity and idiocy, an intermediate form impinging on the other two in turn without overlapping them, and that the crime would often have to become apparent in an event and delimit a sort of no-man's land of lucidity alternating with delusion, which both doctors and lawyers would try to appropriate for themselves. Monomania thus seems merely to have drawn the frontier in the "nerve" medicine based upon the two-fold and complementary assumption that the mind operates in conformity with universal reason and that the social order possesses an intrinsic virtue.

THE RECOURSE TO WRITING

This "stumbling block" of monomania did, however, have considerable theoretical and practical effects, inasmuch as the inherent obscurity of this concept and the doctors' deep-seated uncertainty about it combined to lead to the emergence of the "sociology" of mental illness, which was no longer restricted to identifying signs and registering them on the nosographic chart, but now introduced, and supplemented defective clinical observation with, a quantitative and spatial dimension (statistical surveys by age group, region, and occupation) and above all a temporal dimension in the expanded anamnesis used from now on, involving a retrospective investigation into the madman's personal and family history.[13] Going much further—and

---

idleness) and the social series (education, inebriety, venereal abuses, hunger, misery). As to the impelling factor, it is sudden impulse, usually taking the material form of "the evil spirit, a word, an idea," as patients put it.

[13] Without going so far as to assert that the facts of monomania

here it is that Rivière's memoir is relevant—it created the
conditions for a new exchange of words between doctors,
lawyers, and subject, and, in the last resort, recourse to
writing.[14]

Since the malady could not be recognized by intrinsic
signs, the only recourse was to resort to social coordinates
and the sick man's biography to discover the deeply-em-
bedded basis and remote antecedents of the disease; and,
after the occurrence, the act, the crime, the subject was
asked to write about it in order to put to the test (which
of course included the ordinary corporal bullying in such
forms as the shower, cauterizing with the branding iron,
threats of bodily harm)[15] what remained the most formidable danger and the most subtly ambiguous effect of monomaniac crimes, the possibility of feigning and simulating

---

made the medico-legal consultation possible, it must be recognized, first,
that it would not have taken the form and acquired the impetus it did,
nor would it have been so strongly urged in treatises on forensic
medicine, had it not existed as a form of suspected madness; and,
secondly, that most of the consultations which have come down to us
from the early decades of the 19th century concern cases of possible
monomania. Vastel's report as included in the Rivière dossier is an excellent example of this, and one in which the doctor was prompted, in our
opinion, by prudential considerations to exaggerate delusion and invoke
Rivière's imbecility in the interest of the defense, at a period when the
plea of monomania was becoming more and more embarrassing to doctors,
judges, and prosecutors alike.

[14] Resort to the criminal's writing is already mentioned in Gall's
Treatise: "They say and they write, purposing to destroy themselves: 'I
will do it nevertheless.' Is it credible that these words and writings, which
so well depict these unfortunates' disturbances, have often contributed
to ensuring that their actions were viewed as premeditated and executed
with discernment? Their madness—people said—is merely feigned; a
madman does not say: I am mad, and madness does not reason. This
false and barbaric reasoning may, if care is not taken, send to the
scaffold beings who have nothing but madness to their discredit."

[15] Thus Marc ruled out "neither rigorous nor painful methods in
circumstances in which they may serve to discover the truth, but exercised without infringing the principles of humanity" ("Matériaux pour
l'histoire médico-légale de l'aliénation mentale" in *Annales d'hygiène*,
1829).

madness,[16] which due to the obscurity of the malady and the doctor's uncertainty, was yet another possibility.

It is because of this "stumbling block" that, according to forensic medicine, the disease could, and ought to, be detected during the procedure of *investigation, interrogation*, and *observation*. Investigation involved reconstructing the sick man's previous state, assembling the testimonies of persons who had been in contact with him, checking the precedents and noting the physiognomical signs;[17] interrogation was defined by Brierre as "one of the best methods of getting at the truth when there is some suspicion that

[16] With regard to simulation, Zacchias' old opinion that *"nullus morbus fere est qui facilius et frequentius simulari potest, quam insania"* and the old rule of classical jurisprudence that *"semel furiosus semper praesumitur furiosus"* and *"demens de praeterito praesumitur demens de praesenti"* are combated as early as Fodéré's *Traité du délire* (1817), which states that "to simulate being mad and dissimulate it are the absolute contraries of madness."

Though later, around 1850, it seems that simulation had to be ruled out as a result of anatomo-pathological research, since delusion has a systematic and organic coherence which a sick man cannot know or feign (Brierre de Boismont, *Manuel de médecine légale*, 1835: "The generally held opinion is so mistaken that those who hope to simulate this state infallibly give themselves away"; Morel, "Rapport médical sur un cas de simulation de folie" in *Annales médico-psychologiques*, 1857: "There is no mental defective who is devoid of the notion of cause, the notion of substance, the notion of being"; Billod, "Simulation de la folie" in *Annales médico-psychologiques*, 1860: "What the simulator does not know is that insanity, this disorder of our faculties, is a part of the admirable order which governs everything in this world and yet lends itself to regular classification"), at the period of Rivière's crime the question still seemed open; thus Marc asserted in 1829 that "one of the most serious duties that may devolve on the practitioner in medical jurisprudence is therefore to determine whether the insanity is real or feigned"; for, as Brierre de Boismont was to add later ("De la monomanie ou délire partiel" in *Annales d'hygiène*, 1847), "this variety of insanity, the subject of lively controversy, exists without the slightest doubt, but it is sometimes hard to observe its presence, and it is unquestionably the variety which calls for the exercise of the greatest penetration on the part of the enlightened physician."

[17] The depositions of the witnesses in the Rivière case provide an excellent example of this.

madness is being simulated"; observation is largely based on the evidence of the writing—"You get him to write, you suggest projects to him and, by winning his confidence, you induce him to communicate his chimerical plans and unfounded hatreds; and once you come to know all his motives for his actions, you can gain an accurate idea of his condition" (Brierre de Boismont, *De la monomanie*, pp. 260-1). Secondly, the doctor induced the criminal to write "letters or memoirs to set down his line of defense or complain to the authorities" (Orfila, *Traité*, vol. I, p. 491). Thirdly, "you obtain an account of any of his remarks overheard, his gestures, his acts, and the writings composed solely under the influence of the ideas with which the sick man is preoccupied" (Orfila, *ibid.*, p. 492).

So a charitable "trap"[18] was laid for the criminal to enable him to tell the truth about his act by speaking or writing. The criminal's or "madman's" speech therefore served as final proof when all others had failed. The madman and his speech,[19] the madman and his writing—this would, in the last resort, be the proof of motive for the judge or prosecution and the distinction between truth and simulation for the doctor. Thus we owe Rivière's memoir (requested, as we know, by the prosecution) to the inherent uncertainty of medical knowledge (though this, of course, was not the only cause), the recognition, spoken or unspoken, that the truth of madness found expression in the madman's speech (a complex of forms woven by a secret connivance between the doctors and the lawyers), regardless of what the in-

[18] About this concept of trap Marc could assert that there were cases "in which the monomaniac dissimulates, and every time he is brought back to the subject of his delusion he obstinately evades it because he senses that a *trap* is being set for him and that everything he says on this point will be taken for madness. A monomaniac like this is generally strong-minded and still in possession of a large part of his intellectual faculties" (*De la folie*, 1840, p. 51).

[19] M. Foucault elsewhere shows the connections between writing and crime. I would observe that in what follows Rivière wrote *also* to thwart the trap.

tentions, latent or manifest in the accused, may have been in writing it.[20]

THE UNDECIDABLE

The madman's speech then lodged in the gaps in the doctrine, sensed the trap, and tried to thwart it. For it was in this inherent gap that all the links, all the complicities, all the evasions came together, Rivière's memoir being merely their enigmatic surface. It was this that had to furnish the proof, fill the gap, and make it possible to re-establish knowledge in a certainty regained.

But what in fact happened? The subject who had fallen into a trap set a trap in turn; he behaved so as to raise the doctors' and lawyers' uncertainty to a sort of *undecidable* universal of madness instead of furnishing what was ex-pected—the proof of the true and the false. In the event, the proof doubled back on itself as soon as they thought they had grasped it. One sentence is amply sufficient to demon-strate this: "I was arrested with a bow and though I said I had made it in order to pass for mad, yet it was not ex-actly that."

It was indeed not exactly that; there is more than that. For the equivalence in time and space between the truth of facts and the truth of spirit[21] which seems to govern the

[20] A mere remark here: Letting the madman talk may well be viewed as the theoretical birth certificate of what was later to become psy-choanalytic practice—*pudenda origo* of a need which was purely a police and legal matter to shift on to the madman the onus of the truth of a knowledge which lacked truth and found it a problem. And since analysis was just as incapable as the emergent mental medicine of con-ceiving of an insanity engendered and produced by "reason" and its "order," letting the sick man talk could only be, no matter what the refinements and subtleties of practice and theory, a scrap of knowledge appropriated from the sick man as a sort of surplus value to the profit of the doctors' fragmented and defective knowledge.

[21] To the contemporary doctors a true fact was a non-simulated fact, just as truth of spirit ruled out any intention of simulating on the subject's part.

whole Western metaphysic of the discourse of reason never appears in Rivière's discourse; on the other hand, what there is in it is a continual and indefinite "doubling back" from one term to the other in accordance with a circular equation in which the second term is in practice introduced by the crime.

Truth of facts: falsity of spirit = falsity of facts: truth of spirit.

Was Rivière, inasmuch as he narrated true (non-simulated) facts relating to a period at which he was taken for mad (an opinion adopted and accentuated by Vastel), and inasmuch as he said after the crime that he recovered his reason, only however to announce facts of (real or possible) simulation, and inasmuch as he made most use of reason when he represented himself as possibly "mad," and, when he decided to tell the truth, returned to the savage state which the witnesses considered as a sign of his madness, and, lastly—and this is the asymptotic limit of the equation—inasmuch as he rationally wrote a memoir in which a doctor saw nothing but delusion—was Rivière mad or was he not? Was Rivière, inasmuch as he seemed himself to posit the true question of truth (if one is mad and one pretends to be rational, and if one is rational and one pretends to be mad, what is one in reality?)—was Rivière a simulator or was he not? And the motive he alleged (to deliver his father from women), perfectly logical and coherent as it was in his system—a coherence taken right up to the proof and test of crime—was it so in the system of the judges and prosecutors? The proof that these questions could not be answered is that it was answered only contradictorily, no doubt because, ultimately, Rivière's memoir answered the question with another question:[22] *Is a system*

22 We have merely sketched here the twofold complex of the indefinite doubling back of a certain discourse of "madness" and of the paradoxical exchange which sustains from one question to another the "dialogue" between the criminal madman and those who get him to speak.

in which contradiction is inherent as a condition and cri-
terion of truth and which is sustained by the irreducible act
of the crime true or false?[23]

Thus the additional knowledge of the memoir—and in
this resides its epistemological and political interest to us—
has brought us no reply; it has, however, testified to the fact
that:

(1) Given a certain concept of madness, the question
of true or false remains *undecidable*; what is paralyzed is
not so much the sick man's will as the doctor's and lawyer's
will to truth;

(2) The doctor's knowledge is not a knowledge if he has
to supply the proof by a speech which simply reconfirms,
as if there was any need for that, the impossibility of truth;

(3) More generally, there is an inherent limit to this
pretension to the "scientificity" of medical knowledge so
long as this knowledge reveals itself incapable of thinking
of the relations of dependency and the forms of the en-
gendering of madness on the basis of a certain mode and
certain relations of production, and confines itself, rooted
as it is in an uneasy coexistence, a coexistence periodic and
intermittent, of reason and madness (*beside* a universal and
normative reason and social order), to localizing "artificial
territorialities" for a new naturalization of madness: accidental causes, external lineaments of symptoms, the rises
and falls in the sway of reason, and factors such as heredity,
degeneration, skull dimensions, and so on.

DOING TOO MUCH

It therefore seems as if this additional knowledge and
this surplus value of knowledge not only cannot be appropriated, but have in fact revealed the gap they were

[23] This undecidable factor posited by Rivière's discourse is the
theoretical reason which induced us to discard any temptation to commentary or interpretation, that is to say, any reduction of this discourse
to one or another order of reason.

supposed to fill. This "doing a little more," this "laying it on" to show the little less and to call everything in question again seem to have been Rivière's relation to *labor*, according to Lami Binet's testimony. Let us look again for a moment at this astonishing passage:

"I have worked with Rivière the father for a long time (about five or six years); Rivière the father carted pebbles which I dug from a quarry; his son helped him to put them into a cart; when the father decided the cart was fully enough loaded, he told his son, do not put *any more* stones in; the accused went on as if he had not *heard*, the father repeated it, but to no avail; he had to reach into the cart himself and throw out the stones he thought were *too much*; but as soon as he had moved a little way off from the cart, to get his horses ready to drive away, for instance, Rivière the son *put back* into the cart the stones his father had thrown out."

It is all there, if we look at it closely: the additional work without profit, the exchange of words with no one to address, the calling into question again, and the obstinate starting of the work all over again.

Rivière seems always to have done a little more and a little too much; in his "senseless" child's games when he cut off the heads of cabbages, in his deluded emotional investments in universal history, in the construction of his machines, above all in his crime. It was by doing a little more, by doing too much, that he could exchange the alienating labor of reason for the liberated work of desire.

Perhaps this—who knows?—was his inherent motive, which, because of the flaw in their knowledge, the doctors could not see nor the lawyers hear.

Alexandre Fontana

About the Editor

MICHEL FOUCAULT studied at the Sorbonne, gaining his Licence de Philosophie in 1948, his Licence de Psychologie in 1950, and the Diplôme de Psycho-Pathologie from the University of Paris in 1952. He lectured at the University of Uppsala for four years, and during 1959–1960 was the Director of the Institut Français in Hamburg. He then became Director of the Institut de Philosophie at the Faculté des Lettres in the University of Clermont-Ferrand. He recently was appointed Professor of History and Systems of Thought at the Collège de France.

M. Foucault has lectured in many universities, including those in Copenhagen, Oslo, Lisbon, Madrid, Buffalo, Istanbul, Naples, and Brussels. He writes frequently for French newspapers and reviews, and is an editor of *Critique*.

The first of his books to appear in English was *Madness and Civilization*, which won the Medal of the Centre de la Recherche Scientifique on its publication in France in 1961. *The Order of Things* was published in 1970, *The Archaeology of Knowledge* in 1972, and *The Birth of the Clinic* in 1973.